Robot Surgery

Edited by

Seung Hyuk Baik

Robot Surgery
Edited by Seung Hyuk Baik

Republished by InTech
Janeza Trdine 9, 51000 Rijeka, Croatia

Additional hard copies can be obtained from orders@intechopen.com

Robot Surgery, Edited by Seung Hyuk Baik
p. cm.
ISBN 978-953-7619-77-0

For EU product safety concerns:
IN TECH d.o.o., Prolaz Marije Krucifikse Kozulić 3, 51000 Rijeka, Croatia,
info@intechopen.com or visit our website at intechopen.com.

Preface

Robotic surgery is yet in the early stages even though robotic assisted surgery is increasing continuously. Thus, exact and careful understanding of robotic surgery is necessary because chaos and confusion exist in the early phase of anything. Especially, the confusion may be increased because the robotic equipment, which is used in surgery, is different from the robotic equipment which is used in the automobile factory. The robots in the automobile factory just follow a program. However, the robot in surgery has to follow the surgeon's hand motions. I am convinced that this In-Tech Robotic Surgery book will play an essential role in giving some solutions to the chaos and confusion of robotic surgery.

The In-Tech Surgery book contains 11 chapters and consists of two main sections. The first section explains general concepts and technological aspects of robotic surgery. The second section explains the details of surgery using a robot for each organ system. I hope that all surgeons who are interested in robotic surgery will find the proper knowledge in this book. Moreover, I hope the book will perform as a basic role to create future prospectives. Unfortunately, this book could not cover all areas of robotic assisted surgery such as robotic assisted gastrectomy and pancreaticoduodenectomy. I expect that future editions will cover many more areas of robotic assisted surgery and it can be facilitated by dedicated readers.

Finally, I appreciate all the authors who sacrificed their time and effort to write the book. I must thank my wife NaYoung for her support and also acknowledge MiSun Park's efforts in helping complete the book.

Editor

Seung Hyuk Baik, MD, PhD

Yonsei University, Seoul,

Korea

Contents

SECTION I

1

Classification, Design and Evaluation of Endoscope Robots

Kazuhiro Taniguchi[1], Atsushi Nishikawa[2], Mitsugu Sekimoto[3], Takeharu Kobayashi[4], Kouhei Kazuhara[4], Takaharu Ichihara[4], Naoto Kurashita[4], Shuji Takiguchi[3], Yuichiro Doki[3], Masaki Mori[3], and Fumio Miyazaki[2]
[1]*Graduate School of Engineering, The University of Tokyo,*
[2]*Graduate School of Engineering Science, Osaka University,*
[3]*Graduate School of Medicine, Osaka University,*
[4]*Research & Development Center, Daiken Medical Co., Ltd.*
Japan

1. Introduction

With development of endoscopic surgery and medical robotics, surgery using endoscope robots has become a representative of robotic surgery. This chapter describes classification, design methods and evaluation methods of endoscope robots.
Expectations for a minimally invasive surgery have increased year by year with the dramatic advancement of image diagnosis technology, including CT and MRI. A camera (endoscope) and surgical instruments are inserted into tiny holes made in the patients' abdomen or chest region for surgical procedures. Compared to abdominal or open chest surgery, endoscopic surgery has less pain and has a greater advantage in cosmetic appearance as well as the economic advantages, resulting in its growing popularity. The most distinctive feature of endoscopic surgery is that the surgical field is observed through images taken by an endoscope, rather than the naked eye. The most important element to surgical safety and efficient operating is how well an endoscope reveals the field of view during surgery. Generally, a camera assistant operates the endoscope. The operation of the endoscope needs fine adjustment for the angle of the field of view and the distance of the surgical area as well as correct aiming of the endoscope at the surgical field. Camera assistants sometimes operate the endoscope according to instructions of a surgeon; however, camera assistants need to operate the endoscope using their judgment in understanding the surgeon's intentions so that they can move the endoscope according to how the surgery is progressing moment to moment. The operation of an endoscope by camera assistants requires as much proficiency as that of surgeons. There are not many surgeons who have sufficient proficiency in endoscopic surgery, which requires special techniques. In fact, it is not unusual for surgery to be interrupted due to a camera assistant not being sufficiently proficient in using the endoscope and is unable to obtain the exact field of surgery required.
To solve this problem, "endoscope robots that can hold and position an endoscope instead of a human camera assistant" (Fig. 1) have been developed. Fig. 1(a) shows a usual endoscopic

surgery where a human camera assistant operates an endoscope and Fig. 1(b) shows an endoscopic surgery using an endoscope robot. Among endoscope robots reported so far, Naviot™ (Kobayashi et al., 1999, Tanoue et al., 2006) made by Hitachi in Japan, AESOP™ (Sackier & Wang, 1994) made by Computer Motion (Intuitive Surgical) in the U.S.A and EndoAssist™ (Finlay, 2001) made by Prosurgics in England have been commercialized and widely used. The commercialized endoscope robots operate according to surgeon's instructions with switches by hand or voice recognition technology. There are some robots, still being studied, which automatically position the endoscope while the robot itself interprets the surgeon movements. The endoscope positioning system (Nishikawa et al., 2006, Nishikawa et al., 2008)developed by Nishikawa et al. represents an automatic endoscope positioning robot.

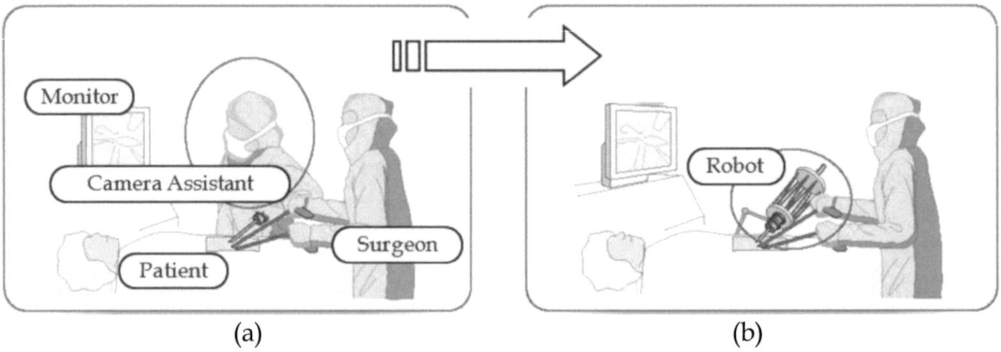

Fig. 1. Endoscopic surgery (a) A human camera assistant operates the endoscope. (b) An endoscope robot operates the endoscope.

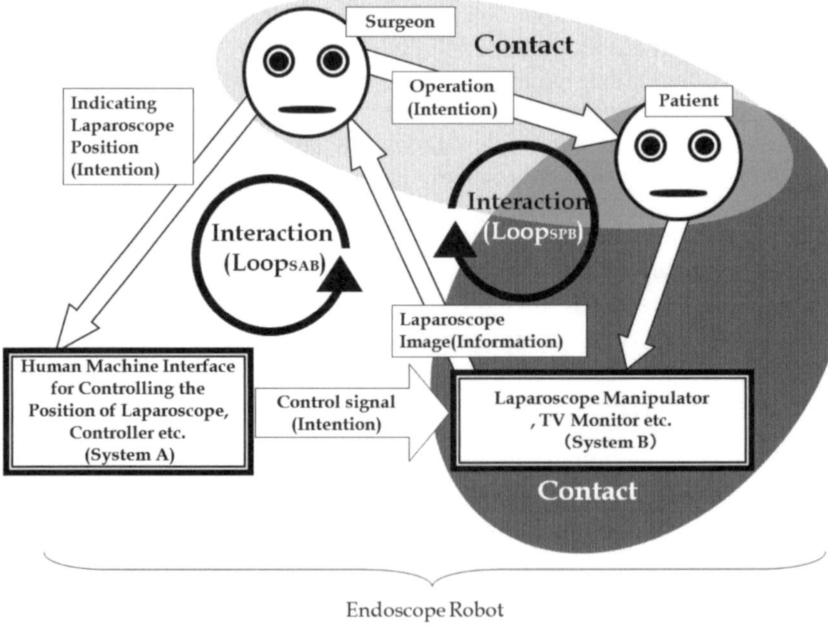

Fig. 2. Endoscope robot as an interactive media

As shown in Fig. 2, we have developed endoscope robots by separating them into two systems: System A, which receives information (intention) from surgeons, and System B, which positions the endoscope and provides information, to the surgeons, including images taken by the endoscope. System A is the human interface and controller and System B is the manipulator, endoscope equipment and navigation equipment. Upon developing endoscope robots, we develop System A and System B separately and evaluate and review them separately. Then, System A and System B are integrated and evaluated comprehensively. When System A and System B are evaluated separately, a manipulator system where System B is simulated is used for System A and a human interface where System A is simulated is used for System B. More specifically, a robot with only necessary degrees of freedom is realized and commercially available endoscope equipment are used for System A and joystick interface is used for System B in most evaluations. In Fig. 2, a loop ($Loop_{SAB}$) of "surgeon → System A → System B → surgeon" interaction is built between an endoscope robot and the surgeon. That is, an endoscope robot is treated as a part of the interactive media. In the endoscope robot, a surgeon works on System A (intention), System A receives the intention from the surgeon and outputs a control signal (intention) to System B. As a result, System B is properly controlled and sends new information to the surgeon. Hence, surgeons can "expand their human abilities" through this interactive media. "Intention" means information to make an effect on items sent and received. We call mutual information flow between humans and the system which is performed to expand human abilities as an interaction loop. Proper information flow in the interaction loop establishes a strong link between humans and robots, resulting in cooperative work between humans and robots more efficient than that between humans and humans.

There is a loop ($Loop_{SPB}$) of "surgeon → patient → System B → surgeon" in Fig. 2. This loop is an interaction loop between surgeons and patients through systems (System B) such as manipulators. Analysis of this interaction loop enables evaluation of surgery or robots.

This chapter focuses on $Loop_{SAB}$ for endoscope robot design methods and on $Loop_{SPB}$ for their evaluation methods.

2. Classification of endoscope robots

Table 1 and Fig. 3 demonstrate classification results of the following 27 kinds of endoscope robots which are commercialized or published in article for referee reading as of September 2009: a) A460 CRS Plus (Hurteau et al., 1994), b)AESOP™ (Sackier & Wang, 1994), c)LARS(Taylor et al., 1995), d)EndoAssist™ (Endosista) (Finlay, 2001), e)Staubli Rx60(Munoz et al., 2000), f)ERM(Munoz et al., 2005), g)LapMan(Polet & Donnez, 2004), h)RES(Mizhuno, 1995), i)Naviot™ (Kobayashi et al., 1999, Tanoue et al., 2006), j)PASEO(Nishikawa et al., 2003), k)HISAR(Funda et al., 1995), l)ViKY(LER)(EndoControl, 2009, Long et al., 2007), m)5-DOFs Laparoscopic Assistant Robot(KaLAR) (Lee et al., 2003), n)FIPS(Buess et al.,2000), o)Imag Trac(Kimura et al., 2000), p)Wide-Angle View Endoscope(Kobayashi et al., 2004), q)Dual-View Endoscopic System(Yamauchi et al., 2002), r)Automatic Tracking And Zooming System(Nakaguchi et al., 2005), s)COVER(Taniguchi et al., 2006), t)P-arm(Sekimoto et al., 2009), u)Free hand(Prosurgics, 2009), v) Robolens (Sarkaret al., 2009), w)Swarup Robotic Arm (SWARM) (Deshpande, 2004), x)MST Laparoscope Manipulator(Szold et al., 2008, NGT, 2009), y)ROBOX(Rininsland, 1999, KIT, 2009, FZK, 2009), z) FELIX (Rininsland, 1999, FZK, 2009), aa) Paramis (Graur et al., 2009).

Endoscope robots are treated as interactive media described in the previous section and separated by $Loop_{SAB}$ and $Loop_{SPB}$. For $Loop_{SAB}$, a human machine interface was examined for System A and a manipulator was examined for System B. Table 1 demonstrates the results of the human machine interface and Fig. 3 indicates the manipulator.

	Loop SAB	Loop SPB
	System A	
a) A460CRS Plus	Remote hand switch	Human
b) AESOP™	Voice recognition, remote hand switch, foot pedal	Product
c) LARS	Tool mounted switch	Animal
d) EndoAssist™ (Endosista)	Head control	Human
e) Staubli Rx60	Voice recognition	Animal
f) ERM	Voice recognition	Human
g) LapMan	Tool mounted switch	Product
h) RES	Head control, equipment tracking , hand and foot switches	Model
i) Naviot™	Tool mounted switch, head pose	Product
j) PASEO	Face gesture	Animal
k) HISAR	Tool mounted switch	Model
l) ViKY(LER)	voice recognition, foot control	Human
m)5-DOFs Laparoscopic Assistant Robot(KaLAR)	Voice, equipment tracking	Animal
n) FIPS endoarm	Tool mounted switch, voice recognition	Model
o) I magTrac	Tool mounted switch, voice recognition	Human
p) Wide-Angle View Endoscope	Remote hand switch	Animal
q) Dual-View Endoscopic System	Remote hand switch	Animal
r) Automatic Traking And Zooming System	Automatic tracking	Animal
s) COVER	Face gesture	Animal
t) P-arm	Joystick, automatic operation, touch screen, voice recognition	Animal
u) FreeHand	Head pose	Product
v) Robolens	Voice recognition	Human
w) Swarup Robotic Arm (SWARM)	Remote controller	Human
x) MST Laparoscope Manipulator	Equipment tracking	Animal
y) ROBOX	Voice recognition, mouse, foot pedal, Equipment tracking	Human
z) FELIX	Voice recognition	Model
aa) Paramis	Voice recognition	Model

Table 1. Classification results of endoscope robots and human machine interface

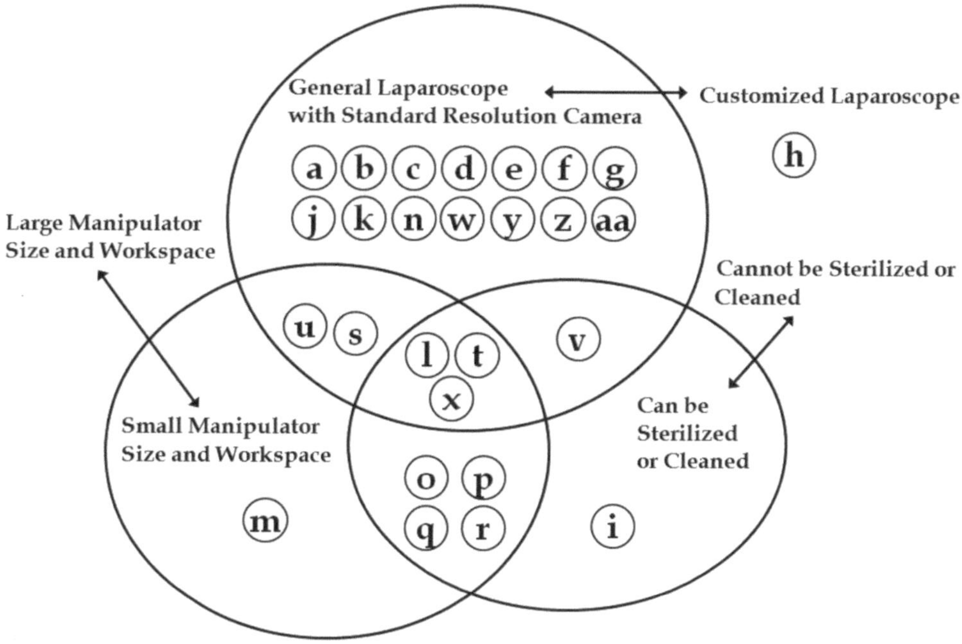

Fig. 3. Classification results of characteristics of endoscope robots and manipulation: A)A460 CRS Plus, b)AESOP, c)LARS, d)EndoAssist(Endosista), e)Staubli Rx60, f)ERM, g)LapMan, h)RES, i)Naviot, j)PASEO, k)HISAR, l) ViKY(LER),m)5-DOFs Laparoscopic Assistant Robot(KaLAR), n)FIPS, o)Imag Trac, p)Wide-Angle View Endoscope , q)Dual-View Endoscopic System, r) Automatic Tracking And Zooming System, s)COVER, t)P-arm, u)FreeHand, v) Robolens, w)Swarup Robotic Arm (SWARM) , x)MST Laparoscope Manipulator, y)ROBOX, z) FELIX , aa) Paramis

Among "safety", "compact and lightweight", "cleanliness" and "usability: popular general endoscopes can be used" which are required on the medical front, "safety" should be independently discussed as a necessary condition for a medical robot; therefore, System B of each endoscope robot is classified according to "compact and lightweight", "cleanliness" and "usability". The definition of "compact and lightweight" is that a manipulator is attached with a general-purpose endoscope holder or an endoscope and manipulator are combined. The definition of "cleanliness" is that the endoscope robot parts which are used in clean fields can be sterilized. Robots that maintain cleanliness using a sterilized drape is classified as unclean. The most popular general endoscopes are OLYMPUS and KARL STORZ, which are commercially available. Table 1 also shows the subject of endoscope robots of $Loop_{SPB}$. We examined whether each endoscope robot has been commercialized, whether an endoscope robot is used in human surgery, whether an endoscope robot is used only on animals, whether an endoscope robot is used only in *in-vitro* experiment or whether an endoscope robot model has been completed and has not been evaluated. We described them as product, human being, animal and model respectively in the table. Fig. 3 shows that endoscope robots satisfying all items are l) ViKY(LER), t)P-arm ,and x)MST Laparoscope Manipulator only. Endoscope robots satisfying two out of three items of "compact and lightweight", "cleanliness" and "usability" are o)Imag Trac, p)Wide-Angle View Endoscope , q)Dual- View Endoscopic System, r) Automatic Tracking And Zooming System, s)COVER, and u)FreeHand. A special endoscope for robots are used in o)Imag Trac, p)Wide-Angle View Endoscope, q)Dual-View Endoscopic System and high resolution CCD camera with a resolution of one million pixel (general pixel is four hundred thousand) is used in r) Automatic Tracking And Zooming System.

3. Design of endoscope robots and implementation examples

This section describes specificity of endoscope robots and required items for endoscope robots based on specificity. Examples of endoscope robots developed based on the required items are desmonstrated. Design of endoscope robots is design of $Loop_{SAB}$ shown in Fig. 2. Information that surgeons output to System A feeds back to surgeons from System B in the form of image taken by the endoscope. A variety of useful systems have been developed for System A of an endoscope robot with remote control techniques, voice recognition, and image processing technology.In contrast, the development for System B has been slow due to the complication of the system with regard to specificity of purpose and the extensive contact it is required to have with patients on the medical front. This section explains System B, especially manupulator design.

3.1 Specificity of endoscope robots

Industrial robots operate under environments where the robots are isolated from humans; however, endoscope robots support surgery coming in contact with patients while the robots and surgeons closely interact. Industrial robots perform work which has been planned in advance under a closed, unvaring environment; however, endoscope robots are used for surgery in the medical front with high entoropy, where mistakes or failures are unacceptable. In addition, even though the surgery methods may be the same, the surgery contents vary in each case since the patients having the surgery vary. Hence, required items for robots of industry and endoscope robots are entirely different. Robots for industry required "high power", "high speed" and "high accuracy". Endoscope robots requires "safety" and "cleaness" since the robots come into physically contact with humans.

Upon designing robots, which work with humans, such as endoscope robots, "robot physical ability" and "robot computational ability" are points for designing the robots. It is necessary to design robots which have enough physical and computational abilities (artificial intelligence) to work with humans. To design a robot which does the housework including cleaning, washing or cooking, very high physical ability and computational ability are necessary for the robot. Physical and computational abilities of endoscope robots can be limited since the robots work with surgeons who have high intelligence for special tasks under special environments. A study group of Nishikawa et al. described before, have given much attention to interaction between humans and robots and realized the automatic operation of endoscope robots (Nishikawa et al., 2006, Nishikawa et al., 2008). For automation, Nishikawa analyzed the relatonship between endoscope images and surgical instruments in actual surgeries, and invented simple computation algorithms for endoscope robots specialized for specific tasks, without attempting to create endoscope robots that could understand the flow of the surgery, context of procedures or reasons behind actions. This algorithm has been designed focusing on the expansion of the ability of surgeons, and has obtained high reliability with introducing the concept of "fluctuation" as a characteristics of living bodies. This can be a good example of information in an interacton loop being optimized between the surgeons and the endoscope robots. To design endoscope robots, it is important to consider the specificity of the endoscope robots and optimize $Loop_{SAB}$ interaction.

3.2 Required items for endoscope robots

Necessary elements for the construction of endoscope robots are broken into "required items", "basic items" and "enhancement items". The required items are necessary conditions for the endoscope robots. The basic items are strongly influential in the basic concepts of endoscope robots, and enhancement items are items that provide additional functions to the endoscope robots.

3.2.1 Required items

The required items are degree of freedom necessary for endoscope operations and safety as a medical equipment. It cannot be called an endoscope robot unless required items are met. First of all, we will describe degree of freedom. As shown in Fig. 4, since an endoscope operation during surgery is performed with insertion / retraction of an endoscope, roll around the insertion direction, and pitch and yaw based on the insertion site, the necessary degree of freedom for endoscope robots are four degrees of freedom. Roll is used to correct the top and bottom of image for direct-viewing endoscope and to observe the back of the organs for a oblique-viewing endoscope. Roll is not always necessary in surgery which targets narrow operation fields such as laparoscopic cholecystectomy. Among robots developed for the purpose of compact and to be lightweight, robots (Taniguchi et al., 2006) with three degrees of freedom with pitch, yaw and inserting, excluding roll, have been developed under conditions where the surgery target positions are limited. Degree of freedom as well as safety are the most important items for design of System B.

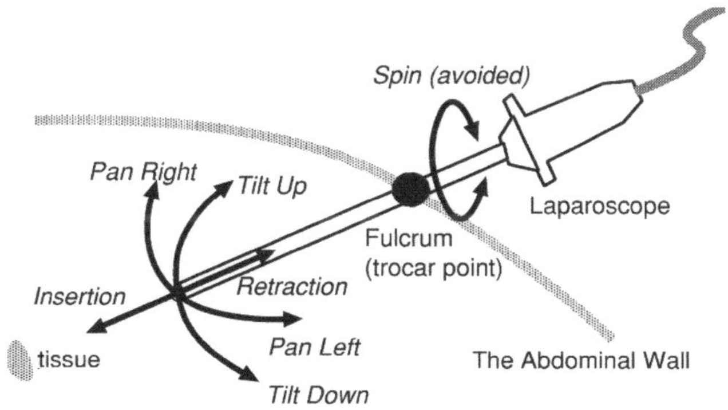

Fig. 4. Movement of endoscope: Since the endoscope is limited due to the insertion site, the endoscope has four degrees of freedom.

Next, we will describe safety. Suggestions on the safe use of medical robots include suggestions by Leveson et al (Leveson & Turner, 1993) learn from "Therac-25 accidents" and suggestions (Taylor & Stoianovici, 2003) by Taylor et al. Referring to the suggestions, we have the following points for securing safety when using endoscope robots.

- It is essential to secure mechanistic safety, and furthermore, the safety is secured by a control program (software) .
- Several completely independent safety devices are used.

- While endoscope robots are being developed, documents are created and managed, and examinations are steadfastly performed and discussed with the results being thoroughly managed. The quality of the products is fastidiously managed.
- Several emergency cease functions are equipped. The emergency cease functions shall be installed at positions where the surgeons or nurses can immediately stop a endoscope robot.
- Considering the environment where medical staff will use the robots, clinicians, medical staff, medical device manufacturers and engineers, in coordination, assess the risks. Opinions from the related meetings are emphasized.
- The systems are designed so that surgeons can respond to stalled or runaway endoscope robots due to robot failure or dramatic environment changes, such as natural disasters, including earthquakes.

Mechanisms to secure the above safety are equipped with System A and System B separately and each relationship shall be clarified.

When study phases progress and practical use of endoscope robots is aimed at, it is necessary to comply with international standards including ISO and IEC on safety and JIS, Europe and U.S.A standards.

The methods to secure safety of endoscope robots which are being studied and developed are described below. AESOP, which were commercialized in the 90's and have been used worldwide, uses two control safety securing methods, "low limit setting" and "control disable function". The low limit setting is a function to secure safety, in which the lowest descendent position of a robot arm is set before surgery and the software controls the arm so it will not descend below the position crushing a patient's body during surgery. The control disable function stops the arm movement when the patient moves, stress is applied to the arm movement, or the magnet for installing the endoscope is dislocated when something hits the tip of the endoscope or shear stress is applied to the endoscope installation portion of the arm. AESOP is safety managed by a control program and mechanical safety is not secured. In addition, safety mechanism of System A and System B is not independent and we judge that safety is not sufficiently secured. Next, we will describe how to secure safety for Naviot™. As methods to secure mechanical safety, "optical zoom mechanism", "five joints link mechanism" and "limitation of degree of freedom" are introduced. In addition, the safety for System A and System B is completely independent. The optical zoom mechanism does not have a direct acting movement toward the interperitoneal direction by endoscopes and there is no possibility of interference with organs. The driving range of five link mechanisms is mechanically limited. Even when the endoscope robots malfunction or operate incorrectly, the robots do not move violently, the upper space of the abdominal cavity is secured and the surgery field is not interrupted. Limiting the degree of freedom and simplifying mechanisms cause less malfunction or incorrect movements. To secure control safety, a "status monitor function" is equipped. This function has function checkout functions before surgery and emergency cease functions when an overload (interference between patients or medical staff and robots) is observed during surgery. In addition, Naviot™ has a measure against electric insulation and an emergency cease switch. With all things considered, it is very safe. Many endoscope robots have been studied and developed, some of which do not secure sufficient safety; only mechanical safety is secured by processing values of a pressure sensor with software, or, only a degree of freedom around the insertion site is mechanically realized, resulting in insufficient safety.

3.2.2 Basic items

The basic items include the dimension of the endoscope robot, methods to secure cleanliness, installation methods and the kinds of endoscopes used. Determining these items lead to determine concepts of endoscope robots, especially in System B. Changing the basic items often leads to changing the basic structure of System B of an endoscope robot. Changing the basic items makes an endoscope robot totally different. First of all, the dimension of endoscope robots is described. In Japan, development of compact and lightweight robots is popular. Compact and lightweight endoscope robots have advantages, such as they can be easily installed, cleanliness can be easily secured or it does not interrupt the surgery. Next, installation area of endoscope robots is described. There are four areas to be installed, the floor near a surgical table in the operating room, hanging from the ceiling near the surgical table, on the surgical table or on the abdomen of the patient. In many studies, the endoscope robot is installed on the floor of the operating room or on the surgical table. Efficiency when an endoscope robot is installed on the abdomen of the patient has been studied recently. It is better to discuss installation positions and installation methods of an endoscope manipulator while considering that a surgical table height or slant is sometimes adjusted during surgery. Then, a method to secure cleanliness is described. There are two kinds of methods to secure cleanliness of the endoscope robots, one of which is to cover the endoscope robot with a sterilized drape and the other is to sterilize only the mechanism used in the clean fields.

A sterilized drape may tear during surgery due to the robot's movement. Covering the robot with a sterilized drape would be a big burden to medical staff. Finally, the kinds of endoscopes used are described. Either commercially available endoscopes or endoscopes developed for a specified endoscope robot are used. We think the former is preferable. Compared to the ones developed for endoscope robots, it is better to use economic and high image quality endoscopes appropriate for the medical front which has been developed by endoscope manufacturers, and apply them to the endoscope robots. This has the advantage when the endoscopes are comprehensively evaluated from a point of view of cleanliness, economic efficiency and securing stability of the field of view.

3.2.3 Enhancement items

Enhancement items include easy installation, re-installation and removal of endoscope robots, high availability (troubleproof), easy operation and easy installation and removal of endoscopes during surgery. Easy installation, re-installation and removal of endoscope robots mean easy preparation for surgery and clean up, leading to improved safety. When emergency situations such as the failure of an endoscope robot, occurs, it is preferable that the endoscope robot is rapidly removed from the operation field and the surgery can be switched to traditional abdominal surgery. Since it takes time to install large endoscope robots and which need sterilization drapes, the dimension of endoscope robots or methods to secure cleanliness influences the ease of installation, re-installation and removal of endoscope robots.

It is necessary to clean the lens at the tip of an endoscope several times during surgery because of blood, mists or tarnish. A function that the endoscope can be easily installed or removed to or from the robot is important to secure stable field of view. A human camera assistant can clean the lens of an endoscope for 20 sec. during surgery; therefore, the same performance is required for endoscope robots.

Operability of endoscope robots depends on System A. To avoid malfunctions it is preferable that System A with which surgeons directly give instructions to the robots, can be viscerally operated and can operate endoscope robots freely without using major equipment. The key to optimize $Loop_{SAB}$ is enhancement items of System A.
It is preferable that endoscope robots be designed considering affordance and the directions on how to use the endoscope, be quickly and easily understood. It is also preferable that special training or skills are not necessary to use endoscope robots and people using them for the first time can use them easily.

3.2.4 Others

The endoscope robots shall be designed so as not to be regarded as an alternative to the human camera assistant, but as an expansion of the surgeon's skill. The surgeons should be made to feel comfortable; reassuring them that they will always be in control of the robots. It is necessary that surgeons viscerally understand all movement of the robots.
Finally, it is understood that developing endoscope robots is not to imitate the hand movements of surgeons. The work done by surgeons follows the hand movement of humans; movement that is not suitable for robots. Upon developing endoscope robots, the goals shall be correctly specified, considering the optimized mechanism, or optimized system to obtain the goals and how to optimize each interaction group ($Loop_{SAB}$ and $Loop_{SPB}$).

3.3 Implementation example of endoscope robot

This section describes P-arm (disposable endoscope positioning robot) that we developed as an implementation example of endoscope robots.

3.3.1 Basic concepts

We mainly focus on "safety", "cleanliness" and "usability" and have defined the basic concept of endoscope robots as follows:

- The robots are equipped with a mechanism that if the endoscope robot, coming into contact with patients or doctors, applies a force that may cause harm, a structure that joins of the mechanism manipulator is dislocated and the force is mechanically released. Even if the joints of the manipulator are dislocated, the endoscope can be positioned (safety).
- Parts that operate in clean fields shall be disposable. Disposable parts enable "secure cleanliness" and "warranty of quality of endoscope robots". Since maintenance is unnecessary, inconvenience to the medical front can be reduced (cleanliness) (quality: safety).
- Endoscope robots shall be compact and lightweight. Endoscope robots shall weight less than the endoscopes (usability).
- Endoscope robots are mounted on the surgical table. A mechanism which can freely change endoscope robots' position and posture on a surgical table according to surgical targets is equipped (usability).
- Generally commercially available endoscopes (direct-view endoscope and oblique-viewing endoscope) can be operated (usability).

The critical matter of having endoscope robots that can be disposable is dependent upon the economic efficiency of the endoscope robots. Disposable endoscope robots require that they can be manufactured at a competitive cost. As a method to realize endoscope robots manufacture at a competitive cost, we decided that "the interface and control equipment of the endoscope robots shall be used repeatedly, and the manipulators used in the clean fields, are to be disposed of after each surgery".

3.3.2 Mechanism of endoscope robot

Fig. 5 shows the endoscope robot that we developed. System A of this robot is composed of a joystick interface and controller (control equipment). System B is composed of a disposable manipulator and general endoscopic device. The disposable parts are the manipulator, the tube and cylinder which send water to an actuator shown in Fig. 6. Since this endoscope robot was developed while System B was studied and developed, the joystick interface was used as a human machine interface so that System B could be easily evaluated and discussed. Human machine interfaces of this robot include automatic operation, voice recognition and a touch screen. Their explanation will be omitted.

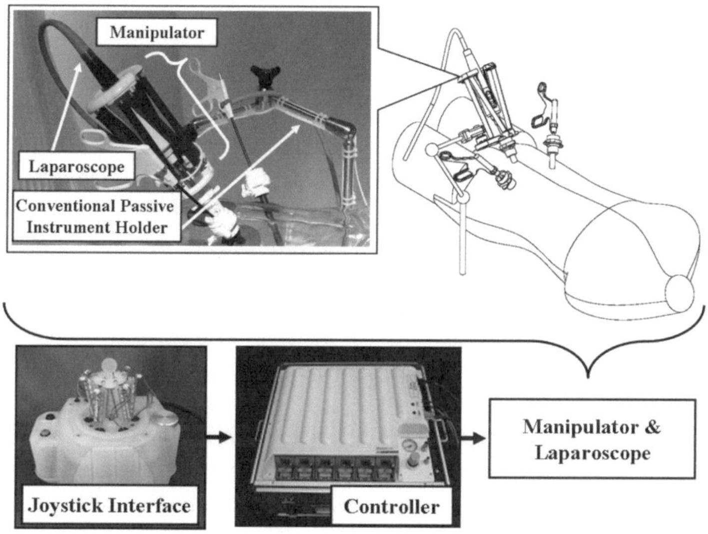

Fig. 5. System configuration

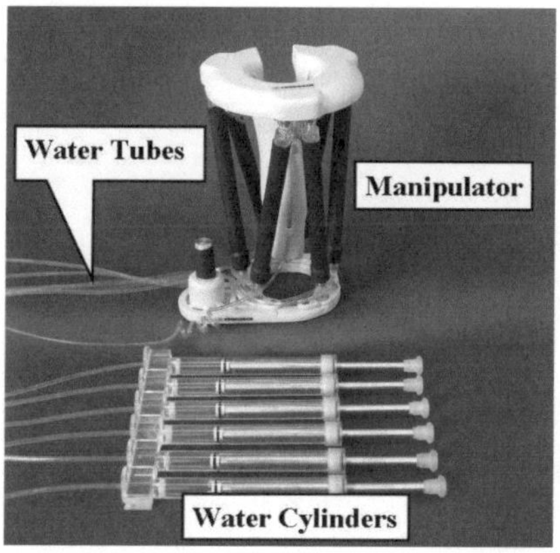

Fig. 6. Disposable part

In our endoscope robot, the manipulator is composed of the Stewart-Gough Platform (six degrees of freedom parallel mechanism) (Tsai, 1999) and a linear actuator we developed and which can be sterilized is used for each element of the parallel mechanism. Our endoscope robot uses redundant six degrees of freedom. There have been some opinions that redundant degrees of freedom are unnecessary from the point of view of safety. This is because the runaway of a controller leads to unexpected movement of a manipulator since many of the endoscope robots developed so far use a serial mechanism or parallel linkage mechanism. Even if one of the actuators goes out of control, the parallel mechanism can suppress the runaway actuator with the other actuators; therefore, redundant degree of freedom will lead to safety. Hence, we selected six degrees of freedom of parallel mechanism focusing on safety. The parallel mechanism uses a smaller space with movement and can be more compact, trimmed weight and simplified, causing low cost compared to the serial mechanism when a tool (including an endoscope) operates in the narrow space such as in the human abdomen. Although high speed and accuracy are noticeable advantages in the parallel mechanism, we pay more attention to safety than high speed or high accuracy.

To enhance ease of installing the endoscope robot, we used a method where it can be installed to the surgical bed using a general abdominoscope holding arm which surgeons are familiar with, instead of using an installation table exclusively for endoscope robots. The advantages to this method are that medical staffs do not have to learn or have training on a new installation method and the endoscope robots can be easily installed or re-installed. Since the existing arm is used, development cost can be reduced, resulting in a competitive cost.

As a method for attaching the endoscope to the manipulator, we developed a way by using a permanent magnet. This method enables the endoscope to be installed during surgery and then, to possibly be removed during the same surgery, for cleaning the lens of the endoscope, resulting in securing the stability of the field of view (Fig.7).

We have developed a medical-use hydraulic disposable linear actuator for endoscope robots. Since this actuator can be sterilized and is disposable, it can be used in clean fields of surgery, without previous sterilizating. This actuator, supplying air of 0.4MPa from the tube to the actuator, applies force to a direction where an actuator is stretched continuously and the water is sent from the cylinder or pump installed outside of the clean field through the tube. Consequently the amount of the water pressure is controlled to shrink the actuator. It

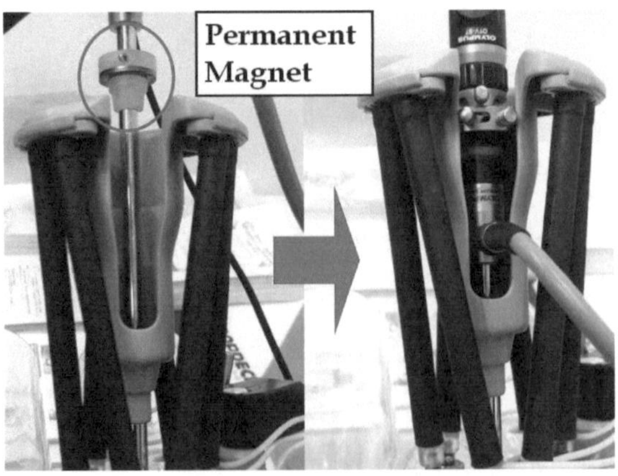

Fig. 7. Endoscope installation and removal mechanism using a permanent magnet

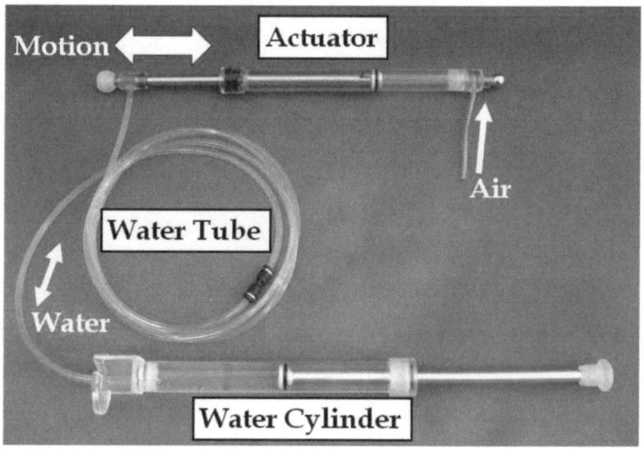

Fig. 8. Hydraulic linear actuator

is completely safe as there is no possibility of ground leakage in the clean field. This actuator measures 185.0 mm in length and 112.5 mm in amount of extension. This actuator maximally stretches when no control is applied to the cylinder (Fig. 8). When it is mounted in a robot, an endoscope is outstretched when no control or setting is performed (default) to the robot. Before surgery, a site for an endoscope is made on the patient's body, an endoscope is inserted into the site and the internal cavity is surveyed with the widest vision; therefore, providing a wide vision as a default can make settings easier and more efficient. Since force is applied to a direction where the endoscope is kept away from viscera, safety is improved.

As described above, the parallel mechanism is very safe. There is no chance of electrification and force is applied to a direction where an endoscope is kept away from the viscera all the time, resulting in extreme safety. As a method to improve the safety of an endoscope further, "shock absorber" and "up to three emergency stop switches" are added. The shock absorber, a permanent magnet spherical bearing is used for connection between the end plate of the manipulator and each actuator. This disconnects the actuators from the endplate and absorbs the shock when an endoscope interferes with organs or the manipulator contacts with a doctor (Fig.9). Since the endoscope robot has redundant six degrees of freedom, four degrees of freedom necessary for the endoscope operation is secured even though up to two actuators are dislocated. Actuators dislocated due to shock can be re-installed at the original position with a single movement due to the permanent magnet spherical bearing. As independent and different systems, three emergency stop devices can be installed. We prepared two kinds of emergency stop devices. One of them is a push-button type installed near the joystick and is used when a camera assistant performs an emergency stop. The other one are foot pedals installed under the foot of the surgeon and assistant. Either of them could operate in case of emergency.

Each parameter of the manipulator is described below. These parameters are set for laparoscopic cholecystectomy.

- Dimension: Base plate radius: 48.5 mm, end plate radius: 63.75 mm, height when all actuators contract: 207 mm
- Weight: About 580 g (The weight of endoscope and camera is not included.)
- Movement: Insertion/retraction: 112.5 mm, movable maximum range: 26 deg
- Movement speed of actuators: 8 mm/sec at a maximum

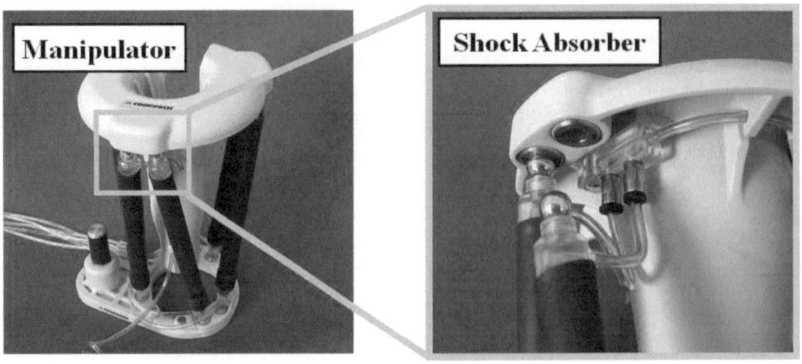

Fig. 9. Shock Absorber

4. Evaluation methods of endoscope robots

4.1 Evaluation methods of endoscope robots

Endoscope robots are evaluated using the information flow of $Loop_{SAB}$ and $Loop_{SPB}$ shown in Fig. 2. At the design stage, $Loop_{SAB}$ is evaluated and $Loop_{SPB}$ is mainly evaluated for test models. At this stage, the evaluation of each system in the $Loop_{SAB}$ is important and it is necessary to evaluate surgery results while facing up patients in the $Loop_{SPB}$ during the test model stages. For $Loop_{SPB}$, information quality, information density, the period when information is output, stability of the Loop, each element of the surgeons, patients and manipulators are evaluated. Information quality indicates the image quality taken by the endoscope, information density indicates the range of the field of view, and the period when the information is output means the surgery time. The state of the surgeons is evaluated by the psychological stress of the surgeons who use the robot. The state of the patients is evaluated by the degree of perfection of the surgery and the state of manipulators is evaluated by the amount of space occupied for movement and the operation experiments over a long period of time.

The followings are details of experiments of test models of endoscope robots with attention to information flow and their evaluation.

- *in-vitro* experiments using animals or human organs: Whether or not the range of the field of view of the endoscope robots (operation range) is sufficient is evaluated. Also, in order to check whether or not the manipulators will obstruct the movement of the surgeons during surgery, the amount of space used when the manipulators operate is evaluated. In addition, the psychological stress of the surgeons who use endoscope robots is evaluated. In this experiment, the evaluation standard is if endoscope robots can be used for laparoscopic cholecystectomy. Surgery time and degree of perfection of the surgery are also evaluated. Pig livers with cholecyst are mainly used in this experiment (amount, quality and period of information and each element).
- *in-vivo* experiment using animals: Details of the evaluation is the same as in *in-vitro* experiments where animals or human organs are used. In these experiment, fluctuation due to bleeding or breathing, particular to a living body, which cannot be evaluated in *in-vitro* experiment are evaluated (amount, quality and period of information and each element)
- Clinical test: Comprehensive evaluation is performed using endoscope robots for laparoscopic cholecystectomy of a human patient (amount, quality and period of information, each element).

- Operation experiments over a long period of time: Durability of endoscope robots is evaluated. As an index time for the extensive operation experiment, we set the duration length, for three times the length of time that a manipulator is continuously used without maintenance (each element).
- Setup experiment: To evaluate if $Loop_{SPB}$ is easily constructed, the length of time for endoscope robot setup is evaluated. Whether medical staff who are using the endoscope robots for the first time can easily set up the robot without error is also evaluated (Loop stability)
- Endoscope lens cleaning experiment: Quality or stability of information in the $Loop_{SPB}$ depends on the cleanliness of the endoscope's lens. During *in-vitro* or *in-vivo* experiments, the time required for cleaning the endoscope lens and how easily the lens can be cleaned is evaluated. The index time for cleaning is 20 sec (quality and stability of information)
- Correspondence experiment in emergencies: Assuming emergency situations such as an endoscope robot becoming out of control, the time required to switch from the surgery using the endoscope robot to surgery without the endoscope robot being used including halting and removal of the endoscope robot is evaluated (Loop stability).
- Evaluation of cleanliness of the endoscope robots: Quality of cleanliness is evaluated after cleaning or sterilization (each element)

For evaluation of $Loop_{SAB}$, the strength of the endoscope robots, the operation range, the space required to operate the manipulators and the accuracy of movement with the human interface are evaluated during computer simulations at the design stages.
The details of each evaluation methods are described below.

4.2 *in-vitro* experiment using pig livers with a cholecyst

Laparoscopic cholecystectomy is normally used to evaluate endoscope robots [Yen et al., 2006, FDA, 2006]. This experiment frequently uses pig organs, not human organs. There are problems in ethical issues when human organs are used and pig organs have a relatively similar structure to human organs anatomically. This experiment simulates the environment by using a liver with a cholecyst to reproduce pseudo *in-vivo* environment and laparoscopic cholecystectomy where the cholecyst is removed from the liver. The experiment is performed in two cases where a camera assistant operates an endoscope and where a robot operates an endoscope and the results are compared. Livers equal to three times the number of experiments are prepared. Among the livers, the ones whose shapes and level of difficulty of surgery are similar are selected. The livers are placed in a surgery training box where an abdominal cavity is simulated to reproduce pseudo *in-vivo* environment. As examples, Fig. 10 shows an *in-vitro* experiment using a pig organ with P-arm as an endoscope robot and Fig. 11 shows an example of the device installation.
Next, specific details of evaluation are described.

- Whether images taken by an endoscope operated by a robot provides the same range of images as those taken by an endoscope operated by a camera assistant is evaluated. We aim at there being no difference in the images taken by endoscopes operated by robots and those operated by camera assistants. Surgeons evaluate whether there is no essential difference in a scale of enlargement of the image taken by endoscopes, the range of field of view and the angle of view for the surgery. Cholecystectomy is separated into three phases, bile duct treatment, cholecyst (body area) removal and treatment of the bottom of the cholecyst. Fig. 12 shows images taken by an endoscope in each phase during the experiment.

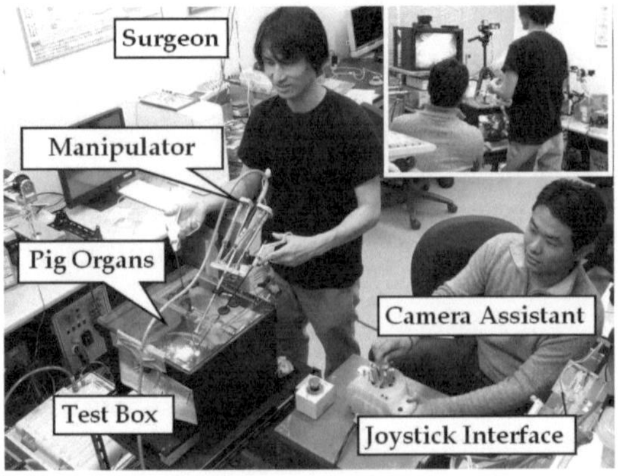

Fig. 10. *in-vitro* experiment

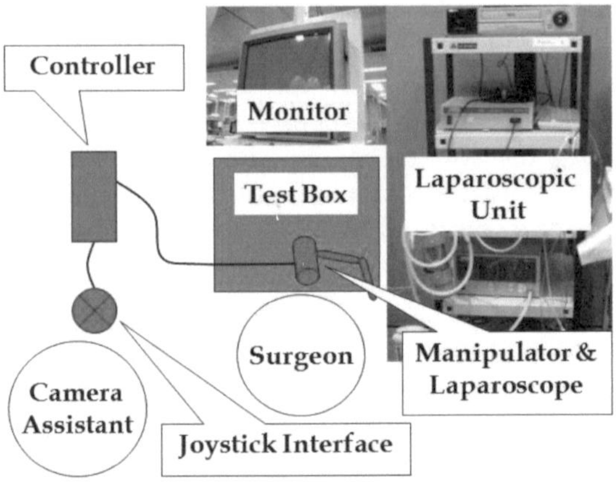

Fig. 11. Installation of devices in *in-vitro* experiment

(a) (b) (c)

Fig. 12. Images taken by an endoscope during *in-vitro* experiment: a) Bile duct treatment, b) cholecyst (body area) removal, c) treatment of the bottom of the cholecyst

- Whether the space occupied by the manipulators obstructs the surgery or not is evaluated. Surgeons operate while they watch a monitor where the images are taken by an endoscope. If manipulators widely move and obstruct the hands of the surgeons, it is difficult for the surgeons to know the movement of the manipulators in advance. Manipulators and the hands of the surgeons are videoed during this experiment to make sure that there is no interference. After the experiment, we investigate whether the manipulators had interrupted the surgeons with questionnaires.

- Surgeons compare cases where the camera assistant operates the endoscope and where the robot operates the endoscope and evaluate whether the operation of an endoscope by the robot is not inferior to that of the camera assistant. Surgeons also evaluate the degree of perfection of the surgery.
- Surgeons' psychological stress during the experiment is measured when a camera assistant operates the endoscope and when a robot operates the endoscope. Whether surgeons have psychological stress or not by using an endoscope robot during surgery is objectively evaluated. The stress is measured using surgeons' salivary component and acceleration pulse wave. To evaluate whether surgeons are subjected to psychological stress due to the use of an endoscope robot during surgery, surgeons' saliva and acceleration pulse wave before and after surgery are measured. Then, they are analyzed and evaluated. Saliva cortisol and saliva α amylase are measured. The details are in a chapter of the In-Tech book"Advances in Human-Robot Interaction" (Taniguchi et al., 2009) for reference.

4.3 *in-vivo* experiment using a pig

Efficiency of endoscope robots are evaluated by performing a laparoscopic cholecystectomy on a pig based on problems including bleeding or fluctuation due to the patient's breathing, which is particular to living bodies. It is better to evaluate laparoscopic assisted distal gastrectomy and laparoscopic anterior resection as an advance surgery which needs a wide range of view. These procedures require a wide operation range and do not use endoscope robots since endoscope robots will interrupt surgery unless they are compact. As an example, Fig. 13 shows an *in-vivo* experiment where a pig is used and P-arm is used as an endoscope robot and Fig. 14 shows the installation location of devices. This laparoscopic cholecystectomy started when a trocar was placed on an anesthetized pig and cholecystectomy was performed and ended when the insertion site was sutured. The process during surgery was the insertion of an endoscope, adjustment of the range of view, movement of the field of view and removal of the cholecyst (gallbladder). Fig. 13 shows an *in-vivo* experiment with one surgeon and one camera assistant and a fixing supporting arm is used to hold the liver instead of a surgery assistant.

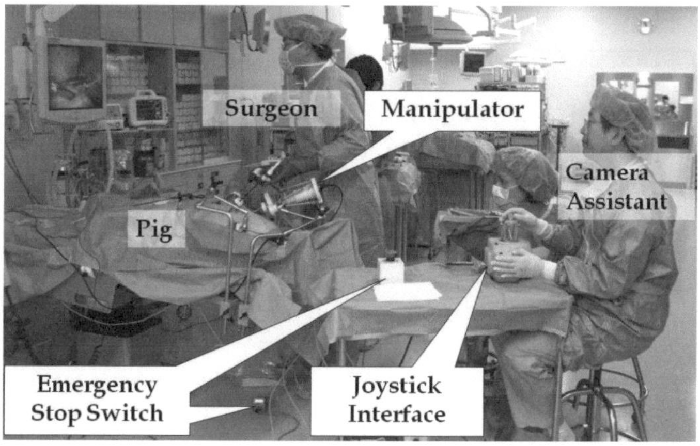

Fig. 13. *in-vivo* experiment

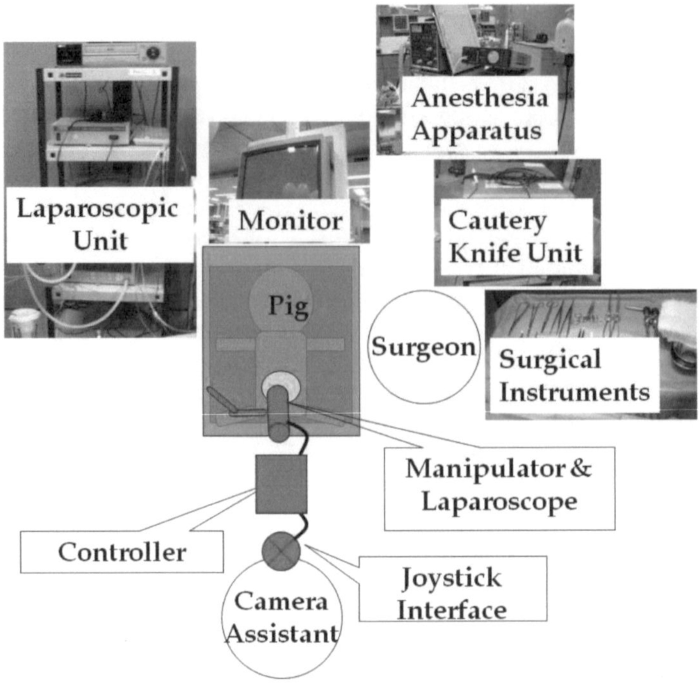

Fig. 14. Device installation for *in-vivo* experiment

Evaluation items for this experiment are the same in the *in-vitro* experiment using a pig liver with cholecyst described in section 4.2. The time for surgery to be measured is from when surgery started with the forceps inserted into the abdominal cavity to when the cholecyst is removed outside of the abdominal cavity (including robot setup time).

Fig. 15 shows images of bile duct treatment, cholecyst (body area) removal and removal of the bottom of cholecyst taken by an endoscope. Surgeons evaluate scale of enlargement, angle of field of view and range of view necessary for cholecystectomy.

Fig. 16 shows images of laparoscopic assisted distal gastrectomy taken by an endoscope. Fig.17 shows laparoscopic anterior resection. The number from 1 to 9 in Fig. 16 and 17 indicates progress of procedures.

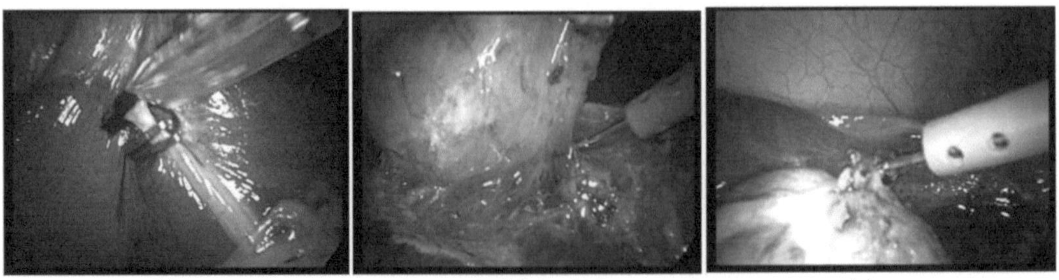

(a) (b) (c)

Fig. 15. Images taken by an endoscope during *in-vivo* experiment A)Laparoscopic image of the bile duct in an experiment, b)Laparoscopic image of the body of gallbladder in an experiment , c)Laparoscopic image of the fundus of gallbladder in an experiment

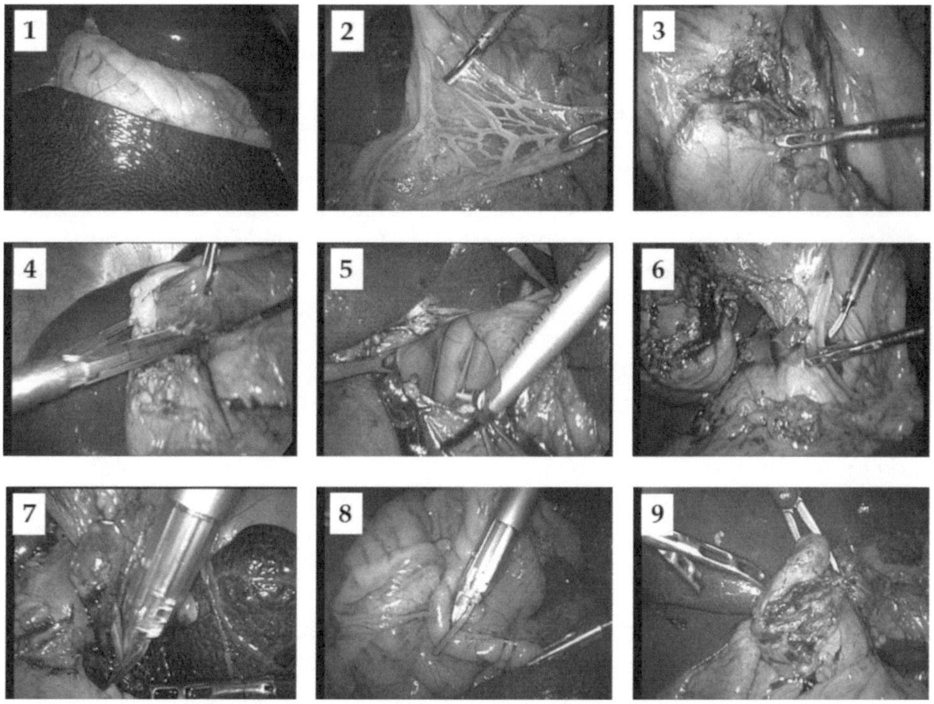

Fig. 16. Laparoscopic image of laparoscopic assisted distal gastrectomy (LADG)

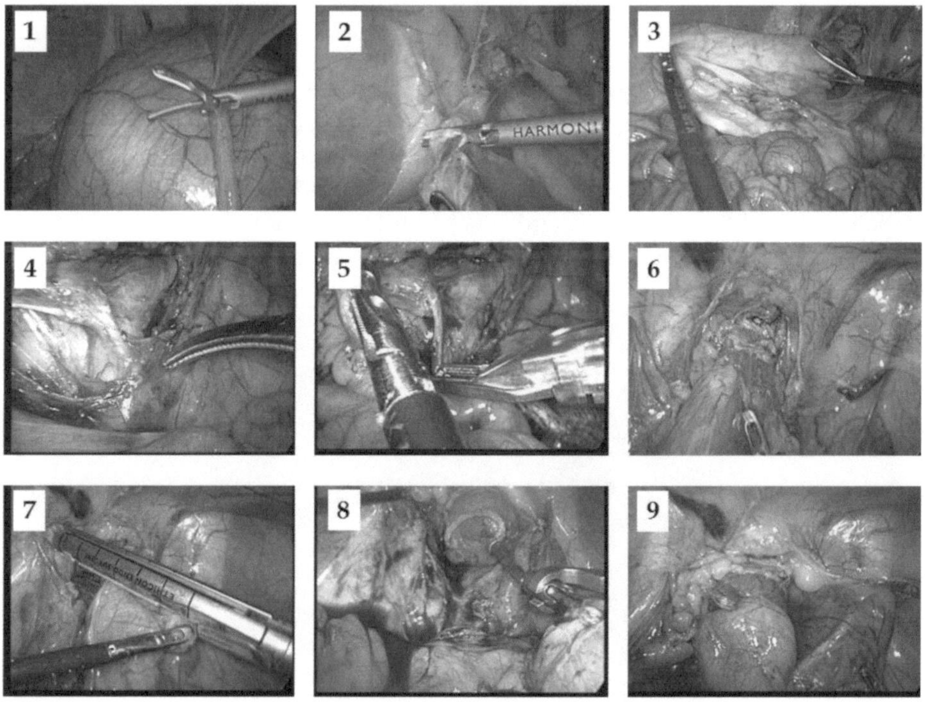

Fig. 17. Laparoscopic image of laparoscopic low anterior resection

4.4 Robot setting experiment, switching experiment from endoscope robot operation to manual operation assuming emergencies such as failure of a robot, endoscope lens cleaning experiment

Details of evaluation items on $Loop_{SPB}$ stability and quality of information are described below.

- Robot setting experiment: The time it takes the surgeons to install the manipulator to the surgical table, the endoscope to the manipulator, and the endoscope to be positioned, is measured. This experiment is performed several times and the learning curve is analyzed and evaluated. It is desirable that the setup be easily performed in a short amount of time and that the time required for setting up should be shorter after the surgeons have become accustomed to the operation ($Loop_{SPB}$ stability)
- Switching experiments from endoscope robot operation to manual operation: This experiment is performed to simulate handling when an emergency such as the failure of an endoscope robot occurs. The following time was measured; the endoscope robot was made to stop by pressing the emergency stop switch and the manipulator was moved, by the holding arm, to an area where the robot does not interrupt the surgery. Then, a normal surgery started where a human camera assistant positions the endoscope holding position. It is desirable that the above procedure is performed within 30 sec. ($Loop_{SPB}$ stability)
- Endoscope lens cleaning experiment: The following time is evaluated; the endoscope is removed from the robot, the endoscope lens is cleaned, the endoscope is re-installed to the endoscope robot and the field of view is secured by the endoscope. The endoscope lens cleaning time when a human camera assistant operates the endoscope is about 20 sec. It is desirable that the lens cleaning time with the robot is also within 20 sec. (quality of information, $Loop_{SPB}$ stability)

4.5 Operation experiment over a long period of time

To discuss the durability of endoscope robots, continuous operation of the robot is performed for longer than three times that of an actual surgery. In this experiment, an endoscope, camera head and optical fibre cable are installed to an endoscope robot and the endoscope is inserted into the trocar which is installed to a human body model to simulate the usage environment of an actual surgery. For the robot movement, a control program

Fig. 18. Operation experiment over a long period of time

developed for operation experiments over a long period of time moves four degree of freedom where speed and movable range is variously changed. Fig. 18 shows this experiment using P-arm as an example.

4.6 Evaluation on cleanliness

Sterilization methods include sterilization drape, gaseous sterilization, autoclave sterilization and electron-ray beam sterilization. When the sterilization drape is used, it is necessary to evaluate whether the sterilization drape does not tear due to the robot operation or the contact with medical staff. When gaseous sterilization, autoclave sterilization or electron-ray beam sterilization is used, specialized institutions evaluate and discuss cleanliness.

4.7 Presenting at exhibitions

Presentations of test models of endoscope robots at medical institute exhibitions should be made to gather opinions from others in the medical field, such as doctors, nurses or ME, It would also be advisable to make presentations of test models of endoscope robots at engineering exhibitions and to obtain opinions from the point of view of engineers.

5. Development into the future

Generally speaking, medical robotics is an academic framework of robots which provide "new eyes and hands" beyond the ability of human surgeons. Medical robots can be classified into treatment robots (surgical CAD/CAM systems), which perform surgery with image guidance and surgical assistant robots (surgical assistant systems), which assist in the treatment by the surgeons. Endoscope robots are classified into the surgical assistant robot [34]. This chapter treated endoscope robots as an interactive media and described the design and evaluation methods of endoscope robots. Our goal was to get a better understanding of endoscope robots while considering endoscope robots as interactive media, since endoscope robots closely interact with humans and assist with the surgery, coming in contact with patients around surgeons. Research and development of endoscope robots is striving for maintenance-free, compact, lightweight, automated, safe, clean and low cost endoscope robots; for the purpose of applying them to advanced surgeries. Diversion to NOTES of endoscope robots or single port surgery is not envisioned in the future. It is possible to make endoscope robots operate surgery devices such as forceps instead of endoscopes; however, easy diversion is a mistake. The reason is that methods to secure the required safety, accuracy or speed are totally different between the operation of an endoscope and the operation of forceps.

Development of endoscope robots has been well-established for the last 20 years and endoscope robots have been commercialized and active on the medical front. This chapter is written hoping that further study and development of endoscope robots spreads to all medical institutions where endoscopic surgery is performed and that endoscope robots will become partners with surgeons, for the benefit of many precious lives.

6. Acknowledgement

This research was supported in part by "Special Coordination Funds for Promoting Science and Technology: *Yuragi* Project" of the Ministry of Education, Culture, Sports, Science and

Technology, Japan, Grant-in-aid for Scientific Research (A) (No. 19206047) of the Japan Society for the Promotion of Science.

7. References

Kobayashi, E.; Masamune, K.; Sakuma, I.; Dohi, T. & Hashimoto, D. (1999). A New Safe Laparoscopic Manipulator System with a Five-Bar Linkage Mechanism and an Optical Zoom. *Computer Aided Surgery*, Vol.4, 182-192.

Tanoue, K.; Yasunaga, T.; Kobayashi, E.; Miyamoto, S.; Sakuma, I.; Dohi, T.; Konishi, K.; Yamaguchi, S.; Kinjo, N.; Takenaka, K.; Maehara Y. & Hashizume, M. (2006). Laparoscopic cholecystectomy using a newly developed laparoscope manipulator for 10 patients with cholelithiasis. *Surgical Endoscopy*, Vol.20, No.5, 753-756, ISSN 0930-2794 (Print) 1432-2218 (Online).

Sackier, J. M. & Wang, Y. (1994). Robotically assisted laparoscopic surgery form concept to development. *Surgical Endoscopy*, Vol.8, No.1, 63-66, ISSN 0930-2794 (Print) 1432-2218 (Online).

Finlay, P. A. (2001). A Robotic Camera Holder for Laparoscopy. Proceedings and Overviews of ICAR2001 Workshop 2 on Medical Robotics. *Proceedings of the 10th International Conference on Advanced Robotics*, 129-132. Aug. 2001, Budapest, Hungary

Nishikawa, A. ; Ito, K. ; Nakagoe, H. ; Taniguchi, K. ; Sekimoto, M.; Takiguchi, S. ; Seki, Y. ; Yasui, M. ; Okada, K. ; Monden, M. & Miyazaki, F. (2006). Automatic Positioning of a Laparoscope by Preoperative Workspace Planning and Intraoperative 3D Instrument Tracking. *MICCAI2006 Workshop proceedings*, Workshop on Medical Robotics:Systems and Technology towards Open Architecture, 82-91.

Nishikawa, A.; Nakagoe, H.; Taniguchi, K.; Yamada, Y.; Sekimoto, M.; Takiguchi, S.; Monden, M. & Miyazaki, F. (2008). How Does the Camera Assistant Decide the Zooming Ratio of Laparoscopic Images? -Analysis and Implementation-. *Proceedings of the 11th International Conference on Medical Image Computing and Computer Assisted Intervention (MICCAI 2008)*, New York, USA, Sep.2008.

Hurteau, R.; DeSantis, S.; Begin, E. & Gagner, M. (1994). Laparoecopic Surgery Assisted by a Robotic Cameraman: Concept and Experimental Results. *Proceedings of IEEE International Conference on Robotics & Automation*, 2286 – 2289.

Taylor, R. H.; Funda, J.; Eldridge, B.; Gomory, S.; Gruben, K.; LaRose, D.; Talamini, M.; Kavoussi, L. & Anderson, J. (1995). A telerobotic assistant for laparoscopic surgery. *IEEE Engineering in Medichine and Biology*, vol.14. no.3, 279 – 288.

Munoz, V. F.; Vara - Thorbeck, C.; De Gabriel, J. G.; Lozano, J. F.; Sanchez-Badajoz, E.; Garcia-Cerezo, A.; Toscane, R. & Jimenez-Garrido, A. (2000). A medical robotic assistant for minimally incasive surgery. *Proceedings of IEEE International Conference on Robotics & Automation*, 2901 – 2906.

Munoz, V. F.; Gomez De Gabriel, J.; Garcia-Morales, I.; Fernandez-Lozano, J. & Morales, J. (2005). Pivoting motion control for a laparoscopic assistant robot and human clinical trials. *Advanced Robotics*, vol.19, no.6, 694 – 712.

Polet, R. & Donnez, J. (2004). Gynecologic laparoscopic surgery with a palm-controlled laparoscope holder. *The Journal of the American Association of Gynecologic Laparoscopists*, 73–78.

Mizhuno, H. (1995). Robotic Endo-Surgery System. *Robot symposium 5th*, 115 - 118 (in Japanese)

Nishikawa, A.; Hosoi, T.; Koara, K.; Negoro, D.; Hikita, A.; Asano, S.; Kakutani, H.; Miyazaki, F.; Sekimoto, M.; Yasui, M.; Miyake, Y.; Takiguchi, S. & Monden, Morito. (2003). FAce MOUSe: A Novel Human-Machine Interface for Controlling the Position of a Laparoscope. *IEEE Transactions on Robotics and Automation*, vol.19, no. 5, 825-841.

Funda, J.; Gruben, K.; Eldridge, B.; Gomory, S. & Taylor R. H. (1995). Control and evaluation of a 7-axis surgical robot for laparoscopy. *Proceedings of IEEE International Conference on Robotics & Automation*, 1477-1484.

EndoControl (2009). http://www.endocontrol-medical.com/ [accessed October 10, 2009]

Long, J. A.; Cinquin, P.; Troccaz, J.; Voros, S.; Berkelman, P.; Descotes, J. L.; Letoublon, C. & Rambeaud. J. J. (2007). Development of Miniaturized Light Endoscope-Holder Robot for Laparoscopic Surgery. *Journal of Endourology*, vol.21, no8, 911-914.

Lee, Y. J.; Kim, J.; Ko, S. Y.; Lee, W. J. & Kwon, D. S. (2003). Design of a Compact Laparoscopic Assistant Robot : KaLAR. *Proceedings of the International Conference on Control Automation and Systems*, 2648-2653.

Buess, G. F.; Arezzo, A.; Schurr, M .O.; Ulmer, F.; Fisher, H.; Gumb, L.; Testa, T. & Nobman, C. (2000). A new remote-controlled endoscope positioning system for endoscopic solo surgery The FIPS Endoarm. *Surgical Endoscopy*, vol.14, 395 - 399.

Kimura, T.; Umehara, Y. & Matsumoto, S. (2000). Laparoscopic cholecystectomy performed by a single surgeon using a visual field tracking camera. *Surgical Endoscopy*, vol.14 , 825 - 829.

Kobayashi, E.; Sakuma, I.; Konishi, K.; Hashizume, M. & Dohi, T. (2004). A robotic wide-angle view endoscope using wedge prisms. *Surgical Endoscopy*, vol.18, 1396-1398.

Yamauchi, Y.; Yamashita, J.; Fukui, Y.; Yokoyama, K.; Sekiya, T.; Ito, E.; Kanai, M.; Fukuyo, T.; Hashimoto, D.; Iseki, H. & Takakura K. (2002). A dual-view endoscope with image shift. *Proceedings of CARS2002*, 183 - 187.

Nakaguchi, T.; Makino H.; Igarashi T.; Kamimura K.; Tsumaru N. & Miyake Y. (2005). An Automatic Tracking and Zooming System for Laparoscopic Surgery. *Transactions of Japanese Society for Medical and Biological Engineeing*, vol. 43, no. 4 685-693.

Taniguchi, K.; Nishikawa, A.; Yohda, T.; Sekimoto, M.; Yasui, M.; Takiguchi, S.; Seki, Y.; Monden, M. & Miyazaki, F. (2006). COVER: Compact Oblique Viewing Endoscope Robot for laparoscopic surgery. *Proceedings of CARS2006*, 207.

Sekimoto, M.; Nishikawa, A.; Taniguchi, K.; Takiguchi, S.; Miyazaki, F.; Doki, Y. & Mori, M. (2009). Development of a Compact Laparoscope Manipulator (P-arm). Surgical Endoscopy, ISSN0930-2794 (Print) 1432-2218 (Online)

Prosurgics (2009). http://www.freehandsurgeon.com/about.php [accessed October 10, 2009]

Sarkar, S.; Abolhassani, M. D.; Farahmand, F.; Ahmadian, A. R. & Saber, R. (2009). Research Activities at the Research Centre for Science and Technology in Medicine, *Iranian J Publ Health*, vol. 38, suppl. 1, 153-157.

Deshpande, S. (2004). http://www.lapindianrobot.com/robot1.htm [accessed October 10, 2009]

Szold, A.; Sholev, M.; Matter, I. (2008). Smart and slim laparoscopic robotic assistant. *Proceedings of the 20th International Conference of Society for Medical Innovation and Technology (SMIT2008)*, 211.

NGT, (2009). http://www.ngtnazareth.com/viewProject.asp?i=14 [accessed October 10, 2009]

Rininsland H. (1999). ARTEMIS: A telemanipulator for cardiac surgery. *EuropeanJournal of Cardio-thoracic Surgery*, vol.16, suppl. 2, 106-111.

KIT, (2009). http://www.iai.fzk.de/www-extern/index.php?id=352&L=1 [accessed October 10, 2009]

FZK, (2009). http://bibliothek.fzk.de/zb/Videolabor/hbm/Tabellen/Jahrg_00_fix.htm [accessed October 10, 2009]

Graur, F.; Plitea, N.; Vlad, L.; Pisla, D.; Vaida, C.; Furcea, L. & Neagos, H. (2009). A Muresan, Experimental laparoscopic cholecystectomy using paramis parallel robot, *Proceedings of the 21st International Conference of Society for Medical Innovation and Technology (SMIT2009).*

Leveson, N. G. & Turner, C. S. (1993). An Investigation of the Therac-25 Accidents. *IEEE Computer*, vol.26, no.7, 18-41.

Taylor, R. H. & Stoianovici, D. (2003). Medical Robotics in Computer-Integrated Surgery *IEEE Transactions on Robotics and Automation*, vol. 19, no. 5, 765-781.

Tsai, L. W. (1999). Robot Analysis: The Mechanics of Serial and Parallel Manipulators. *Wiley*.

Yen, D.; Roxolana, H. & Neil, O. (2006). US FDA regulation of computerized and robotics surgical systems. *Proceedings of CARS2006.*

FDA, (2006). http://www.jscas.org/guideline/FDA_CARS2006_Talk.pdf [accessed October 10, 2009]

Taniguchi, K.; Nishikawa, A.; Sugino, T.; Aoyagi, S.; Sekimoto, M.; Takiguchi, S.; Okada, K.; Monden, M. & Miyazaki, F.(2009). Method for objectively evaluating psychological stress resulting when humans interact with robots. In-Tech book: Advances in Human-Robot Interaction, IN-TECH Education and Publishing.

2

Extreme Telesurgery

Tamás Haidegger and Zoltán Benyó
Budapest University of Technology and Economics
Hungary

1. Introduction

The technological development of the last decades resulted in the rise of entirely new paradigms in healthcare. Within interventional medicine, first Minimally Invasive Surgery (MIS) and later robot-assisted surgery redefined the standards of clinical care. The concept of telemedicine dates back to the early 1970s, and in the late '80s, the idea of surgical robotics was born on the principle to provide active telepresence to surgeons. With the help of mechatronic devices physicians were first able to affect remote patients with the Green telepresence system in 1991. Soon after, many new research projects were initiated, creating a set of instruments for telesurgery. Visionary surgeons created networks for telesurgical patient care, demonstrated trans-continental surgery and performed procedures in weightlessness. The U.S. Army has always been interested in this technology for the battlefield, and currently the Telemedicine and Advanced Technology Research Center (TATRC) enforces research to test and extend the reach of remote healthcare. However, due to the high business risk, not many surgical robots succeeded to pass clinical trials, and barely some become profitable.

Beyond intercontinental operations, probably the most extreme field of application is medical support of long duration space missions. With a possible foundation of an extra-planetary human outpost either on the Moon or on Mars, space agencies are carefully looking for effective and affordable solutions for life-support and medical care. Teleoperated surgical robots have the potential to shape the future of extreme healthcare.

Besides the apparent advantages, there are some serious challenges of robotic healthcare that must be dealt with. The primary difficulty with teleoperation over large distances or beyond Earth orbit is communication lag time. Even in the case of intercontinental teleoperation—assuming the usage of commercial communication lines—latency can be in the order of several hundred milliseconds. While military satellite networks show better performance, these are not accessible for regular use. Surgery robot control communication protocols must be robust and false-tolerant, while advanced virtualization and augmented reality techniques should help the human operators to better adapt to the special challenges. A novel virtual reality based, extended surgical environment control concept is proposed. To meet safety standards and requirements in space, a three-layered architecture is recommended to provide the highest quality of telepresence with the provisional exploration missions. Today's extreme telesurgery concept may well find a way to common civil applications for the benefit of many patients.

2. Concept of telemedicine and telesurgery

2.1 Advanced medical technology

Telemedicine allows physicians to treat patients geologically separated from themselves. Pilot networks have been installed and tested in the second half of the 20th century, and the first intercontinental procedures were conducted in the 1990s (Rosser et al., 2007).

Telemedicine in general can be broken down to three main categories based on the timing and synchrony of the connection. Store-and-forward telemedicine means there is only one way communication at a time, the remote physician evaluate medical information offline, and sends those back to the original site at another time. Next, remote monitoring enables medical professionals to collect information about patients from a distance with different modality sensors. Finally, interactive telemedicine services provide real-time communication between the two sites, which might be extended with different forms of interactions, achieving real telepresence.

According to the functionality, three levels of telepresence can be defined within telemedicine based on the actual capabilities of the physician at the remote location. If instant and unlimited access is provided to the medical site, that is real-time teleoperation (or telesurgery, in the case of surgical procedure). Telementoring means the use of telecommunications technology—including the internet—to support and guide locally operating medics. Consultancy telemedicine (or telehealth consultancy) requires only limited access to the remote site, and as a result, the distant group cannot use real-time services or information updates.

The advantages of telemedicine are various, in the case of short-distance operations, the technology involved can mean great added value, such as an externally controlled tool holder or surgical robot (Herman 2005). In long-distance telementoring, the time/cost effectiveness and the provided higher level of medical care are the most important benefits, while in extreme telemedicine, such as space exploration it may be the only available form of adequate medical aid.

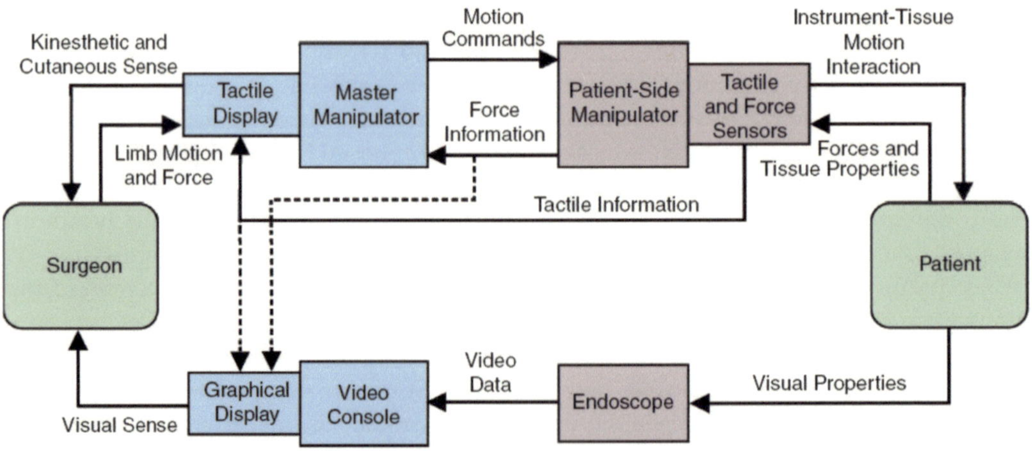

Fig. 1. Integration of different modality feedback information to the concept of telesurgery. Interaction is only possible through a system of sensors and human-machine interfaces. Modified from (Hager et al., 2008).

Beyond the possibility to observe the remote site, the quality of telepresence has always been paramount for the surgeons to be able to perform a procedure. The availability of different modalities combined, such as 2D/3D visual, tactile/haptic, acoustic, etc. has been proved to dramatically increase human performance. Figure 1 shows the integration of different modalities to the control diagram of telesurgery concept. Currently, the dominant form of sensory feedback is visual, as that provides highest density of information. The resolution of video cameras has been increasing in the past years, and currently full HD resolution is available with most systems, accompanied with a high fidelity 3D stereoscopic view. Although haptic feedback was provided with the first robot prototypes, the commercially available systems miss this modality due to the complexity (and additional cost) of the hardware and the challenges to provide life-like tactile feedback to the surgeon.

2.2 History of telehealth

There have been several experiments conducted in the past two decades to verify the usability of remote health care paradigms. Due to the fact that surgeons navigate based on a camera image, telementoring techniques are well applicable in laparoscopy, MIS. It is considered to be one of the most important breakthroughs in medicine in the past decades (Ballantyne, 2007). In 1997, laparoscopic colectomy and laparoscopic Nissen fundoplications were the first procedures performed with the aid of professional telementoring, from over 8 km distance (Rosser et al., 1997). The same group performed the first international telementoring between the John Hopkins Medical Institute (Baltimore, MD) and Innsbruck, Austria and Bangkok, Thailand (Lee et al., 1998). In 1999, they telementored from Maryland five laparoscopic hernia repairs, performed on board of the USS Abraham Lincoln aircraft carrier in California (Cubano et al. 1999). Later, several intercontinental telementorig experiments have been performed, mainly from the USA to Italy, France, Singapore, Nepal and Brazil (Fabrizio et al., 2000).

The U.S. Department of Defense (DoD) got interested in the feasibility of telesurgery even earlier; aimed to develop a system that allows the combat surgeons to perform life saving operations on wounded soldiers from a safe distance (Satava, 1995). The idea of robotic support in space dates back to the early '70s, proposed in a study for the National Aeronautics and Space Administration (NASA) to provide surgical care for astronauts with remote controlled robots (Alexander, 1973). This is particularly desirable, as the specific, high level medical education of the flight surgeons might be impossible to achieve. Proficiency in MIS, laparoscopic surgery requires extreme amount of practice, and maintenance of skills is only possible with continuous training.

3. Robotic telesurgery

In most of the cases, mechatronic systems and cameras are the remote hands and eyes of the surgeon, and therefore key elements of the operation. Out of the 370 international surgical robotic projects listed in the Medical Robotic Database (MeRoDa, 2009), there are several dozens with the capability of teleoperation.

In general, robots can be involved in medical procedures with differnet level of autonomy (Nathoo et al. 2005). Many of the developed systems only serve as a robust tool holding equipment, once directed to the desired position. Systems that are able to perform fully automated procedures—such as CT-based biopsy or drilling—are called autonomous, or supervisory controlled. (A human supervisor would always be present to intervene if deviation occurs compared to the surgical plan.) This can be combined with the classic tools of image guided surgery, once the robot is registered to the patient.

When the robot is entirely remote-controlled, and the surgeon is absolutely in charge of the motion of the robot, we call it a teleoperated system. These complex systems typically consist of three parts; one or more slave manipulators, a master controller and a sensory (e.g. vision) system providing feedback to the user. Based on the gathered visual (and haptic, acoustic, etc.) information, the surgeon guides the arm by moving the controller and closely watching its effect.
By modifying the teleoperation control paradigm, we can introduce cooperative (also called compliant) control. It means that the surgeon is directly giving the control signals to the machine through a force sensor, performing hands-on operation.

3.1 First telesurgery systems

Funded by the DoD, the first prototype of telesurgery robot was developed at Stanford Research International (SRI) (Menlo Park, CA) called the Green Telepresence System (Green et al., 1991). It was assembled by 1991, primarily aimed for open surgery. The idea to use it with MIS came with the rapid spread of laparoscopic technique. A series of ex-vivo and in-vivo trials were performed by 1995 (Bowersox et al., 1996).
NASA Jet Propulsion Laboratory (JPL) (Pasadena, CA) also started to develop a system in the early times, and by 1993 they created the RAMS (Robot-Assisted Microsurgery System), targeting high-precision ophthalmic procedures (Schenker et al., 1995).
Based on the experience at SRI and NASA, the Defense Advanced Research Projects Agency (DARPA) of DoD initiated the Trauma Pod project in 1994. The main goal was to "enhance battlefield casualty care by developing autonomous and semi-autonomous mobile platforms through the integration of tele-robotic and robotic medical systems. The initial phase has successfully automated functions typically performed by the scrub nurse and circulating nurse… The next phase of the program will develop methods for autonomous airway control and intravenous access... Finally, these systems will be miniaturized and incorporated into a tactical platform capable of operating in a battlefield or mass casualty environment." (Trauma Pod, 2009). The robots developed with the help of DARPA have already been tested under extreme circumstances, in weightlessness and at NASA Aquarius underwater habitat.

3.2 Commercialized systems

The most well known commercialized robots are the da Vinci Surgical System from Intuitive Surgical Inc. (Sunnyvale, CA) and the discontinued Zeus from Computer Motion Inc. (Santa Barbara, CA). While these robots inherited the structure and features that make them capable of performing telesurgical operations, most commonly they are used for on-site surgery. Their primary advantage is easing the complexity of laparoscopic procedures, providing better visualization, control and ergonomics to the surgeon, and higher precision to the patient.
Presently, the market leader (and the only available) complete teleoperated robot is the da Vinci, created with roughly 500M USD investment. The patient side consists of two or three tendon-driven, 6+1 degree of freedom (DOF) slave manipulators. These are designed with a Remote Center of Motion (RCM) kinematics, resulting in an inherent safety regarding the stability of the entry port. The camera holder arm allows 3 DOF navigation controlled with the same master interface. The system provides high quality 3D vision with stereo-endoscopes, adjustable tremor filtering (~6 Hz) and motion scaling (1:1 – 1:5).

In 1995, Intuitive licensed technology from NASA, SRI, IBM and several universities, and by 1997, the first prototype—Lenny—was developed for animal trials. Next, Mona was made for the very first human trials involving vascular and gynaecological procedures in the Saint-BlasiusHospital (Dendermonde, Belgium) in March 1997. As the system was originally intended for cardio-vascular (beating-heart) surgery, specific clinical trials were performed in Paris and Leipzig in May 1998 (Ballantyne et al., 2004). Based on the initial experience, the market-ready version of the robot (named da Vinci honouring the great inventor) got advanced control and ergonomic features compared to the Mona. Final clinical tests began in 1999, and the U.S. Food and Drug Administration (FDA) approved the system for general laparoscopic surgery (gallbladder, gastroesophageal reflux and gynecologic surgery) in July 2000, followed by many other approvals. Once the system was on the market, Intuitive continued perfecting it, and the second generation—the da Vinci S—was released in 2006 (Figure 2). The latest version, the da Vinci Si became available in April 2009 with improved full HD camera system, advanced ergonomic features, and most importantly, the possibility to use two consoles for assisted surgery.

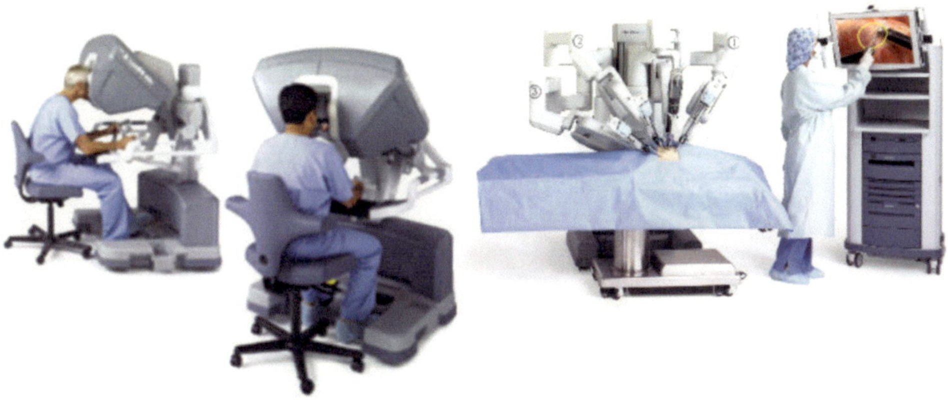

Fig. 2. Master controllers and the patient side manipulators of the new da Vinci Si surgical system. (Photo: Intuitive Surgical Inc.)

Currently, there are more than 1300 da Vinci units around the world, ¾ of them in the U.S. The number of procedures performed is well over 300,000, the most successful application of the robot became prostatectomy. Around 70% of all radical prostate removal procedures were performed robotically in the U.S. in 2008.

The concept of the da Vinci theoretically allows remote teleoperation, but that has not been the primary focus of Intuitive. The previous versions of the robot used a proprietary short-distance communication protocol through optic fibre to connect the master and the slave, while the latest Si facilitates further displacement of the two units. In 2005, TATRC presented collaborative telerobotic surgery on animals with modified da Vinci consoles, being able to overtake a master controller with a remote one through public internet connection (Flynn, 2005). During the experiment, the average roundtrip latency was 500 ms from Denver to Sunnyvale, which was disturbing for the physicians.

Another similar robot was the Zeus Telesurgical System developed by Computer Motion Inc. (Santa Barbara, CA). It was based on the AESOP (Automated Endoscopic System for Optimal Positioning) camera holder arm (FDA approved in December 1993). The Zeus received FDA clearance in 2001. The Zeus was controlled in master-slave setup, and used

UDP/IP (User Datagram Protocol over Internet Protocol) for communication. This facilitated various experimental telesurgery procedures as described later (Kumar & Marescaux, 2008). After long litigation with Intuitive over mutual intellectually property violations, the whole company was bought by Intuitive, and first the production, then the support of the Zeus system was suspended.

3.3 Light-weight prototypes

Although some systems never got commercialized, they were created with the aim to facilitate extreme telesurgery. NASA JPL and MicroDexterity Systems Inc. (Albuquerque, NM) developed the RAMS (Robot-Assisted Micro-Surgery) system (Das et al., 1998). The RAMS consists of two 6 DOF arms, equipped with 6 DOF tip-force sensors, providing haptic feedback to the operator (Figure 3). It used the concept of telesurgery for control; however, the operator sat right next to the slave arms. The robot was originally aimed for ophthalmic procedures, especially for laser retina surgery. It is capable of 1:100 scaling (achieving 10 micron accuracy), tremor filtering (8-14 Hz) and eye tracking. Currently the prototype rests idle at JPL, as the project was discontinued.

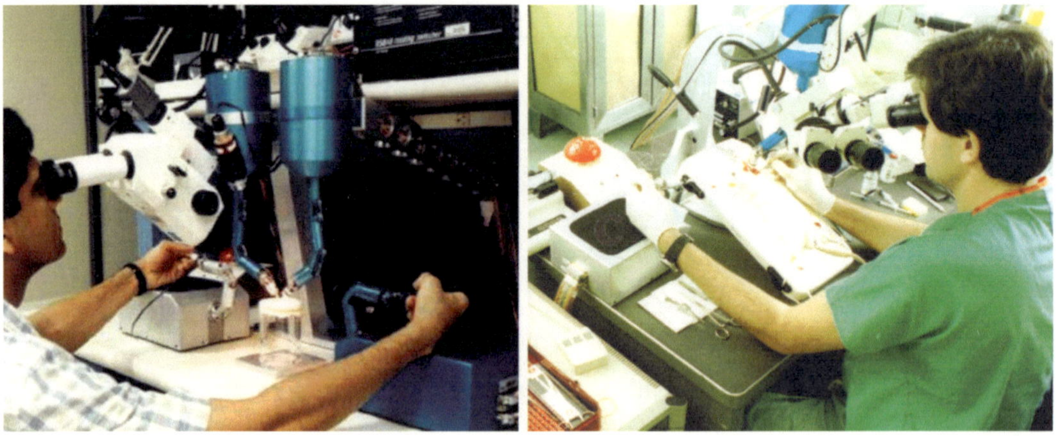

Fig. 3. The RAMS robot developed at NASA JPL in laboratory trials and in-vivo animal tests in 1998. (Photo: NASA)

Doctors and scientists at the BioRobotics Lab., University of Washington (Seattle, WA) have developed a portable surgical robot that can be a compromised solution to install on spacecrafts with its 22 kg overall mass (Rosen & Hannaford, 2006). The DARPA supported robot—called Raven—works along the same principle as the da Vinci. It has two articulated, tendon driven arms, each holding a stainless steel shaft for different surgical tools. It can easily be assembled even by non-engineers, and its communication links have been designed for long distance remote-control. The system has participated in multiple field tests, and now several units are being built for large scale clinical trials (Lum et al., 2009).
Realizing the importance of a light, but stiff structure, SRI started to develop the M7 in 1998 (Figure 3.). The system weights only 15 kg, but able to exert significant forces compared to its size. It is equipped with two 7 DOF arms, motion scaling (1:10), tremor filtering and haptic feedback. The end-effectors can be changed very rapidly, and even laser tissue welding tool can be mounted. The controller has been designed to operate under extremely different atmospheric conditions, e.g. it only contains solid-state memory drives. The

software of the M7 has been updated lately to better suit the requirements of teleoperation and communication via Ethernet link. The M7 performed the world's first automated ultrasound guided tumor biopsy in 2007.
The German Aerospace Center (DLR) Institute of Robotics and Mechatronics (Wessling, Germany) has already built several generations of light-weight robotic arms for ground and space applications. They have also taken part in many telerobotic space experiments in the past decades. The KineMedic and the most recent MIRO 7 DOF surgical robots are considered for real teleoperation—even in extreme locations—as one arm is only 10 kg and capably of handling 30 N payload with high accuracy (Hagn et al., 2008).
Small scale, in-body robots offer great advantages, as they are always remote controlled, opening the possibility of spatial displacement of the physician from the patient. Engineers at the University of Nebraska (Lincoln, NE) together with the physicians of the local Medical Center developed a special mobile in-vivo wheeled robot for biopsy (Rentschler et al., 2006). Equipped with a camera, the coin-sized robot can enter the abdominal cavity through one small incision and move teleoperated around the organs. The robot is able to traverse the abdominal organs without causing any damage, therefore reduces patient trauma. More recently, the group has developed various swallowable robots that can be controlled with external magnets.
The CRIM group at Scuola Superiore Sant'Anna (Pisa, Italy) leads a European Union FP7 founded international research collaboration to develop tethered, partially autonomous robots to perform surgery in the endolumen (Menciassi & Dario, 2009). Another EU project—Vector—aims for the creation of effective capsule robots for local surgical procedures throughout the GI tract (Eirik et al., 2009).

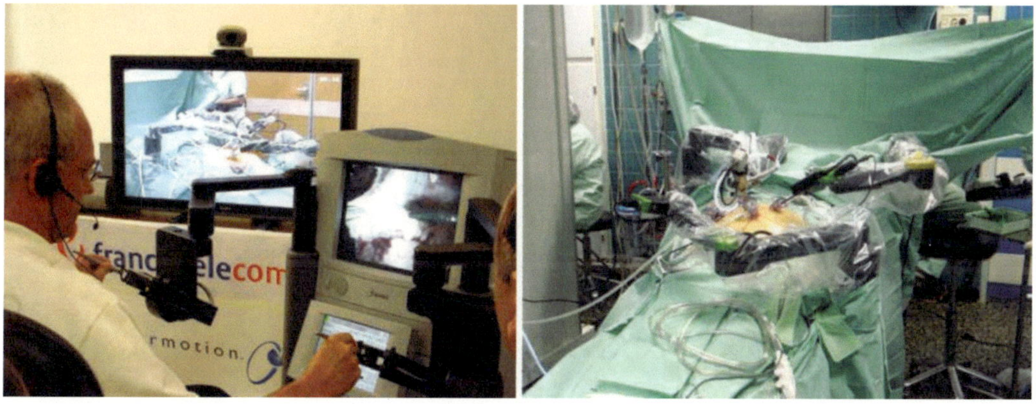

Fig. 4. The Zeus robot during the first intercontinental surgery, the colecystectomy was performed on the patient in Strasbourg from New York. (Photo: IRCAD)

4. Remarkable experiments

4.1 Long distance telesurgery

The Zeus robot proved to be a solid platform to test and experiment different telesurgical scenarios. Between 1994 and 2003 the French Institut de Recherche contre les Cancers de l'Appareil Digestif (IRCAD) (Strasbourg, France) and Computer Motion Inc. worked together in several experiments to learn about the feasibility of long distance telesurgery and effects of latency, signal quality degradation. After six porcine surgeries, the first transatlantic human procedure—the Lindbergh operation—was performed with a Zeus 7. September, 2001 (Marescaux et al., 2002). The surgeons were controlling the robot from New York, while the patient laid 7,000 km away in Strasbourg (Figure 4). Based on previous research (Fabrizio et al., 2000), it was estimated that the time delay between the master consol and the robot should be less than 330 ms to perform the operation safely, while above 700 ms, the operator may have real difficulties controlling the Zeus. A high quality, dedicated 10 Mbps ATM fibre optic link was provided by France Telecom, transmitting not just the control signals and video feedback, but also servicing the video conferencing facilities, and an average of 155 ms communication lag time was experienced. Out of that roughly 85 ms was the communication lag through the transmission, and 70 ms the coding and decoding of the video signals.

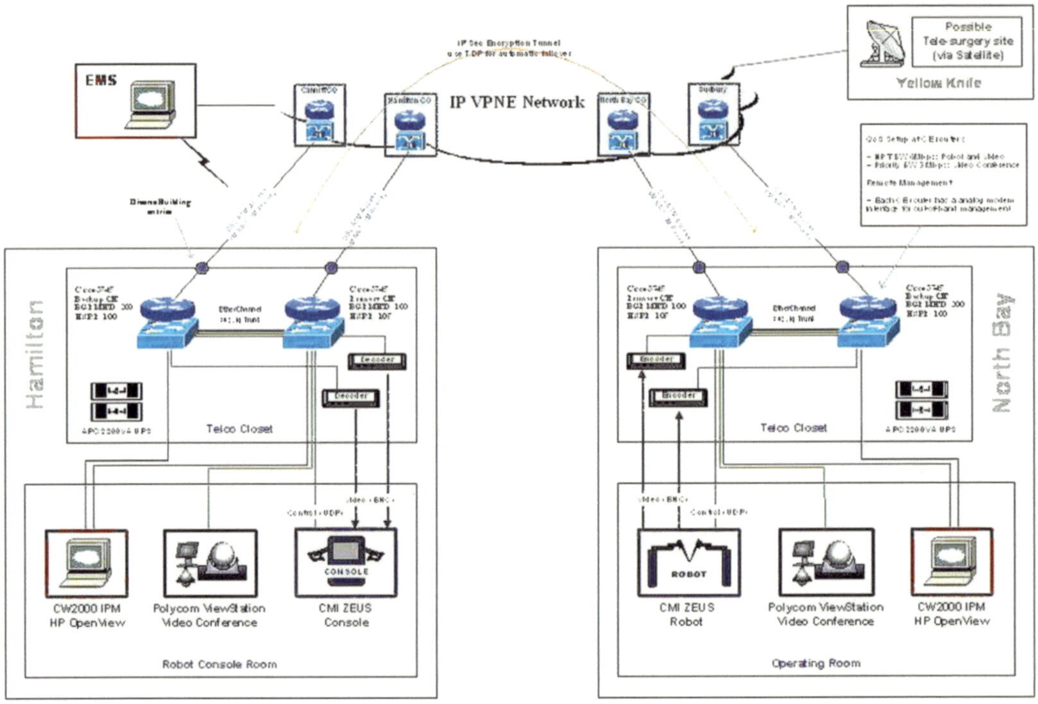

Fig. 5. Network Route Director (NRD) designed for CMAS by Bell research in 2002 to support the telesurgical network in Canada.

In Canada, the world's first regular telerobotic surgical service network was build and managed routinely between the Centre for Minimal Access Surgery (CMAS), a McMaster University Centre (Hamilton, Ontario) and a community hospital in North Bay some 400 km away, using the Zeus robot (Anvari, 2005). The average latency recorded was about 150 ms using commercial high-speed internet link Virtual Private Network (VPN) protocol (Figure 5). CMAS performed 22 telerobotic cases with North Bay General Hospital and over 35 telementoring cases with North Bay General Hospital, Ontario and the Complexe Hospitalier La Sagamie, Quebec. The network was eater extended to include more centers in Canada. While the FDA only permitted the single case of telesurgery of the Lindbergh operation in the USA, Canadian health authorities cleared the methodology for routine procedures.

A remotely-controlled catheter guiding device guided by a robot was used in Milan in 2006 to automatically perform heart ablation, initiated and supervised by a group of professionals from Boston, MA. The robot uses high magnetic fields to direct the catheter to the desired location, taking advantage of the pre-operative CT scans of the patient and real time electromagnetic navigation. Initial trials were performed on 40 patients before the telesurgical experiment took place. The novelty of the system was that it could create the surgical plan on its own based on an anatomical atlas including 10,000 patients (Pappone et al., 2006).

4.1 Underwater trials

NASA has conducted several experiments to examine the effect of latency on human performance in the case of telesurgery and telementoring. The NASA Extreme Environment Mission Operations (NEEMO) take place on the world's only permanent undersea laboratory, Aquarius. It operates a few kilometers away from Key Largo in the Florida Keys National Marine Sanctuary, 19 meters below the sea surface. A special buoy provides connections for electricity, life support and communication, and a shore-based control center supports the habitat and the crew. Twelve NEEMO projects have been organized since 2001, and three were focusing on teleoperation recently.

The 7th NEEMO project took place in October 2004. The mission objectives included a series of simulated medical procedures with an AESOP robot, using teleoperation and telementoring (Thirsk et al., 2007). The four crew members (one with surgical experience, one physician without significant experience and two aquanauts without any medical background) had to perform five test conditions: ultrasonic examination of abdominal organs and structures, ultrasonic-guided abscess drainage, repair of vascular injury, cystoscopy, renal stone removal and laparoscopic cholecystectomy. The AESOP was controlled from the CMAS (Ontario, Canada) 2,500 km away. A Multi-protocol Label Switching (MPLS) VPN was established, with a minimum bandwidth of 5 Mbps. The signal delay was tuned between 100 ms and 2 s to observe the effects of latency. High latency resulted in extreme degradation of performance: a single knot tying took 10 minutes to accomplish. The results showed that the non-trained crew members were also able to perform satisfyingly by exactly following the guidance of the skilled telementor. They even outperformed the non-surgeon physician, but fell behind the trained surgeon. Scientists also compared effectiveness of the telementoring and the quality of teleoperated robotic procedures. Even though the teleoperation got slightly higher grades, it took a lot more time to complete (Doarn et al., 2009).

During the 9th NEEMO in April 2006 the crew had to assemble and install an M7 robot, and perform real-time abdominal surgery on a patient simulator. Throughout the procedure a microwave satellite connection was used, and time delay went up to 3 s to mimic the Moon-Earth communication links. Each of the four astronauts had to train at least 2 hours with the wheeled in-vivo robots designed at the University of Nebraska. In another experiment, pre-established two-way telecom links were used for telementoring. The crew had to prove the effectiveness of telemedicine through the assessment and diagnosis of extremity injuries and surgical management of fractures. The effects of fatigue and different stressors on the human crew's performance in extreme environments were also measured. Latency was set up to 750 ms in these experiments. The significant performance degradation of the microwave connection was noticed during stormy weather, causing a jitter in latency up to 1 s (Doarn et al., 2009).

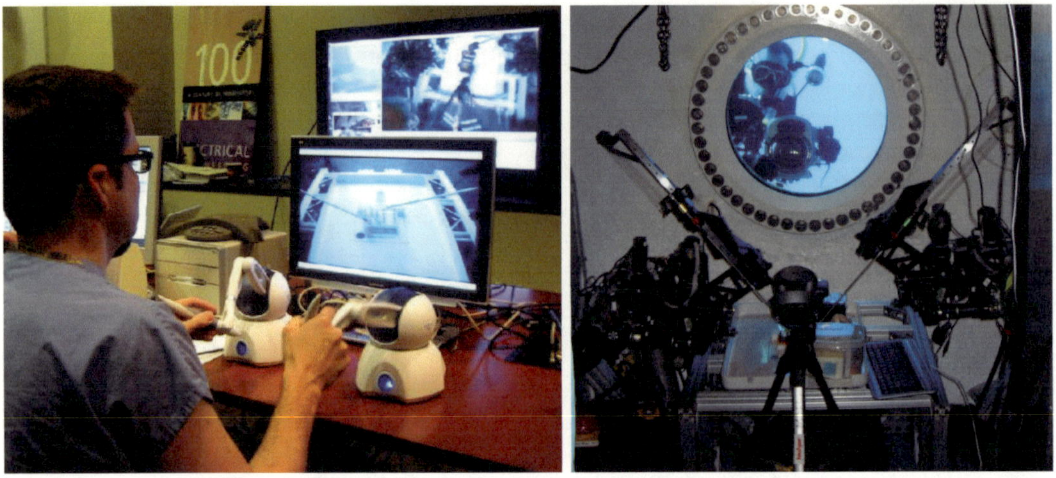

Fig. 6. The Raven robot performing FLS tasks on board of NASA Aquarius in Florida, while guided by a surgeon from Seattle. (Photo: University of Washington)

The 12th NEEMO project ran in May 2007, and one of its primary goals was to measure the feasibility of telesurgery with the Raven and the M7 robots (Figure 6). NASA sent a flight surgeon, two astronauts and a physician into the ocean. Suing operations were performed on a phantom in simulated zero gravity environment to measure the capabilities of surgeons controlling the robots from Seattle. This time the Aquarius was connected to the mainland through a Spectra 5.4 GHz Wireless Bridge, allowing for a minimum of 30 Mbps bandwidth, and average latency of 70 ms. The HaiVision CODEC was used for video compression giving very good quality, but also introduced significant latency, up to 1 sec.

A group of three professionals guided the robot using commercial internet connection, and the communication lag time was increased till up to 1 s. Several simple tasks were performed, as part of the Fundamentals of Laparoscopic Surgery (FLS). The M7 demonstrated the first image-guided autonomous surgery (using a portable ultra sound system). It was live broadcasted at the American Telemedicine Conference 2007 (Nashville, TN). The M7 was able to insert the needle into a tissue phantom by itself.

4.2 Surgery in space

To facilitate exploration missions beyond Earth, space agencies have always been pushing for more advanced telehealth concepts. Surgical experiments (laparotomy and celiotomy on rabbits) were first reported from Russian cosmonauts in 1967. The first survival procedure was performed on STS-90 Neurolab mission on rats in 1998 (Campbell el al., 2001). The world's first human operation was a cyst removal from a patient's arm, on board of the European Space Agency's Airbus A-300 Zero-G aircraft. The plane performed 25 parabola curves, providing 20–25 s of weightlessness every time (New Scientist Space & AFP, 2006). ESA had plans to perform teleoperation in 2008 with a robot controlled through satellite connection, but the mission was postponed. NASA had its first zero gravity robotic surgery experiment in late September 2007 (Kamler, 2007). On a DC-9 hyperbolic aircraft suturing tasks were performed with the M7 (Figure 7). The performance of classical and teleoperated robotic knob tying was measured. Both the master and the slave devices were equipped with acceleration compensators, otherwise it would have been almost impossible to succeed with the tasks. The results showed that humans can still better adapt to extreme environments, however, advanced robotic solutions do not fall far behind.

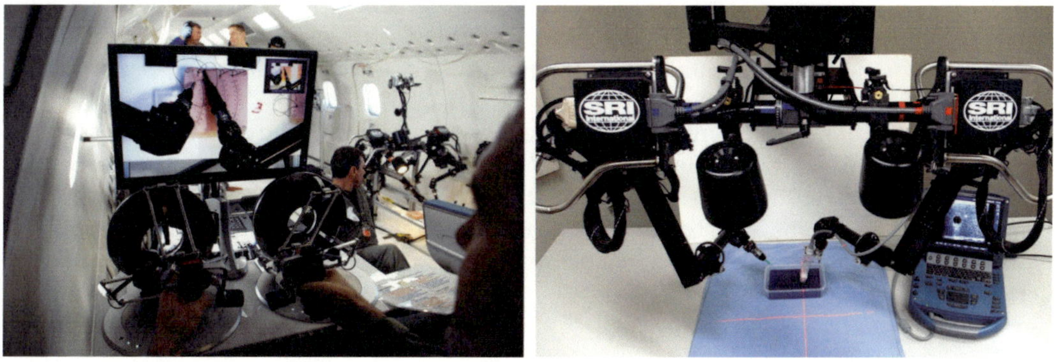

Fig. 7. The M7 on board of a NASA parabolic flight, and the robot performing autonomous ultrasound-guided tissue biopsy. (Photo: NASA, SRI)

5. Challenges in teleoperation

Effectiveness of surgical care heavily relies on the prompt delivery of treatment, and extreme teleoperation serves this principle. Beyond the obvious challenges of reduced medical equipment, constrained resources and probably limited experience of the on-site staff, several technical difficulties arise with extreme telesurgery.

Significant delay in the sensor feedback can totally distract the surgeon and cause serious safety hazard, as examined by different research groups. Engineering methods have been developed to overcome the difficulties originating from the absence of communication infrastructure, unpredictable propagation condition changes and hardware failures. The U.S. Robotics roadmap points to robotic telesurgery as a major focus of research in order to improve quality of care (Christensen et al., 2009). It calls for engineering solutions to ensure natural interaction between the human operator and the remote robot through specific patient models, from whole-body level to tissue characteristics. This would allow for advanced off-site surgical planning, automated guidance and also for realistic training opportunity.

5.1 Effect of latency

The primary difficulty with teleoperation over large distances or low quality network infrastructure is the communication lag time. The continuous development of the internet backbone infrastructure has resulted in a significant reduction of typical delays. Using commercial services, delay may be around 85 ms, across the United States, and lag time might be anywhere from 20-400 ms world-wide. Due to the Transmission Control Protocol (TCP/IP) and the routing algorithms latency can vary over trials, and this further degrades user performance.

Satellite based internet connections can use a fleet of Low or Medium Earth Orbit (LEO/MEO) satellites such as the commercial constellations of Orbcom, Globalstar or Iridium. Typical roundtrip delays are 40 ms, but the bandwidth is only 64 kbps per channel. Currently developing O3b Networks (scheduled for deployment late 2010) would provide 1 Gbps with approximately 125 ms lag time. Geosynchronous satellites provide higher latency due to their 36,000 km altitude above the equator. Round trip latency is 540-700 ms typically. Understandably, designated military satellites can provide a lot faster communication channel, the minimum latency per satellite hop is expected to be 4.3–7.8 ms one way (Berlocher, 2009). Despite the recent improvement in surface line speed, satellite communication has the potential to overcome ground lines primarily in speed, with a reasonable quality of service and availability.

Beyond Earth orbit radio and microwave frequency signals propagate at almost the speed of light in space, however already in the range of long distance manned space missions, several minutes of latency can be experienced. Planet Mars orbits 56,000,000 km to 399,000,000 km from Earth which means a 6.5 to 44 minutes of delay in transmission. In addition, for about two weeks every synodic period, direct communication can be blocked, as the Sun stays in between Earth and Mars, direct.

5.2 Adaptation to latency

Most humans are capable of adapting to sensory feedback latency up 500 ms (Anvari, 2004) and some experiments suggest that individuals might be able to perform tasks even with a consistent 1000 ms delay (Lum et al., 2008). Researchers showed that varying latency significantly reduces the operators' performance both with robotic telesurgery and virtual reality (VR) applications (Thomson et al., 1999). It is advisable to use the consistent, maximum latency of system to achieve performance continuity. General approach to handle latency is to slow down the surgeons' movements, allowing time for the visual feedback to confirm the intended move. However, in extreme cases this prevents the effective work and firm reaction to unexpected events. The on-site medical assistant can also help with imminent moves and minor tasks (Hanly et al., 2009).

While keeping the stereo vision system's two video channels synchronized is crucial for high quality performance, other modalities might be useful delivered earlier. By reflecting e.g. forces sooner back to the operator (bypassing the time video coding/decoding takes), they can improve their ability to compensate for latency. The compression and decompression of the video stream can be reduced by the use of novel CODECs and state-of–the-art computing hardware, but it still takes significant time, generally 100-700 ms.

Approaching from the control theory point of view, several strategies have been developed to overcome the difficulties on the master side. One solution is to realize communication delays as force reflection for the human operator (Nohmi, 2003). It feels as if the remote manipulator was controlled through a virtually coupled spring, applying adequate forces. This method can be well used to provide information on the remote manipulator's movement while there is no real feedback due to the latency, however it is not precise enough (and may alter the surgeons decisions by occasionally providing unreal forces) to approve it for surgical applications.

When humans are adapting to asynchronous sensory feedback, they tend to create a virtual representation of the remote site to predict the consequences of their moves and project the tools ahead. A similar concept has been proposed for virtual reality based simulators (Frank, 1986). This has been successfully extended with sensory fusion for VR control (Kadavasal & Oliver, 2007), where the operator controls the model of the remote system in a virtual environment, and the lag time between the simulated and the real setup is handled by the environment model. We propose to apply this concept to telesurgery, where robot commands could be sent to a simulator that predicts the dynamic state of the virtual surgical site, including the robot's position, and acceleration along with the patient's body and tissue properties and reactions (Figure 8). The optimal control of the robot is calculated autonomously with high frequency on the patient site, while the Intelligent Surgical Interpreter provides an interface to the master controller. Sensory updates are processed by the simulators at the surgeon site, and the virtual environment is updated according to the new measurements. This framework allows the smooth integration of different modalities, but require a very precise 3D model of the patient, gained from pre-operative MRI, CT and PET scanning. The models might be continuously updated through intra-operative imaging techniques. A variety of operations and possible outcomes could be simulated and analyzed before the actual surgery takes place, reducing the risk of complications.

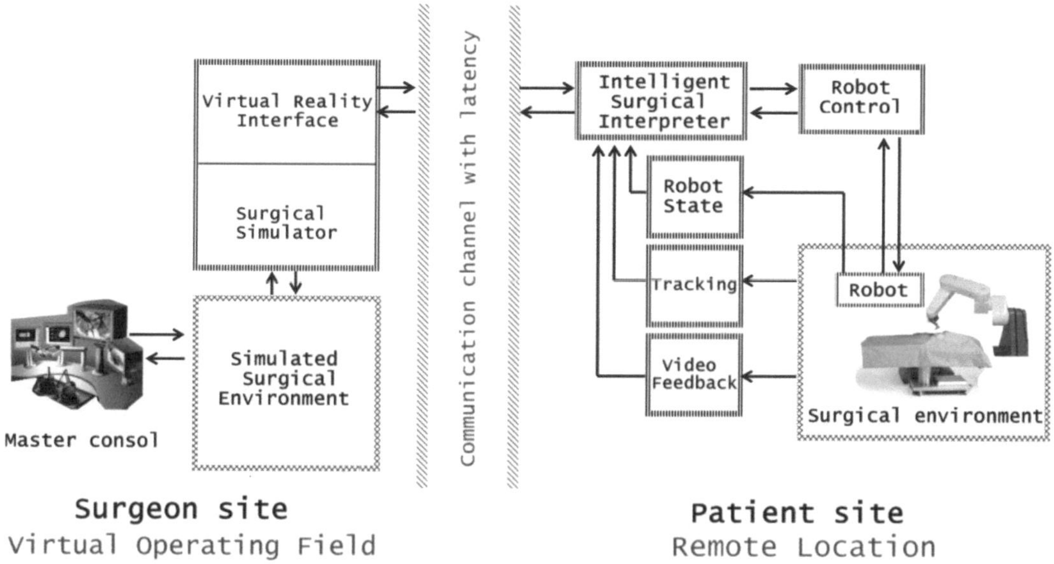

Fig. 8. The concept of virtual reality extended control of surgical robots in order to locally deal with the disturbing effects of latency.

5.3 Communication protocol

Further difficulties may arise with the data protocol of the robots that links the master consol and the slave arms. Presently, the majority of telepresence systems communicate through Transmission Control Protocol (TCP) that is used along with the Internet Protocol (IP) to send data in the form of individual units-packets. Another common type is the User Datagram Protocol (UDP), a connectionless protocol that—like the TCP—runs on top of IP networks. UDP/IP provides very few error recovery services, offering instead a direct way to send and receive datagrams. Asynchronous Transfer Mode (ATM/AAL1), which encodes data traffic into small fixed sized packets is also frequently used, but lacks advanced security services, just as the UDP/IP. In the case of communication breakdown, the recovery time may be critical, therefore redesigned gateway architecture should be added to allow TCP transfers to survive a long duration blockage.

The Zeus and the da Vinci were designed to discard each packet that has any sort of internal error; they do not correct bit-level errors. If several packets are lost, or there is a breakdown, the robots suspend their operation. To meet the special communication requirements

through satellites, the Space Communications Protocol Standards (SCPS) was developed and tested by DoD and NASA (Wang & Horan, 2009). SCPS uses similar architecture to TCP/IP, but it is more effective in handling latency created by long distance transmissions and the noise associated with wireless links. The SCPS exists as a full ISO standard, and also meets the U.S. Military Standards.
To ensure superior quality visual and tactile feedback, high sampling rate must be used on the patient site (app. 1 ms). Along with the high definition video feedback this has a significant bandwidth demand. Under regular circumstances a 10 Mbps connection is already suitable for teleoperation, however in the case of high definition, multimodal equipment, a 40 Mbps two-channel link would be required (Spearing & Regan, 2005). This may not cause much problem on the International Space Station (ISS) that was equipped with a 150 Mbps connection in 2005, but in the case of a Mars mission, NASA only plans to develop a 5 Mbps connection as a part of the new space communication architecture relying on the reconfigurable Space Telecommunications Radio System (STRS), and upgrade it to 20 Mbps by 2020 (Reinhart & Johnson, 2008).

6. Long duration space mission support

While advanced internet based communication networks enables effective telesurgery all over the Earth (with the discomfort of latency), serious technological problems arise in the case of long-haul space exploration missions. Space medicine and health care have always been a critical issue for aerospace agencies and several comprehensive studies reckon with the technological capabilities and challenges (Campbell & Billica, 2008).
Despite the current financial difficulties, the overall goal and future direction in exploration is towards the continuous human presence on the Moon and on Mars. The previously proposed MARS mission by NASA would have required the support of a 6 member crew for 18 months. The team's designed healthcare module is a subsystem within the prefabricated habitat providing 15.9 m^2 space, and 2,500 kg payload (Drake, 2009). The presently used communication systems have serious limitations concerning the achievable minimum communication lag time, maximum bandwidth and robustness. Based on recent experiments illustrated above, we have a better understanding of the effects and drawbacks of extreme long distance telesmedicine that also apply for telementoring. As long as a new level of machine automation is not reached, it seems inevitable to have a flight surgeon on board of the spacecraft, to adapt to any unforeseeable event. Flight surgeons should receive special training for a better command over computer integrated surgical technology to be provided on board. The rest of the crew should also undergo comprehensive medical training to attain the skills required to monitor any surgical procedure, and to interact in the case of immediate danger. It is also important to practice the skills with the surgery robot throughout the mission, even if no accident occurs.
Based on the pre-described conditions, difficulties and system requirements, a three-layered mission architecture is proposed to achieve the highest degree of performance possible, by combining robotic and human surgery (Figure 9). Depending on the physical distance between the space ship and the ground control centre, different telepresence technologies may end up with the best result. Basically, with the accession of the latency, real-time control strategies and communication techniques' effectiveness decreases significantly. By adaptively switching, different levels of surgical service can be provided throughout the mission.

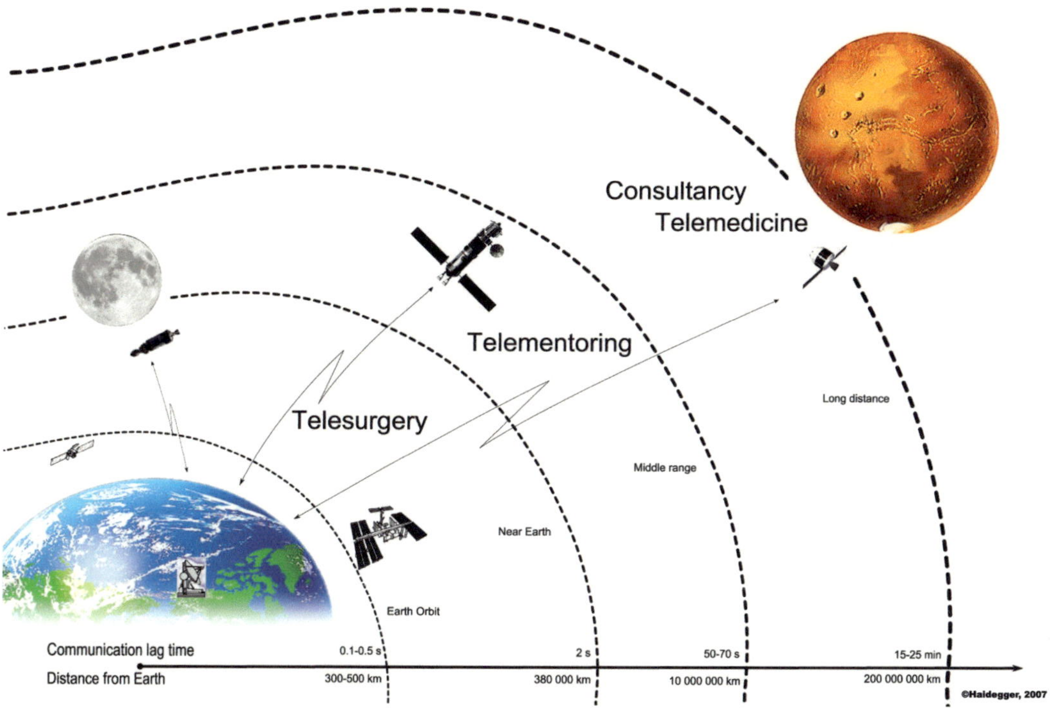

Fig. 9. Concept of telehealth support to provide maximum level of available medical care to astronauts during long distance exploration missions.

Mainly within the range of 380,000 km (app. the Earth-Moon average distance), regular telesurgery techniques can be used in space to provide medical support in the case of emergency. Leaving the Earth orbit, special control strategies have to be applied, to extend the feasibility of telesurgery up to a maximum of 2 s of delay. With robot assisted surgery, a shared control approach should be followed, integrating high-fidelity automated functions into the robot, to extend the capabilities of the human surgeon. For example, to automatically follow the movements of the organs (the beating heart and breathing lung), the robots should be equipped with adequate visual and force sensors, and the precise control algorithms have to be built in on the slave side. Assuming the minimum expertise of the crew to be equivalent of Emergency Medical Technician in these missions, telepresence systems should only rely on assistance and support from the crew. Successful methods have been developed recently to provide automatic movement compensation (Ortmaier et al., 2006). This concept could be most beneficial for long duration on-orbit missions, primarily on board of the ISS. Presently, there is no other option than the immediate evacuation of the affected astronaut, which poses bigger health risk and huge costs.

Flying further from the Earth and having reached the limits of pseudo real-time communication, the procedures should be performed by the flight surgeon, or by any other trained astronaut, under the telementoring guidance of the master surgeons on the ground. Telementoring requires exchange of still images, motion video, digital image editing, voice conferencing, electronic chat and data file transfer. As showed by the NASA undersea experiments (Thirsk et al, 2007), telementoring can be an effective alternative to direct teleoperation, allowing the controller to perform the tasks based on the visual and voice commands of the ground centre. With adequate training and practice, the astronauts with a basic surgical training should be able to successfully accomplish complete procedures. As tested on USS Abraham Lincoln carrier in 1998, 9.6 28.8 kbps connection can already be enough to transfer images at 2-4 fps speed (Cubano et al. 1999). Telementoring may extend the boundaries of telepresence, as it can still be effective with a 50-70 s delay (within the range of app. 10,000,000 km). Upon this phase, the built-in semi-automatic functions of the surgical robot may have a significant role to improve the overall quality of the surgery. Motion scaling, adaptive tremor filtering, the automated following of the organ's movement, automated suturing could significantly improve the less practiced crew members' performance on one hand, while special security measures could also be applied. On the other hand, the setting of virtual boundaries for the robot, tool limitations and speed constraints may reduce the risk of accidents. Astronauts should also benefit from advanced imaging technologies (e.g.: accurately matched anatomic atlases for better navigation around the organs.) With the use of augmented reality systems, live and virtual images can be merged in real time to make the operation even smoother. Surgical malpractice can be reduced significantly by applying safe zones (virtual fixtures) that allow the robot to operate only within the predefined area (Lin et al., 2006). The safeguard teleoperation concept developed originally for mobile space robots could be useful in surgery. The robot can autonomously perform the routine tasks with the real time supervision of a human, however in the case of any malfunction or sudden events, the human operator can take over the control.

There is no crisp boundary between the application of telementoring and consultancy telemedicine. Above a certain signal delay, the terrestrial medical support crew will not be able to react in time to unforeseeable events during the procedure; the flight surgeon will be left alone for longer and longer periods. Above around one minute of delay, it is inconvenient and impractical for the crew to wait for the guidance of the ground after every step, and in some cases, it would endanger the success of the operation. For these missions, the physician must be trained to conduct the operation and make decisions on its own.

It was shown during the NEEMO missions that the general performance of telesurgery is higher than of the telemedicine, and a team of experts may do better than flight surgeons. Therefore depending on the feasibility, telesurgery should be preferred over telementoring.

With a complete remote controlled robot on board of a vessel, high quality surgical assistance could be provided for long duration space missions. Besides, the astronauts would be able to conduct several material and life science experiments and research, using the robots for micro-manipulations, and assist post-operative interventions. Advanced system design will help to deal with signal delays and to extend human capabilities.

7. Conclusion

In the case of telepresence surgery, intercontinental procedures, space missions and other highly complex exploration tasks and telehealth may mean the only sustainable solution to provide complete medical support. Telemedicine gains increasing importance as technology provides new and more effective means of telepresence to gain access to distant places. Medical robotic systems are already able to widely extend the human surgeons' capabilities, to provide high fidelity support for a great variety of procedures. The new generation of robots will lead to a breakthrough in general healthcare.

Extensive effort has been put into the exploration of this new domain of telemedicine, as reviewed in this chapter. To meet the special requirements, completely new and innovative structures are built for long distance telesurgery. The most extreme example of teleoperation is in space applications. Long duration missions and venturing beyond Earth orbit mean new technological challenges, especially considering life-support systems. By integrating cutting-edge mechatronic equipment, semi-autonomous robots could ensure the medical support for a 2-3-year-long mission through telehealth technology. With the combination of real-time teleoperation, telementoring and consultancy telemedicine, the overall mission safety can be greatly increased, assuming a limited level of autonomy to improve the usability. The next few years of research will lead to breakthroughs in the interdisciplinary field of Computer-Integrated Surgery, opening further opportunities for telesurgical application. Robots and smart tools controlled through communication networks are soon to answer the special needs of remote patients.

8. Acknowledgment

The research was supported by the National Office for Research and Technology (NKTH), Hungarian National Scientific Research Foundation grants OTKA T69055, CK80316.

9. References

Alexander, A.D. (1973). Impacts of Telemation on Modern Society, *Proc. of Human Factors and Ergonomics Society Annual Meeting*, Vol., 17, No., 2, 1973 , pp.299-304

Anvari, M. (2004). Robot-Assisted Remote Telepresence Surgery, *Surgical Innovation*, Vol.,11, No., 2, pp.123-128

Ballantyne, G.H.; J. Marescaux & P. C. Giulianotti (eds.) (2004). Primer of Robotic & Telerobotic Surgery, Lippincott Williams & Wilkins, 2004, ISBN 0-7817-4844-5

Ballantyne, G.H. (2007). The Future of Telerobotic Surgery, Chapter 18 in Patel, V.R. (editor), *Robotic Urologic Surgery*, 2007, pp.199-206, ISBN: 978-1-84628-545-5

Berlocher, G. (2009). Minimizing Latency in Satellite Networks, *Via Satellite*, Published at: www.viasatellite.com, September 2009, Accessed: September 2009

Bowersox, J.C.; Shah, A.; Jensen, J.; Hill, J.M.; Cordts, P.R. & Green, P.S. (1996). Vascular applications of telepresence Initial feasibility studies in swine surgery, *Journal of Vascular Surgery*, Vol., 23, Issue 2, February 1996, pp.281-287

Campbell, M.R.; Kirkpatrick, A.W; Billica, R.D.; Johnston, S.L.; Jennings, R.; Short, D.; Hamilton, D. & Dulchavsky, S.A. (2001). Endoscopic surgery in weightlessness: The investigation of basic principles for surgery in space, *Journal of Surgical Endoscopy*, Vol., 15, pp.1413–1418

Campbell, M.R. & Billica, R.D. (2008). Surgical Capabilities, Chapter 6 in Barratt, M.R.; Pool, S.L. (eds.), *Principles of Clinical Medicine for Space Flight*, Springer, 2008, ISBN: 978-0-387-98842-9

Christensen, H.I. et al. (2009). A Roadmap for US Robotics: From Internet to Robotics, Available online: http://www.us-robotics.us/reports/CCC%20Report.pdf Accessed: September, 2009

Cubano, M., Poulose, B.K., Talamini, M.A., Stewart, R., Antosek, L.E., Lentz, R., Nibe, R., Kutka, M.F. & Mendoza-Sagaon, M. (1999). Long distance telementoring: A novel tool for laparoscopy aboard the USS Abraham Lincoln, *Surgical Endoscopy*, Vol., 13., No., 7., 1999, pp.673-678, ISSN 0930-2794

Das, H.; Ohm T.; Boswell, C.; Steele, R. & Rodriguez, G. (1998). Robot Assisted MicroSurgery Development at JPL; *Technical Report*, NASA JPL, Pasadena

Doarn, C.R.; Anvari, M.; Low, T. & Broderick, T.J. (2009). Evaluation of Teleoperated Surgical Robots in an Enclosed Undersea Environment, *Journal of Telemedicine and e-Health*, Vol., 15 No., 4, May 2009, pp.325-335

Drake, B.G. (editor) (2009). Human Exploration of Mars Design Reference Architecture 5.0, *Mars Architecture Steering Group, NASA HQ*, July 2009, NASA/SP–2009–566

Eirik, L.; Johansen, B.; Gjelsvik, T. & Langø T. (2009). Ultrasound based localisation of wireless microrobotic endoscopic capsule for the GI tract, *Proc. 21st Conference of the Society for Medical Innovation and Technology (SMIT2009)*, Sinaia, Romania

Fabrizio, M.D.; Lee, B.R.; Chan, D.Y.; Stoianovici, D.; Jarrett, T.W.; Yang, C. & Kavoussi, L.R. (2000). Effect of time delay on surgical performance during telesurgical manipulation, *Journal of Endourology*, Vol. 14, No. 2, March 2000

Flynn, E. (2005). Telesurgery in the United States, *Homeland Defense J.*, June 2005, pp.24-28

Frank, L.H., (1986). Effects of visual display and motion system delays on operator performance and uneasiness in a driving simulator, *PhD Thesis*, Virginia Polytechnic Institute and State University, 1986

Green, P.E.; Piantanida, T.A.; Hill, J.W.; Simon, I.B. & Satava, R.M. (1991). Telepresence: dexterous procedures in a virtual operating field (Abstr), *American Journal of Surgery*, Issue 57, 1991, pp.192

Hager, G.D.; Okamura, A.M.; Kazanzides, P.; Whitcomb, L.; Fichtinger, G.; Taylor, R. (2008). Surgical and Interventional Robotics Part III; *IEEE Robotics & Automation Magazine*, Vol., 15, Issue 4, December 2008, pp. 84-94

Hagn, U., Nickl, M.; Jorg, S.; Passig, G.; Bahls, T.; Nothhelfer, A.; Hacker, F.; Le-Tien, L.; Albu-Schaffer, A.; Konietschke, R.; Grebenstein, M.; Warpup, R.; Haslinger, R.; Frommberger, M. & Hirzinger, G. (2008). The DLR MIRO: a versatile lightweight robot for surgical applications, International Journal of Industrial Robot, Vol., 35 No., 4, pp.324–336

Hanly, E.J. & Broderick, T.J. (2005). Telerobotic Surgery, *Operative Techniques in General Surgery*, Vol., 7, Issue 4, December 2005, pp.170-181

Herman, B.C. (2005). On the Role of Three Dimensional Visualization for Surgical Applications in Interactive Human Machine Systems, *Master thesis*, Computer Science, The Johns Hopkins University, May 2005

Kadavasal, M.S. & Oliver, J.H. (2007). Sensor Enhanced Virtual Reality Teleoperation in Dynamic Environment, *Proc. of IEEE Virtual Reality Conference (VR'07)*, pp.297-298, Charlotte, NC

Kamler, K. (2007). How I Survived a Zero-G Robot Operating Room: Extreme Surgeon; *Popular Mechanics*—online edition, November 2007

Kumar, S. & Marescaux, J. (eds.) (2008). Telesurgery, Springer, 2008, ISBN 978-3-540-72998-3

Lee, B.R.; Caddedu, J.A.; Janetschek, G.; Schulam, P.; Docimo, S.G.; Moore, R.G.; Partin, A.W. & Kavoussi, L.R. (1998). International surgical telementoring: our initial experience, *Studies in health technology and informatics*, Issue 50, 1998, pp.41-47

Lin, H.C.; Marayong, P.; Mills, K.; Karam, R.; Kazanzides, P.; Okamura, A. & Hager, G.D. (2006). Portability and Applicability of Virtual Fixtures Across Medical and

Manufacturing Tasks. *Proc. of the 2006 IEEE International Conference on Robotics and Automation*, pp. 225-330, Orlando, FL

Lum, M.J.H.; Rosen, J.; Lendvay, T.S.; Wright, A.S.; Sinanan, M.N. & Hannaford, B. (2008). TeleRobotic Fundamentals of Laparoscopic Surgery (FLS): Effects of Time Delay - Pilot Study, Proc. of 30th Annual International IEEE EMBS Conference Vancouver, Canada, August 2008

Lum, M.J.H.; Friedman, D.C.W.; Sankaranarayanan, G.; King, H.; Fodero, K.; Leuschke, R.; Hannaford, B.; Rosen, J. & Sinanan, M.N. (2009). The RAVEN: Design and Validation of a Telesurgery System, *International Journal of Robotics Research,* Vol., 28; No., 9, pp.1183-1197

Marescaux, J.; Leroy, J.; Rubino, F.; Vix, M.; Simone, M. &. Mutter, D. (2002). Transcontinental Robot-Assisted Remote Telesurgery: Feasibility and Potential Applications; *Annals of Surgery*, Vol. 235, No. 4., pp.487-492

Menciassi, A. & Dario, P. (2009). Miniaturized Robotic Devices for Endoluminal Diagnosis and Surgery: A Single-Module and a Multiple-Module Approach, Proc. of the 31st Annual International Conference of the IEEE Engineering in Medicine and Biology Society (EMBS), Minneapolis, MN, August 2009

MeRoDa (2009). Medical Robotics Database, http://www.ma.uni-heidelberg.de/apps/ /ortho/meroda/ Accessed: September 2009

Nathoo, N.; Cavusoglu, M.C.; Vogelbaum, M.A. & Barnett, G.H. (2005). In Touch with Robotics: Neurosurgery for the Future, *Journal of Neurosurgery,* Vol., 56. No., 3., March 2005, pp.421-433, ISSN 1524-4040

New Scientist Space & AFP (2006). Doctors remove tumor in first zero-g surgery; *New Scientist*, 27. September, 2006

Nohmi, M. (2003). Space Teleoperation Using Force Reflection of Communication Time Delay; *Proc. of IEEE/RSJ Intl. Conf. on Intelligent Robots and Systems,* Las Vegas, NV

Ortomaier, T.; Groger, M.; Boehm, D.H.; Falk, V. & Hirzinger, G. (2006). Motion Estimation in Beating Heart Surgery; *IEEE Trans. on Biomedical Engineering,* Vol. 52., No. 10., October 2005, pp. 1729-1740, ISSN: 0018-9294

Pappone, C.; Vicedomini, G.; Manguso, F.; Gugliotta, F.; Mazzone, P.; Gulletta, S.; Sora, N.; Sala, S.; Marzi, A.; Augello, A.; Livolsi, L.; Santagostino, A. & Santinelli, V. (2006). Robotic Magnetic Navigation for Atrial Fibrillation Ablation, *Journal of the American College of Cardiology*, Vol., 47, No., 7, 2006, ISSN 0735-1097

Reinhart, R.C. & Johnson, S.K. (2008). SDR/STRS Flight Experiment and the Role of SDR-Based Communication and Navigation Systems Communications Division, *IDGA 6th Annual Software Radio Summit,* Vienna, VA, February 2008

Rentschler, M.; Dumpert, J.; Platt, S.; Oleynikov, D.; Farritor, S. & Iagnemma, K. (2006). Mobile In Vivo Biopsy Robot, *Proc. of the 2006 IEEE International Conference on Robotics and Automation*, pp. 4155-4160, Orlando, FL

Rosen, J. & Hannaford, B. (2006). Doc at a distance, *IEEE Spectrum Magazine*, Vol. 8., No. 10., October 2006, pp.34-39

Rosser Jr., J.C.; Wood, M.; Payne, J.H.; Fullum, T.M.; Lisehora G.B.; Rosser, L.E.; Barcia, P.J. & Savalgi, R.S. (1997). Telementoring. A practical option in surgical training, *Surgical Endoscopy,* Vol., 11., No., 8., August 1997, pp.852–855, ISSN 0930-2794

Rosser Jr., J.C.; Young, S.M. & Klonsky, J. (2007). Telementoring: an application whose time has come, *Surgical Endoscopy*, Vol., 21., No., 8., August 2007, pp.1458–1463, ISSN 0930-2794

Satava, R.M. (1995). Virtual reality, telesurgery, and the new world order of medicine. *Journal of Image Guided Surgery*, Issue 1, 1995, pp.12–16

Schenker, P.S.; Das, H. & Ohm, T.R. (1995). A New Robot for High Dexterity Microsurgery, *Proc. of the First International Conference on Computer Vision, Virtual Reality and Robotics in Medicine, Springer Lecture Notes In Computer Science (LNCS)*, Vol., 90, 1995, pp.115-122, ISBN:3-540-59120-6

Spearing, R. & Regan, M. (2005). 4.0 NASA Communication and Navigation Capability Roadmap, *Executive Summary*, 2005

Thirsk, R.; Williams, D. & Anvari, M. (2007). NEEMO 7 undersea mission, *Acta Astronautica*, Vol. 60., Issue 4-7, February - April 2007, pp.512-517

Thomson, J.M.; Ottensmeyer, M.P & Sheridan, T.B. (1999). Human Factors in Telesurgery: Effects of Time Delay and Asynchrony in Video and Control Feedback with Local Manipulative Assistance, *Telemedicine journal*, Vol., 5, No., 2, pp.129-137

Trauma Pod (2009). http://www.darpa.mil/dso/thrusts/bio/tactbio_med/traumapod//index.htm Accessed: September, 2009

Wang, R. & Horan, S. (2009). Protocol Testing of SCPS-TP over NASA's ACTS Asymmetric Links, IEEE Transactions on Aerospace and Electronic Systems, Vol., 45, Issue 2, April 2009, pp.790-798, ISSN: 0018-9251

3

Telementoring and Telesurgery: Future or Fiction?

Vitor da Silva, Tom McGregor, Reiza Rayman, Patrick PW Luke
CSTAR, Department of Surgery and Biomedical Physics
The University of Western Ontario, Schulich School of Medicine
London, Ontario,
Canada

1. Introduction

Over the last two decades, minimally invasive surgery (MIS) has emerged as an attractive alternative to traditional open surgical procedures. MIS has been shown to provide excellent surgical outcomes with the added benefit of decreased procedure-related morbidity. Minimal bleeding, reduced blood transfusion rates, shorter hospitalization, and shorter recovery times are all proven advantages for laparoscopic procedures. [1-3] However, many MIS procedures are more technically challenging than the traditional open counterpart, and the learning curve to proficiency is markedly steeper than standard open procedures. Several factors including establishing adequate access, two dimensional vision, decreased depth perception, restricted instrument maneuverability, decreased dexterity and dampened tactile feedback are all unique limitations that make laparoscopic surgery challenging for surgeons trained in traditional open approaches. To the laparoscopically naïve surgeon, this translates into a loss of confidence in performing a procedure in which they were previously skilled. Appropriate training and education are therefore essential for a surgeon to develop the necessary skills required in order to comfortably perform a surgery adequately and safely. Unfortunately, resources are limited. Time, monetary and geographical constraints often limit the ubiquitous dissemination of new surgical knowledge, skills and techniques. The inability to provide adequate training opportunities and support for surgeons in the community continues to be the limiting factors determining the success and widespread availability of laparoscopic surgeries.

Thankfully, with the ever-increasing push to incorporate technological advances into the medical field, we are now able to overcome these barriers. In this chapter we outline how the recent progress in technology and telecommunication has led to the advent of telemedicine - an ingenious solution to our current problem, which will allow for the widespread availability of MIS and improve patient care.

2. What is telemedicine?

Defined as "medical care at a distance", telemedicine is a broad term referring to a physician's ability to practice medicine and directly influence patient care without being physically at the bedside. The underlying principle of telemedicine involves advanced telecommunication systems for data acquisition, processing and display allowing the physician or health care worker to transfer their expertise from a remote location. This opens the door for a wealth of applications, transcending geographical barriers when participating in patient care. Of particular interest to our discussion are the two main branches of telemedicine for surgeons – telementoring and telesurgery.

3. Telementoring

As cutting edge technology evolves, new surgical techniques are developed. This has occurred with the development of laparoscopy, laser, and robotic surgery. Surgeons already established in their community or academic practices have limited time to re-train or take sabbaticals to learn new skills necessary to carry out novel complex operative procedures. In part, this may have contributed to prolonged operative times and alarmingly high complication rates associated with the early development in laparoscopic radical prostatectomy (LRP) [4]. In general, the ability to efficiently train a surgeon to become facile at LRP has requires fellowship training, or recruitment of an experienced surgical mentor. However, when local expertise is not available, it is a challenge to recruit a mentor to teach novel operative techniques, as there rarely exists an established remunerative or academic reward to lure the mentors away from their regular patient-care and academic activities in order to travel and teach others. Therefore, telementoring has been developed to allow long-distance training utilizing mentors from a different hospital, city or continent.

Telementoring involves procedural guidance of one professional by another from a distance using telecommunications. This has involved interactions involving audio dialogue, video telestration (video tablet and pen), and even guidance of a camera or laparoscope with a surgical robot such as Aesop™ (Computer Motion, Santa Barbara, CA). In order to send audiovisual data, connections using WAN (wide area network), LAN (local area network), integrated services digital network (ISDN) or internet protocol (IP) links have been utilized. Security has been established through virtual private networks (VPNe) to prevent others to access and manipulate connections.

At first, telementoring was developed by surgeons from the Johns Hopkins University group utilizing rudimentary teleconferencing audiovisual equipment and a video sketch pad to provide telestration (Cody Sketchpad, Chryon Corp., Melville, NY). Trainees were provided mentorship from the staff surgeons situated 1000 feet away [5]. This developed into telementoring studies involving the USS Abraham Lincoln Aircraft Carrier Battle Group. Five laparoscopic inguinal hernia repairs were performed under telementored guidance from land-based surgeons from Maryland and California [6]. This established the ability to perform long-distance telementoring across bodies of water in times of war. Furthermore, Kavoussi's group utilized the Aesop™ robot as well as the Socrates telestration system (Intuitive Surgical) to telementor 17 urologic operations (including laparoscopic nephrectomy) between Baltimore, Maryland to Rome, Italy. However, the procedures were associated with a half second image delay between sites, and a high technical failure rate (5/17) due to an inability to establish connections through their 4 ISDN lines during times of heavy traffic [7;8].

In its early development, most of the procedures utilizing telementoring have required that an experienced surgeon was situated at the patient's operative tableside. Accordingly, in March 2003, our group from London, Ontario, Canada harnessed SOCRATES™ and AESOP™ telerobotic technology through 4 ISDN lines to successfully telementor laparoscopic nephrectomy and pyeloplasty with the mentor situated over 200 km away. Since our intent was to test the ISDN connections and the robotic platforms, we ensured that the bedside surgeon was equally as experienced as the mentor, and could complete the operation in case of communicative technical failure.

Subsequently, our group has prospectively tested telementoring in a 'real-world' situation, with a truly 'inexperienced' trainee with a 'complex' new procedure. As we have stated in the past, LRP is one of the most technically challenging operations in urology, with a steep learning curve associated with prolonged operative times, complications and poor oncologic outcomes during the early development of the procedure [4]. It has been stated that surgeons need to complete 50-300 cases in order to obtain operative proficiency for LRP. For the first time, we described the experience utilizing long-distance telementoring to facilitate the performance of the LRP with a trainee surgeon naïve to LRP. It should be mentioned, however, that although the trainee had never performed LRP, he had a high volume laparoscopic surgical practice. Utilizing an ISDN telecommunications network, the LRP-naïve trainee observed 6 LRP performed by a trainer located 200 km away from Hamilton to London Ontario (group1) (Figure 1). Using the same network, the trainee performed 6 LRP under the supervision of the remote trainer (group 2). The next six LRP procedures were performed by the trainee independently (group 3). The trainer and trainee were able to communicate back and forth using audio equipment and visual demonstration of anatomy and techniques were communicated via a pen and tablet video screen. The audiovisual feeds were facilitated by simple Polycom technology and ISDN lines. Due to weather issues, telecommunications failed in 1 case. Audiovisual communication was excellent and although visual delays were experienced, this did not greatly impact upon the success of the cases. The median operative times for the three groups were 200 min, 285 min vs. 250 min respectively (p = NS between groups 2 and 3). Median blood loss was not different between groups and no blood transfusions were performed. No anastomotic leaks, open conversion or intraoperative complications occurred. Of the patients with confined disease (pT2), only one patient had a local positive surgical margin (group 2) with all patients having undetectable disease at 1 year. At the 1 year follow-up mark, 11/12 patients in group 2 and 3 have achieved complete urinary continence. Of 8 patients in the groups 2 and 3 that underwent bilateral nerve sparing, 38% of patients achieved potency by 12 months. It was concluded that telementoring could be performed to teach complex operative procedures such as LRP to surgeons. Similarly, Schlacta's group from our centre had successfully trained less-experienced community-based general surgeons (through direct local and telementoring) to perform laparoscopic colon surgery. Although 33% of cases were converted to standard open procedures, the group concluded that there was excellent incorporation of laparoscopic colon surgery into this community-based practice [9].

We conclude that performance of telementoring is feasible and that it is possible to teach complex operations with current technology. We also believe that telementoring does not need to be limited to MIS procedures. Although the majority of hospital administrators are facile with teleconferencing, and telemedicine has been explored by a number of physician groups for patient care and education, surgeons have been slow to adapt to the same technology. We have shown that telementoring using ISDN lines is feasible and relatively inexpensive, utilizing existing communication lines. However, its eventual adaptation in healthcare will depend on further education and an evolution in surgical thinking.

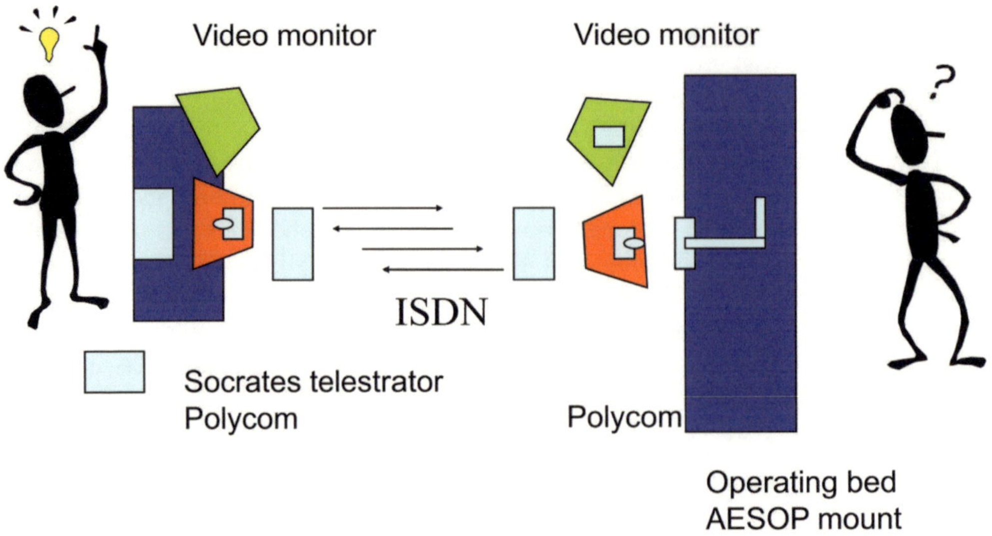

Fig. 1. Telementoring set-up. The set up in our telementoring procedures involved 4 ISDN lines as well as audiovisual Polycoms, and video screen telestrator. The AESOP laparoscope holding robot was used during early, but not later clinical use. The mentor is pictured on the left while the trainee along-side the OR table is pictured on the right hand side.

4. Telesurgery

Telesurgery involves a surgical procedure with the surgeon being situated remotely from the patient. The history of telesurgery dates back to the first commercial application in laparoscopy. The Automated Endoscopic System for Optimal Positioning (AESOP™) was FDA approved in the United States in 1993 and was used solely to guide the laparoscope. When it was initially introduced, the surgeon controlled the robotic arm either manually or remotely with hand or foot switches. Later versions were modified and equipped with voice controls. Although the use of has been associated with 'telementoring procedures', its development gave way to the complex three armed robotic technology that integrated instrument manipulating arms as well.

The manufacturer of the AESOP™, Computer Motion Inc., would later introduce the three armed ZEUS™ robotic system onto the U.S. market in 1998. Concurrently, Intuitive Surgical (Sunnyvale, California) released yet another 3-arm surgical robot, the da Vinci®. Developed from technology designed by NASA, the da Vinci® was originally intended for use by the U.S military, but was quickly adopted for civilian use. In 2003, a merger between Computer Motion Inc. and Intuitive surgical paved the way for the da Vinci® robot, along with it's newly FDA approved EndoWrist™ technology, to dominate the surgical robot market worldwide. The large majority of published literature on robotic-assisted surgery to date, has employed the use of the da Vinci® system. Currently, it is the only commercially available surgical robotic system.

The da Vinci® consists of separate components. The surgeon sits at the console where he/she is able to visualize the surgical field in 3D and operate several hand and foot controls. The surgeon's motions are processed by a computer system and relayed to the robotic arms. The robot has three arms. The central arm holds the camera and 2-3 outer arms hold the surgical instruments, which articulate at the EndoWrist™. This allows the instruments to move with seven degrees of freedom and two degrees of axial rotation, eliminating many of the difficulties associated with standard laparoscopic procedures.

Initially, commercial surgical robots were intended to perform minimally invasive cardiac procedures. However, since the initial description for robot assisted closed-chest coronary artery bypass grafting at our centre in 1999 [10], applications for robotic surgery have been rapidly growing. Since its inception, robotic surgery has not only expanded to other cardiac surgical procedures such as left internal mammary artery take-down and mitral valve repair, but also several gastrointestinal, gynecological and urological procedures. These included: cholecystectomy, Nissen fundoplication, Heller myotomy, pancreatectomy, hepaticojejunostomy, gastric banding, distal gastrectomy, Roux-en-Y gastric bypass, colectomy, tubal re-anastamosis, hysterectomy, nephrectomy, pyeloplasty, adrenalectomy, aneurysm repair and radical prostatectomy, among others. Due to the increased precision and dexterity that the robot contributes to the case, the robot has been exploited for radical prostatectomy more than any other procedure, since it has allowed laparoscopically naïve surgeons to perform laparoscopic suturing to perform critical anastomotic maneuvers with relative ease. We have shown that the robot improves the performance of experienced laparoscopic surgeons as well [11].

Of relevance to telesurgery, these robotic platforms were designed using connections that permitted surgery to be performed with the surgeon at a console remote from the bedside robot and patient. In fact, the original intent was to permit the surgeon to perform surgery just as easily in another room, another building, another continent, or in outer space. Indeed, any surgical procedure with the surgeon sitting remotely from the patient could be considered remote telesurgery. However, it is the possibility of performing long-distance telesurgery that stirs the imagination.

Most notably, in 2001, Marescaux et al. revolutionized surgery by performing a trans-Atlantic robotic assisted cholecystectomy using the ZEUS™ robot [12]. The surgeon and console were located in New York, and the patient and effector arms were in Strausbourg, France. Asynchronous transfer mode (ATM) technology was used to establish connections via high-speed terrestrial fiberoptic networks with a bandwidth of 10Mb/s. These connections were reserved exclusively for the procedure that ran a round-trip distance of 14000 km. Although there was a lag time of 155 ms, the laparoscopic cholecystectomy was completed without incident over 54 minutes. It should be noted that although audiovisual interactions and robotic arm movements were performed through the trans-Atlantic connections, the application of 'electrocautery' to dissect the gall bladder, placement of clips, introduction of the ports, and closure of port-sites had to be performed by the bed-side assistants. As well, laparoscopic cholecystectomy is a relatively simple laparoscopic procedure and could have been easily completed by the bed side surgeons with greater ease and in less time. Although the cost of this solitary operation was astronomical, it demonstrated that 'real world' long-distance telesurgery was feasible, and if the lag time could be limited to <155 ms, surgeons could perform simple procedures from their home base, even if the patient was on a battlefield or in the far reaches of space.

The next natural step in the evolution of telerobotics was to employ this technology to help train and certify surgeons in 'real world' distant or remote communities. This would allow an expertly trained surgeon at a central location to provide assistance and collaboration during a new or challenging procedure to a less experienced surgeon in the community. This would also provide community surgeons in remote areas a means to gain advanced laparoscopic skills, as well as provide patients access to tertiary care level surgical procedures without having to travel.

Although this concept seems intuitive, reports of these practical applications are rare and the anticipated adoption of this technology into the current day clinical practice remains sporadic. Reasons for this may include: the amount of time and organization involved at both sites, financial burdens of the technology and equipment, and a lack of a dedicated and safe network with sufficient bandwidth to transmit such data.

Another group in Ontario, Canada has demonstrated their successful integration of telesurgery into clinical practice. Anvari et. al. [13] used telesurgery on a routine basis to both assist and mentor surgeries requiring advanced laparoscopic skills at a remote hospital over 300 miles away. Commencing in February 2003, one year after the trans-Atlantic cholecystectomy by Marescaux, Anvari was able to provide a "Telerobotic Surgical Service"; using telesurgery, he successfully completed 21 laparoscopic procedures over a two-year period. All surgeries were successful with no major intraoperative complications, including no open conversions. Surgical outcomes were equivalent to those of the same laparoscopic procedures performed at a tertiary center. The array of surgeries performed included: 13 fundoplications, 3 sigmoid resections, 2 right hemicolectomies, 1 anterior resection, and 2 inguinal hernia repairs. The amount of time spent by each surgeon performing the surgical dissection in each case was equally allocated between mentor and trainee. Furthermore, both surgeons were able to operate together using the same surgical footprint, swapping roles seamlessly throughout the procedure.

The group utilized a commercially available network (15 Mbps of bandwidth) to connect the two hospitals. An overall latency of 135-140 ms was incurred, but surgeons were able to compensate with this delay. The Zeus™ surgical system used in all cases, with the console in Hamilton and the operating arms at the operative bedside in North Bay, Ontario.

Overall, the work by Anvari demonstrated that routine telesurgery is feasible, although the full extent of its role as an adjunct to telementoring remains to be determined. As the cost of surgical systems decrease and reliable data networks become more available, barriers preventing the routine use of telesurgery may fall, allowing a more broad involvement in future surgical practice.

5. Limitations of telesurgery

Although successful clinical telerobotic surgery has been accomplished, most cases were simple and did not require extensive dissection, suturing and knot tying. Delays incurred through transmission of telesurgical data through the communication circuits and codecs result in slowing of surgeon movement to account for asynchrony in motor output and visual input. It was not clear whether there was a temporal delay (latency) incurred by distance that would preclude the ability of the surgeon to compensate for visual-motor asynchrony, leading to excessive errors and abandonment of relatively complex procedures.

Utilizing a Zeus™ robot and real-time, internet protocol virtual private network (IP-VPNe) as well as satellite links, 18 porcine pyeloplasty procedures were performed by our group. The pyeloplasty procedure was used as our operative model, since it requires fine operative suturing with requirements of knot tying to accomplish 'water tight' anastomotic competence. The IP-VPNe network consisted of two redundant 17 Mbps IP connections at the surgeon console and two redundant 17 Mbps connections at the operative subject side cart (in London, Ontario), providing highly available WAN access to the Bell Canada VPNe Core network within our test laboratory. The WAN connections were then looped back at the Bell Canada central office in Halifax Nova Scotia, which added 4150 km round trip distance between surgeon and surgical subject sides (both in London, Ontario) (Figure 2). The satellite network was privately partitioned with 10 Mbps bandwith. The routing was a round trip connection from London to Toronto, Ontario, to a telecommunications satellite (Telesat Canada) operating in the Ku band (12-14 GHz) and back to London Ontario, traversing a distance of 71,000 km [14].

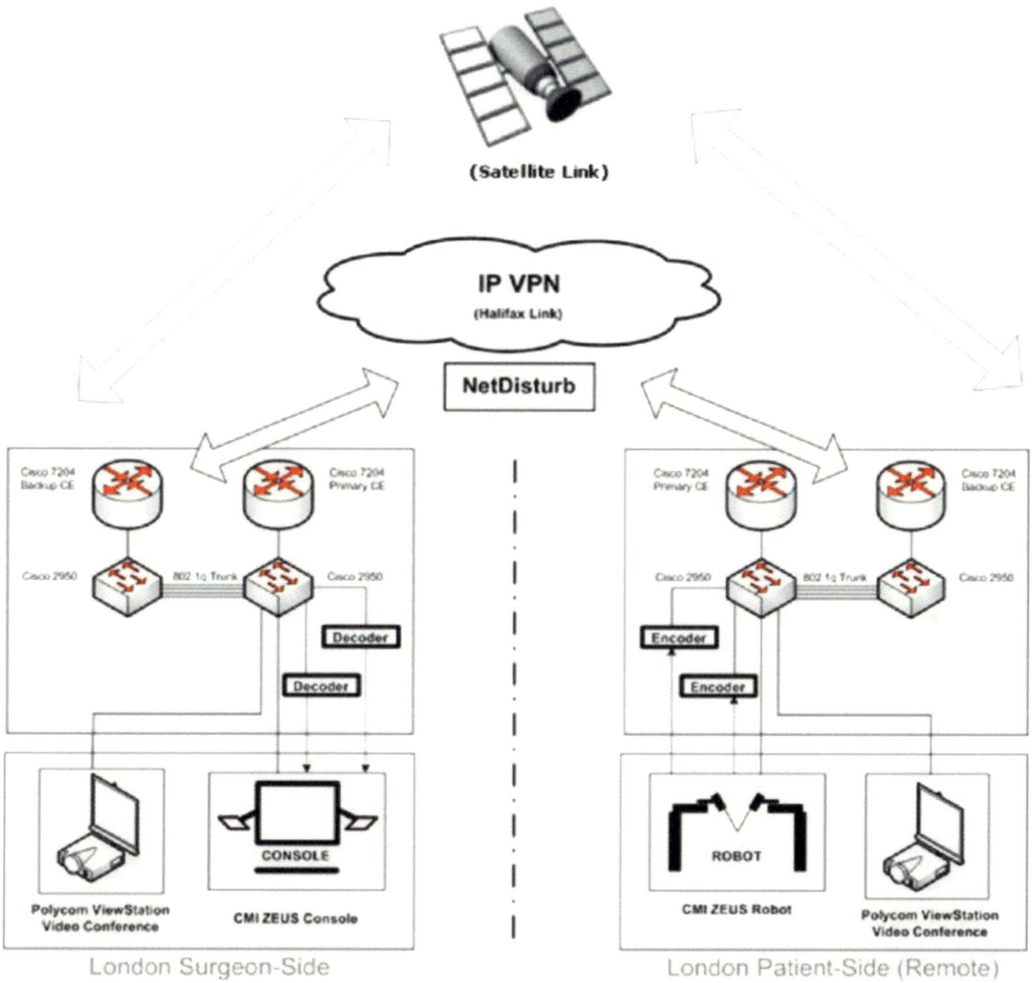

Fig. 2. Hardware set-up of the London-Halifax and satellite telesurgery loops. These loops were used to facilitate telesurgical experimental procedures. This permitted all experiments to be performed in one location, despite telesurgical routes over 4000 km long. Left hand side of figure outlines surgeon console and associated connections, right hand side illustrates telesurgical accessory surgeon console and patient side cart with associated connections.

Network latencies encountered during the trial were 66.3 +/- 1.5 ms for landline and 560.7 +/- 16.5 ms for satellite. During the procedures through landline, VPNe and satellite, fluid robotic motion and faithful visual rendering of the operative field was achieved. Network bandwidth was measured, requiring only 23 Mbps of budgeted 45 Mbps required during the procedures. Operative duration with real-time connection (41.3 +/- 15.0 min) was not significantly different vs. VPNe landline (47.0+/-24.1 min) vs. satellite (51.8+/-4.7 min). The anastomotic competence of the pyeloplasty procedures were excellent in all groups as well [14]. Although it was subjectively more challenging to perform pyeloplasty in the landline and satellite groups, it was shown that complex operative procedures requiring delicate suturing and knot tying could be accomplished using long-distance landline and satellite connections. The fact that operative times and errors were similar between groups indicate that surgeons experienced in telesurgery and robotics are capable in adapting to an operative environment in which latency and network jitter affect the human-machine interface.

Using the same 4150 km 'London to Halifax to London' loop, the ability to perform telesurgery in the same porcine pyeloplasty model was assessed 1 year later using the advanced da Vinci® robotic platform. A maximum of 23 Mbps of budgeted 45 Mbps were required for telesurgical operations, but 3-D stereoscopic vision was lost from the long-distance cases vs. the direct connection controls. Network latencies were similar at 66.1+/-1.5 ms. Network jitter ranged from 0-5 ms and no network failures occurred. With the da Vinci® procedures, operative times were significantly faster than with the Zeus™ procedures, but it was also apparent that with the use of more efficient robotic technology, the long-distance IP-VPNe operations took significantly more time vs. direct cable links (20.7+/-4.7 min vs 10.9+/-1.1 min, $p<0.01$). As well, there were no anastomotic discrepancies in any cases performed (total 12) [15]. We concluded that as robotic technology advanced, surgeries became more facile and the detriment of network latency and jitter were more apparent in our later trials. However, the impact of losing 3-D vision through the VPNe network as it related with operative time is not known.

6. The limits of bandwidth and latency

Our labs performed a series of experiments to quantify maximal tolerable latency during typical surgical maneuvers. Using randomized latencies, task times were significantly higher compared with zero delay at latency times of 500 ms and above ($p<0.01$; Figure 3) [16]. As noted earlier, the root cause of this delay are related with the encoding and decoding processes rather than the physical separation distance between operating sites. Already, we have seen significant progress in codec speed and capacity rates facilitating transmission of dual high definition signals.

Communities without broadband access may need to rely upon satellite communication to support telemedicine. In order to quantify telesurgery applications, our group performed porcine internal mammary artery (IMA) dissection using both IP and satellite networks described earlier [16-18]. There was no significant difference in the time to perform IMA dissection (p = NS). Using a multi-criteria Global Rating Scale, we found that there was also no significant difference in the quality of surgical performance. Bandwidth of the satellite feed was progressively pared down to identify a failure point for the video signal. Telesurgery was no longer possible at bandwidth of approximately 4 Mb/s or less, as determined by the operator and an experienced robotics observer team (Figure 4)[19].

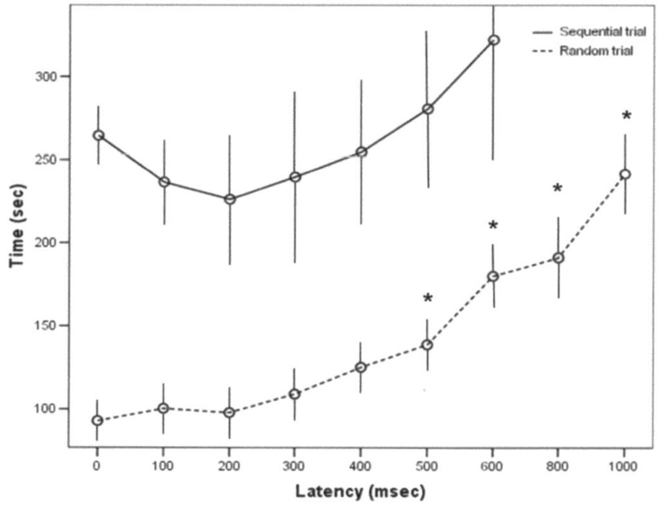

Fig. 3. Overall time for task completion of dry lab objects for sequential and random delay trials at differing latencies. Random trial times were significantly greater compared to zero latency at 500 ms and beyond (repeated measures ANOVA, * $p < 0.001$)

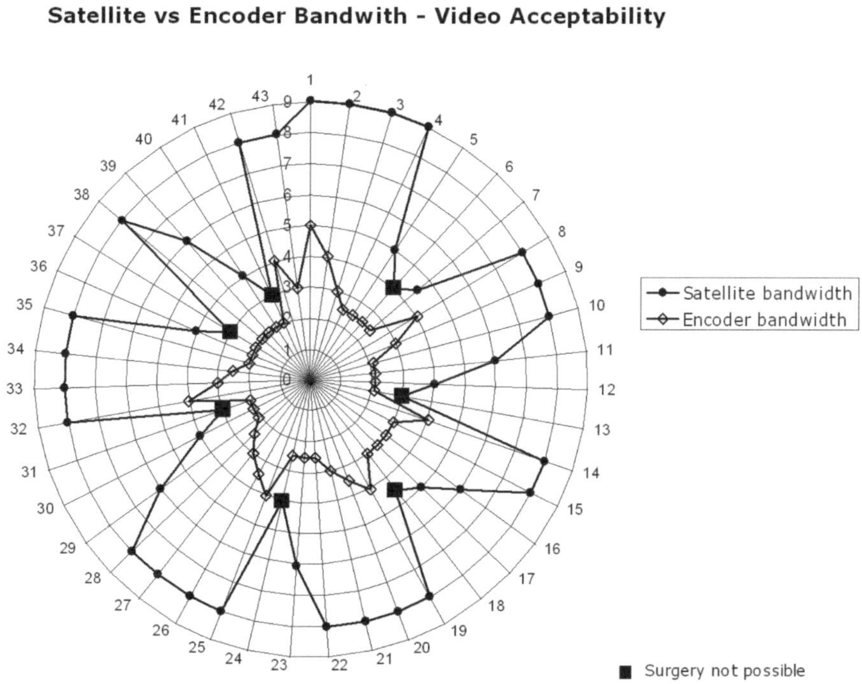

Fig. 4. Satellite and encoder bandwidths were sequentially decreased to identify a minimum level for telesurgery. The bandwidth 'pipe' is shown as concentric circles (9–0 Mb/s). Changes in bandwidth combinations using 7 pigs are seen radially in the 43 spokes. ■, satellite bandwidths at which surgery was no longer possible (approximately 4 Mb/s)

7. Pitfalls

Although the performance of complex operations from a distance has been shown to be feasible using existing technology, the provision of VPNe lines capable of supporting 48 Mbps was expensive ($30,000/ month). There are also issues regarding the medico-legal aspects of performing telesurgery. For example, who assumes the primary medico-legal responsibility for the long-distance procedure? Is it assigned to the bedside surgeon or the experienced surgeon based from afar? What happens if the telecommunication system fails? Are encrypted VPNe systems truly protected from individuals that are capable of 'hacking' into IP lines? There are other issues that exist for the telementor. How do we decide who is credentialed to be a mentor and how do we assign responsibility if the case goes awry? If the most experienced surgeon needs to assume responsibility, then it may be impossible to find any experts that would take on the responsibility of primary patient care without established and reliable financial or academic reward.

8. Future of telesurgery

Technologically, telesurgery will become more facile as network latency becomes reduced through the use of more efficient codecs and the advancement of surgical robotics. However, the development of telesurgery is contingent upon surgeon acceptance, need, and development of routine use, which would be associated with reduce costs. In fact, there may come a time that a surgeon performing robotic surgery may find a colleague to assist in a challenging operation through telesurgical operation of a fourth robotic arm. It would be as simple as dialing up a senior colleague to facilitate the operative procedure. Using telesurgery, that senior colleague may be dialed into an operation that is taking place a thousand miles away.

9. Conclusion

In conclusion, telementoring has been shown to be feasible, inexpensive and an effective tool to facilitate the development of surgical training in remote locations. Currently, its major limitations reside within limited access to trainers, perceived need, and the slow trickle of technology into the operating room. Long distance telesurgery, despite network latency and jitter, has been shown to be feasible, effective but very expensive. It requires significant amount of resources, including a robot in the remote centre, and bedside assistants that are capable of providing a fallback plan in case of technical failure. Ongoing clinical needs and evolving robotic and telecommunication technology are currently being evaluated.

10. References

[1] Beasley KA, Al Omar M, Shaikh A, Bochinski D, Khakhar A, Izawa JI et al. Laparoscopic versus open partial nephrectomy. Urology 2004; 64(3):458-461.

[2] Binsaleh S, Luke PP, Nguan C, Kapoor A. Comparison of laparoscopic and open nephrectomy for adult polycystic kidney disease: operative challenges and technique. Can J Urol 2006; 13(6):3340-3345.

[3] Portis AJ, Clayman RV. Should laparoscopy be the standard approach used for radical nephrectomy? Curr Urol Rep 2001; 2(2):165-170.
[4] Chin JL, Luke PP, Pautler SE. Initial experience with robotic-assisted laparoscopic radical prostatectomy in the Canadian health care system. Can Urol Assoc J 2007; 1(2):97-101.
[5] Moore RG, Adams JB, Partin AW, Docimo SG, Kavoussi LR. Telementoring of laparoscopic procedures: initial clinical experience. Surg Endosc 1996; 10(2):107-110.
[6] Cubano M, Poulose BK, Talamini MA, Stewart R, Antosek LE, Lentz R et al. Long distance telementoring. A novel tool for laparoscopy aboard the USS Abraham Lincoln. Surg Endosc 1999; 13(7):673-678.
[7] Bove P, Stoianovici D, Micali S, Patriciu A, Grassi N, Jarrett TW et al. Is telesurgery a new reality? Our experience with laparoscopic and percutaneous procedures. J Endourol 2003; 17(3):137-142.
[8] Micali S, Virgili G, Vannozzi E, Grassi N, Jarrett TW, Bauer JJ et al. Feasibility of telementoring between Baltimore (USA) and Rome (Italy): the first five cases. J Endourol 2000; 14(6):493-496.
[9] Schlachta CM, Lefebvre KL, Sorsdahl AK, Jayaraman S. Mentoring and telementoring leads to effective incorporation of laparoscopic colon surgery. Surg Endosc 2009.
[10] Boyd WD, Rayman R, Desai ND, Menkis AH, Dobkowski W, Ganapathy S et al. Closed-chest coronary artery bypass grafting on the beating heart with the use of a computer-enhanced surgical robotic system. J Thorac Cardiovasc Surg 2000; 120(4):807-809.
[11] Nguan C, Kwan K, Al Omar M, Beasley KA, Luke PP. Robotic pyeloplasty: experience with three robotic platforms. Can J Urol 2007; 14(3):3571-3576.
[12] Marescaux J, Leroy J, Gagner M, Rubino F, Mutter D, Vix M et al. Transatlantic robot-assisted telesurgery. Nature 2001; 413(6854):379-380.
[13] Anvari M, McKinley C, Stein H. Establishment of the world's first telerobotic remote surgical service: for provision of advanced laparoscopic surgery in a rural community. Ann Surg 2005; 241(3):460-464.
[14] Nguan CY, Morady R, Wang C, Harrison D, Browning D, Rayman R et al. Robotic pyeloplasty using internet protocol and satellite network-based telesurgery. Int J Med Robot 2008; 4(1):10-14.
[15] Nguan C, Miller B, Patel R, Luke PP, Schlachta CM. Pre-clinical remote telesurgery trial of a da Vinci telesurgery prototype. Int J Med Robot 2008; 4(4):304-309.
[16] Rayman R, Primak S, Patel R, Moallem M, Morady R, Tavakoli M et al. Effects of latency on telesurgery: an experimental study. Med Image Comput Comput Assist Interv Int Conf Med Image Comput Comput Assist Interv 2005; 8(Pt 2):57-64.
[17] Rayman R, Croome K, Galbraith N, McClure R, Morady R, Peterson S et al. Robotic telesurgery: a real-world comparison of ground- and satellite-based internet performance. Int J Med Robot 2007; 3(2):111-116.
[18] Rayman R, Croome K, Galbraith N, McClure R, Morady R, Peterson S et al. Long-distance robotic telesurgery: a feasibility study for care in remote environments. Int J Med Robot 2006; 2(3):216-224.

[19] Rayman R, Croome K, Galbraith N, McClure R, Morady R, Peterson S et al. Long-distance robotic telesurgery: a feasibility study for care in remote environments. Int J Med Robot 2006; 2(3):216-224.

4

Simulation Model for the Dynamics Analysis of a Surgical Assistance Robot

Hans-Christian Schneider and Juergen Wahrburg
University of Siegen, Center for Sensor Systems (ZESS)
Germany

1. Introduction

MODI*CAS* (modular interactive Computer Assisted Surgery) represents an integral solution for the software-based combination of a surgical planning software, an optical localization device and a haptic sensor with a mechatronic manipulator in order to support surgical interventions. One key feature of the integral system is to accurately and precisely align any surgical instrument, according to the preoperative planning, in relation to the bony structure of the patient and to intraoperatively ensure the alignment to remain constant all the time. This is made possible due to the automatically controlled tracking of small patient movements in real time. As a result of developed calibration algorithms, the stationary precision and accuracy of the whole system is mainly defined by the measurement characteristics of the applied localization device. Moreover, the actual exploratory focus lies on the enhancement of the dynamic behaviour, especially on the reduction of the dynamic tracking error without concurrently degrading the stationary properties. The following chapter describes the development and use of an offline simulation environment for the analysis and the enhancement of the MODI*CAS* patient tracking system dynamics. At first, the functional principle of the tracking procedure is discussed. Furthermore, the physical modelling of all relevant system characteristics and the identification of the system parameters are described. Additionally, the model behaviour is verified against measurements from the real surgical assistance system. It is shown, that the offline model properly simulates the behaviour of the real system. As an example of use, a comparison of three tracking control strategies is shown on the basis of the developed and identified model. In the future, further simulations will be performed, in order to understand how various system parameters like lags, measurement noise or calibration errors may influence the overall tracking performance. The results will lead to a conclusion about the actual technical constraints and to an outlook on how such system can be further advanced in the future.

2. The modiCAS surgical assistance robot

The concept of the MODI*CAS* surgical assistance system, as shown in Fig. 1 during a clinical trial, has been already introduced in Castillo Cruces *et al.* (2008). The major goal of its concept is to combine a robot manipulator {*rbs*} with a common surgical navigation or localization system {*ots*} respectively to one integral unit (Fig. 2). To be precise, we use a PA10 Series General Purpose Robot from MITSUBISHI HEAVY INDUSTRIES (MHI) as manipulator and a NDI POLARIS P4 Optical Tracking System {*ots*} as localizer. This integrated device helps the surgeon to accurately and precisely align any surgical instrument {*ttp*} relatively to the patient's anatomy {*arb*}, exactly as defined in the computer assisted preoperative planning.

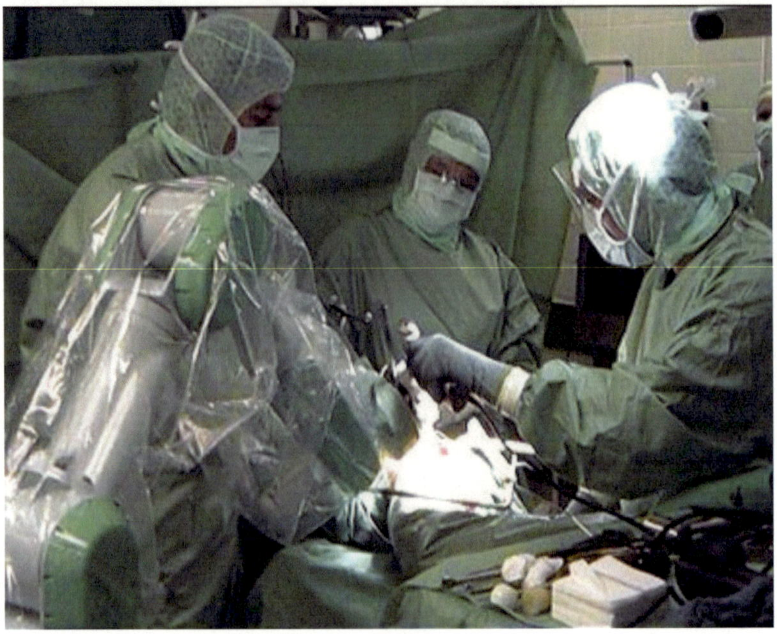

Fig. 1. Clinical trial utilizing the MODI*CAS* assistance robot for total hip arthroplasty implantation

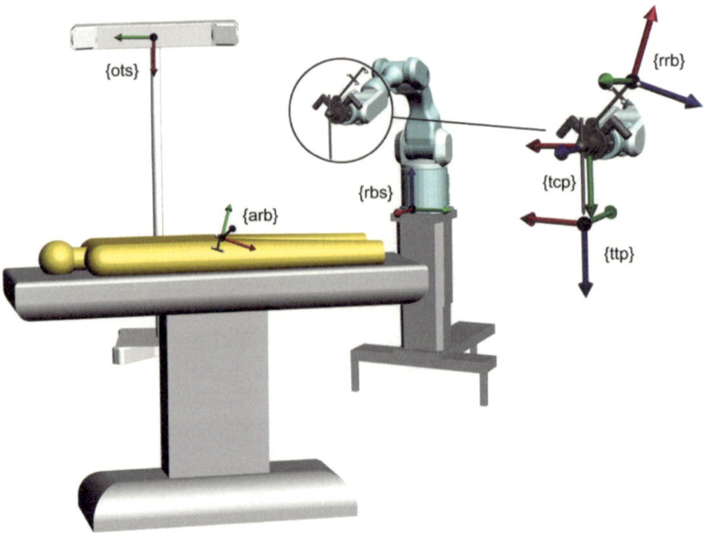

Fig. 2. Coordinate systems – {ots} localizer (optical tracking system), {arb} patient (aim reference body), {rrb} (robot reference body) {rbs} robot base, {tcp} robot wrist (tool center point), {ttp} tool tip

Utilizing a robot manipulator for such positioning tasks offers significant advantages in contrast to pure navigation systems. First, a robot manipulator guided by a precise localization system can position any surgical instrument with a very high precision for a long period of time, without tremor, exhaustion or the possibility of slipping. Second, the surgeon, who is released from the monotonous but straining positioning task, can fully concentrate on the main focus of the intervention, for instance what force he applies to the bony structure when he mills or drills using any wrist-mounted, manually controlled instrument.

One key feature of the MODI*CAS* assistance system is that it does not behave fully autonomously but highly interactively in order to cooperatively assist the surgeon. Therefore, much development work has been concentrated on the cooperative haptic interaction interface, as described in Castillo Cruces *et al.* (2008).

One further research and development goal is to make a rigid fixation of the patient unnecessary by integrating an online tracking function that automatically updates the pose of the aligned instrument in real time if the patient moves. Reducing the dynamic error without degrading the stationary precision of such tracking functionality is a challenging task. In practice, the reachable dynamics and precision are bounded by technical constraints of the system components. Thus, the robot control must be carefully adopted to those system parameters. A reliable simulation model of the whole tracking procedure will be helpful to get a better understanding of the patient tracking principle and the influence of various system parameters on the tracking quality. The development of such a model and the identification of its dynamic parameters, as well as one example of use, will be the focus of this article.

3. Real time tracking of patient's movements by the robot

Due to the fact that the MODI*CAS* patient tracking procedure is carried out by the use of an optical tracking system, it can be characterized as a so called *'visual servoing system'*, like already described in Weiss *et al.* (1987). In the past, *visual servoing* approaches have been categorized in detail, depending on the type of e.g. camera or control principle. A generalized overview is given in Kragic & Christensen (2002). This section will illustrate how the MODI*CAS* patient tracking procedure works, by categorizing it and establishing its kind of implementation.

The PA10 robot arm from MHI is shipped as a modular system that allows three different ways of interfacing. The easiest way is to use a dedicated MOTION CONTROL BOARD (MHI MCB) that carries out the entire basic functionality which is typically provided with common industrial robots e.g. like forward and inverse kinematics calculations, control in cartesian or joint space and trajectory path planning. The MHI MCB was utilized within the first generation of the MODI*CAS* assistance system in order to fulfill the general proof of principle of the overall MODI*CAS* concept. The experiences with that first prototype emphasized the necessity of interfacing the robot on a lower level in order to implement new desired features. For instance, such features are a singularity robust haptic interface, virtual motion constraints, calibrated kinematics or in general the possibility to influence the dynamic behaviour of the controlled robot in a more direct way. For such purpose, the robot can be interfaced through direct joint control. Either in torque mode, where control commands are directly interpreted by the robot as joint torque commands and straightly turned into motor currents. Or in velocity mode, where the control commands are

interpreted as velocity commands and the tracking of the velocity command trajectories is carried out jointwise by internal PI Controllers per each servo. Even though promising approaches are existing in literature concerning model-based computed torque control of a PA10 robot (Kennedy & Desai (2004), Bompos *et al.* (2007)), one global development strategy for the actual MODI*CAS* prototype was fixed to retain a cascade control structure for joint angle control, where the servodriver-internal PI velocity controllers robustly compensate disturbances or physical effects like e.g. gravity, coriolis force and friction, respectively.
If the robot kinematics, describing the geometric relation between the joint angles and the robot wrist pose, are exactly calibrated and further the geometric relation between the base coordinate frames of camera $\{ots\}$ and robot $\{rbs\}$ is also exactly known and rigidly fixed, then it would be possible to omit the optical tracking of the robot wrist $\{rrb\}$. Only the optical tracking of the patient's pose $\{arb\}$ would be necessary in order to generate a corresponding joint angle command vector $\vec{q}_c = f\left(T_{arb}^{ots}\right)$ for the robot controller in order to track patient's movements. Such assembly is defined in Kragic & Christensen (2002) as *'endpoint open loop'* configuration.
Certainly, common uncalibrated robot manipulators have significant kinematic errors. Due to manufacturing tolerances, the real kinematics differ from their nominal model. This leads to a reduced positioning precision depending on the dimension of kinematic errors, even if the manipulator has a good repeatability (Bruyninckx & Shutter (2001)). Further it is extremely challenging to permanently guarantee an exactly fixed geometric relationship between the base coordinate systems of the robot and the camera, if the camera acts from an observer perspective (outside-in or stand-alone, as defined in Kragic & Christensen (2002), respectively). Therefore, within the MODI*CAS* tracking procedure, the robot wrist is optically tracked as well. That facilitates the compensation of kinematic errors or changes in the geometric relationship between the camera's and the robot's base frame. Due to the additional optical tracking of the robot wrist or end effector respectively, such assembly is defined as *'end point closed loop'* configuration.
In principle, due to the optically closed loop, an underlying feedback from the robot's joint encoders is not essentially required to perform visual servoing. Omitting such joint encoder feedback would lead to a so called *'direct visual servoing'* system, where the dynamic control of the robot is carried out directly through the optical feedback loop.
Due to the fact that typical surgical optical tracking systems like the NDI-POLARIS have a relatively low bandwidth in contrast to common robot joint encoders, it is reasonable to use a so called *look and move* approach. Here, the potential of precise but maybe slow optical sensors to compensate kinematic errors is profitably combined with the higher bandwidth of the joint encoders by retaining the joint encoder feedback.
By the reason that surgical optical tracking systems commonly deliver full position and orientation of all tracked elements in the three-dimensional space, the robot control can be performed *'position based'*. The opposite of *position based* is *'image based'*, where the control law is directly based on raw image features instead of fully determined 3D pose data.
Finally, due to the utilization of a stereo vision system which is not rigidly fixed to the robot wrist (like inside-out or eye in hand systems, as defined in Kragic & Christensen (2002), respectively), but acts from an observer perspective (Fig. 2), we can classify the MODI*CAS* patient tracking approach as *position based dynamic look and move using outside-in stereovision in endpoint closed loop configuration.*

A block diagram of the MODICAS patient tracking principle is illustrated in Fig. 3. Here, the robot is dynamically controlled in joint space. Due to that it is interfaced in velocity mode, all joints are velocity-controlled by their servodriver-internal PI controllers that cannot be modified. However, the overlying joint angle control loops may be customized in order to adapt the dynamic behaviour at the best to the desired patient tracking functionality. Available input signals for implementing any desired joint angle controllers are the joint angle command vector $\vec{q}_c$, the joint angle feedback vector $\vec{q}$ and the joint velocity feedback vector $\dot{\vec{q}}$.
In order to follow patient's movements, the control input for the decentralized joint control of the robot must represent the joint angle vector

$$\vec{q}_c = IK\left(T_{arb}^{rbs} \times T_{tcp}^{arb}\right), \tag{1}$$

where the inverse kinematics *IK* give the joint angle vector $\vec{q}_c$ that corresponds to that robot arm configuration T_{tcp}^{rbs} where the robot wrist strikes a desired pose T_{tcp}^{arb} relatively to the patient's reference pose T_{arb}^{rbs}.
If the determination of the patient's pose is carried out through an *outside-in* localization system in *endpoint closed loop configuration,* then the tracking algorithm results in a direct geometric coordinate transformation equation such that

$$\vec{q}_c = IK\left(\underbrace{T_{tcp}^{rbs}}_{FK(\vec{q})} \times \underbrace{\underbrace{\left[T_{rrb}^{ots} \times T_{tcp}^{rrb}\right]^{-1}}_{actual\ T_{tcp}^{ots}} \times \underbrace{T_{arb}^{ots} \times T_{tcp}^{arb}}_{desired\ T_{tcp}^{ots}}}_{\underline{E}}\right), \tag{2}$$

where *FK* are the forward kinematics calculated on the basis of the actual robot joint angle measurements $\vec{q}$; T_{tcp}^{rrb} is a constant matrix derived from the robot to localizer calibration; T_{tcp}^{arb} is the desired constant pose or trajectory of the robot wrist relatively to the patient reference frame; T_{rrb}^{ots}, T_{arb}^{ots} are the frames of the optically measured reference bodies and $\underline{E}$ is the optically determined pose error matrix.
Primally when the optically measured pose of the robot wrist is exactly the same as the desired one relatively to the optically measured pose of the patient, then the equation

$$\underline{E} = \left[T_{rrb}^{ots} \times T_{tcp}^{rrb}\right]^{-1} \times T_{arb}^{ots} \times T_{tcp}^{arb} = \underline{I}, \tag{3}$$

where $\underline{I}$ is the identity matrix, is fulfilled, such that the system is compensated and the actually measured joint angles are directly fed through as setpoint values

$$\vec{q}_c = IK\left(FK\left(\vec{q}\right) \times \underline{I}\right). \tag{4}$$

However, if any pose error $\underline{E}$ occurs due to displacement of the patient $\{arb\}$, the localizer $\{ots\}$ or the robot base $\{rbs\}$ or due to kinematic uncertainties, the tracking algorithm geometrically calculates the desired robot wrist pose that is needed to fulfill equation 3. The dynamic compensation rather takes place in joint space and is carried out through the joint angle controllers. Thus, a manipulation of the tracking dynamics is exclusively carried out by adapting these joint angle controllers.

The functional separation of the tracking procedure into a geometrically setpoint determination and into a dynamic control exclusively in joint space facilitates the use of classical approaches from control theory for each joint in order to design a fast and robust tracking controller.

4. Simulation model describing the real time tracking procedure

Regarding the objective of tuning the MODI*CAS* tracking procedure at the best, a reliable model-based environment, that exactly represents the real world, facilitates watching process variables or changing parameters that are not observable or manipulable respectively within the real system, yet. For instance, such model-based environment allows experiments e.g. regarding the questions, how far the tracking procedure may be improved with upcoming faster localization systems that are not available yet, or how far miscalibration or kinematic errors affect the system stability without the presence of any accidental risk. The following sections illustrate the dynamic model that has been developed with the objectives to perform a detailled offline analysis of the MODI*CAS* patient tracking procedure and to find the best system tuning in view of all current and persisting technical constraints.

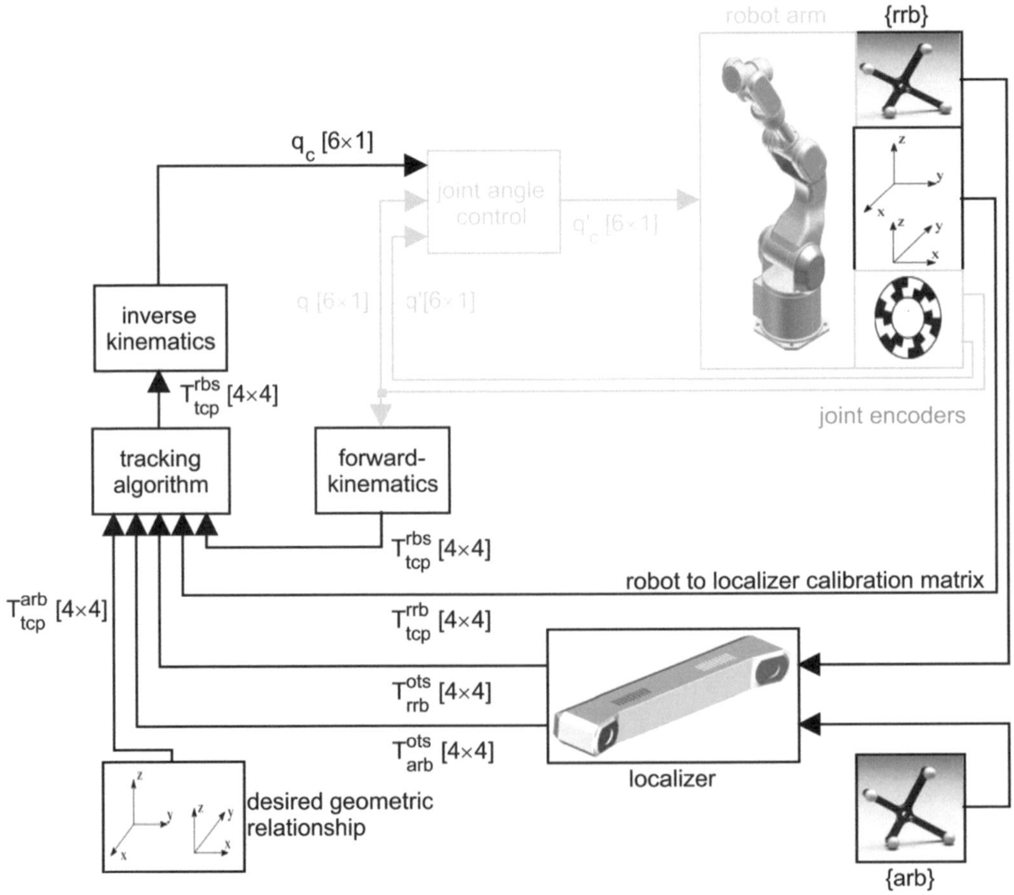

Fig. 3. Block diagram of the MODI*CAS* real time patient tracking procedure

4.1 Global model structure

The global structure of the offline model is directly derived from the block diagram in Fig. 3 which describes the tracking procedure. The forward and inverse kinematics as well as the tracking algorithm itself are straightly copied from the real control software that previously has been implemented within the MODI*CAS* real time control development environment. This environment has been introduced in Schneider & Wahrburg (2008).

4.2 Robot model

The model of the robot arm itself consists of a stiff kinematic model and six structurally identical dynamic joint models with individual joint specific parameters.

The kinematic model, as well as the nominal model in the robot controller, are based on the so called *321-kinematic structure* which is further described in Bruyninckx & Shutter (2001). Due to some simplifying conventions concerning the kinematic structure, the *321-kinematics* model saves some geometric parameters and thus significant computational load in contrast to a common *Denavit-Hartenberg* model. As a result of that simplification, a full identification and thus an exact simulation of the real kinematic errors will not be possible as long as the 321- kinematics model is used. For that purpose, a full implementation of the *Denavit-Hartenberg* convention would be necessary. However, for simple experiments on how kinematic uncertainties affect the behaviour of the tracking procedure, it is sufficient to merely simulate joint angle offsets as well as link length errors (Fig. 4).

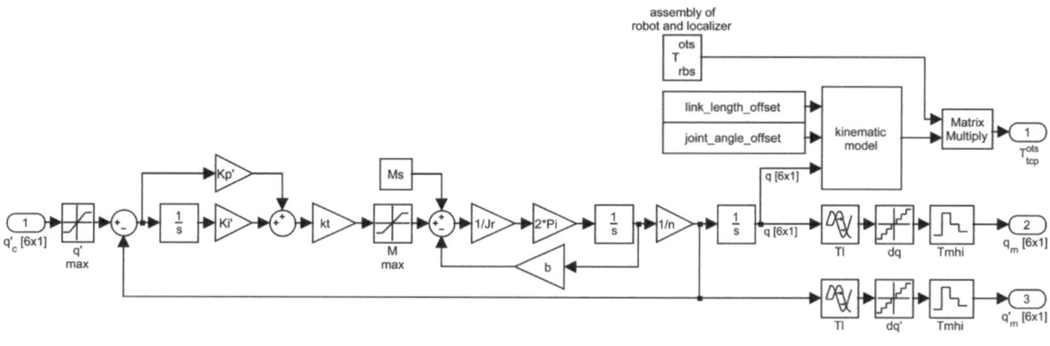

Fig. 4. Robot model - kinematics and joint servo dynamics

Regarding the dynamics, any disturbances or physical effects like e.g. gravity, that act on the gear sides of the real robot joints, are strongly reduced at the motor sides through high gear ratios and therefore relatively small in relation to the inertias of the joint servo rotors. Further, due to the fact that, within the MODI*CAS* system, the PA10 robot is interfaced in velocity mode, such effects are quickly compensated through the servodriver-internal PI velocity controllers. Therefore, it is adequate to model every joint drive as a simple PI-controlled dc-motor as it is illustrated in Fig. 4, in order to authentically simulate the dominant dynamic behaviour of the robot arm in velocity mode. All joint model parameters are listed in Tab. 1.

Those parameters that cannot be determined straightly from available technical data sheets of the robot, are identified by fitting the velocity step response of every joint model into its corresponding measurement from the real system. The estimation of the unknown parameters is carried out through `fmincon()` from the MATLAB OPTIMIZATION TOOLBOX

$\dot{q}_{max}$	maximum velocity command input	$[\frac{rad}{s}]$
M_{max}	maximum torque	$[Nm]$
K_p'	proportional gain of velocity controller	$[\frac{As}{rad}]$
K_i'	integral gain of velocity controller	$[\frac{As}{rad}]$
k_t	motor constant	$[\frac{Nm}{A}]$
J_r	cummulative moment of inertia in the powertrain	$[kg \cdot m^2]$
T_l	joint encoder output lag	$[s]$
dq	joint encoder angle resolution	$[\frac{rad}{digit}]$
$d\dot{q}$	joint encoder angular velocity resolution	$[\frac{rad}{s \cdot digit}]$
T_{mhi}	sample time of the robot interface in velocity mode	$[s]$
b	viscous friction	$[\frac{Nms}{rad}]$
M_s	disturbance torque	$[Nm]$
n	gear ratio	

Tab. 1. parameters of one joint model

which manipulates all unknown parameters within user defined constraints and performs a simulation per each parameter set, until a quality function, defined as

$$Q = \frac{a_1}{n}\sum_{i=1}^{n}\left[q_{ms}(i) - q_{sm}(i)\right]^2 + \frac{a_2}{n}\sum_{i=1}^{n}\left[\dot{q}_{ms}(i) - \dot{q}_{sm}(i)\right]^2, \quad (5)$$

reaches a minimum, where q_{ms} is the measured and q_{sm} the simulated joint angle, $\dot{q}_{ms}$ is the measured and $\dot{q}_{sm}$ the simulated angular velocity and a_1, a_2 are manipulable weighting gains.

Fig. 5 shows the result of the described identification procedure, exemplarily for the first shoulder joint of the robot ($S1$). Due to the simple structure of the joint model, the torque curve is strongly idealized. However, the model reproduces the angle and angular velocity trajectories of the real joint drive very well, if stimulated with the same velocity command like the real one. In order to check if these characteristics are reproducible over the full workspace of the robot, independently from payload, robot arm configuration or input signals, several verification tests were done. Exemplarily, Fig. 6 shows a verification result where, due to a changed robot arm configuration (see Fig. 7), a lower moment of inertia acts on the joint $S1$ and further the velocity command is 0.1 $\frac{rad}{s}$ higher than during the identification process. The simulation is carried out using exactly the same parameters as in the experiment illustrated in Fig. 5. Even though the real torque characteristics differ between the two experiments due to a changed moment of inertia acting on joint $S1$, the simulated angle and angular velocity trajectories always exactly represent the corresponding measurements from the real joint drive. Thus, the developed dynamic joint models are fully adequate to simulate the dynamic behaviour of the robot within the tracking procedure.

4.3 Localizer model

At the actual state of development, the localizer model merely simulates the time performance of the NDI-POLARIS-System and normally distributed spatial measurement noise, whereas the sampling time ΔT_{ots} as well as the measurement lag t_{lots} can be globally changed and the standard deviation for each component of a measured pose (x,y,z,α,β,γ) can

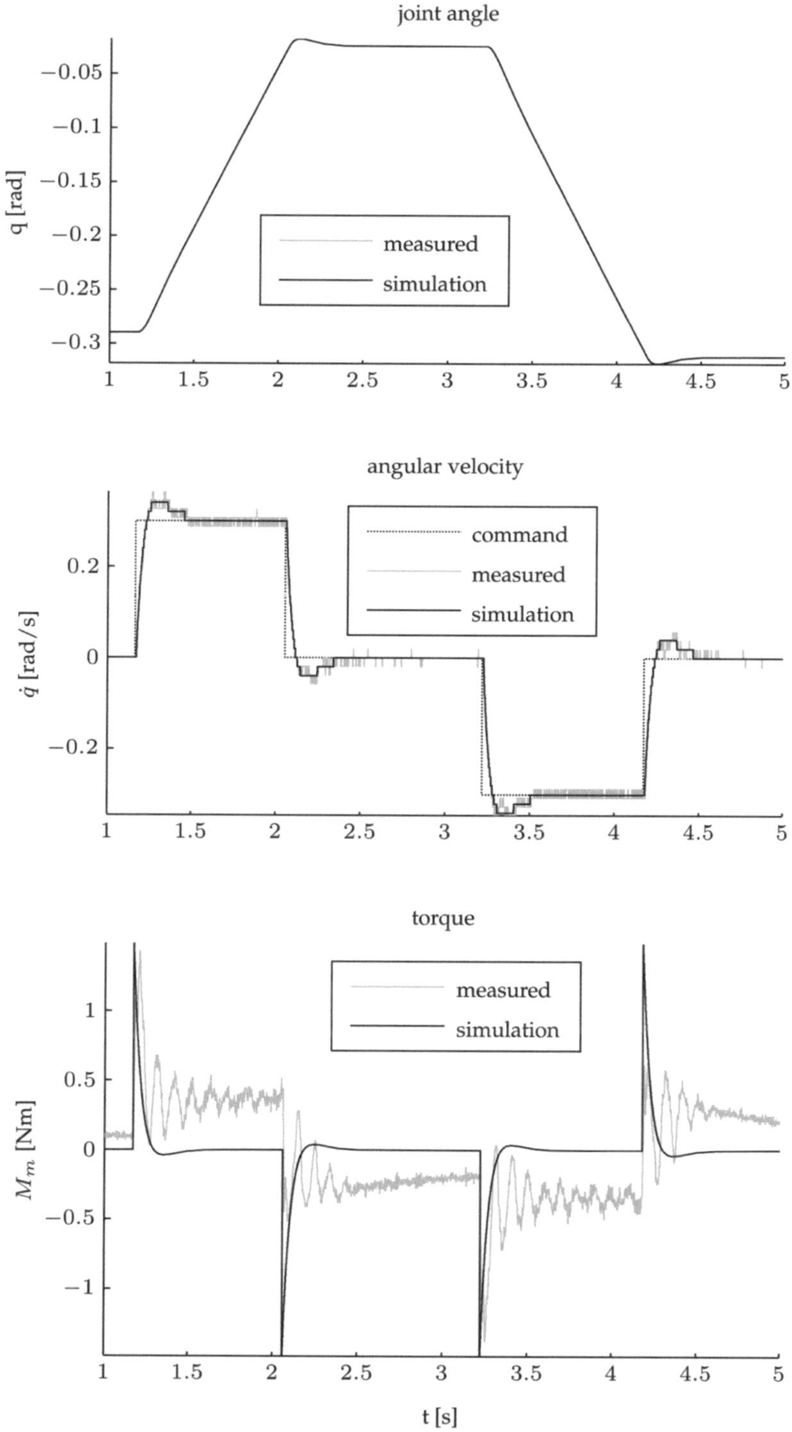

Fig. 5. Simulation results using the identified servo model compared to real measurements (dataset for identification), exemplary for the first shoulder joint ($S1$)

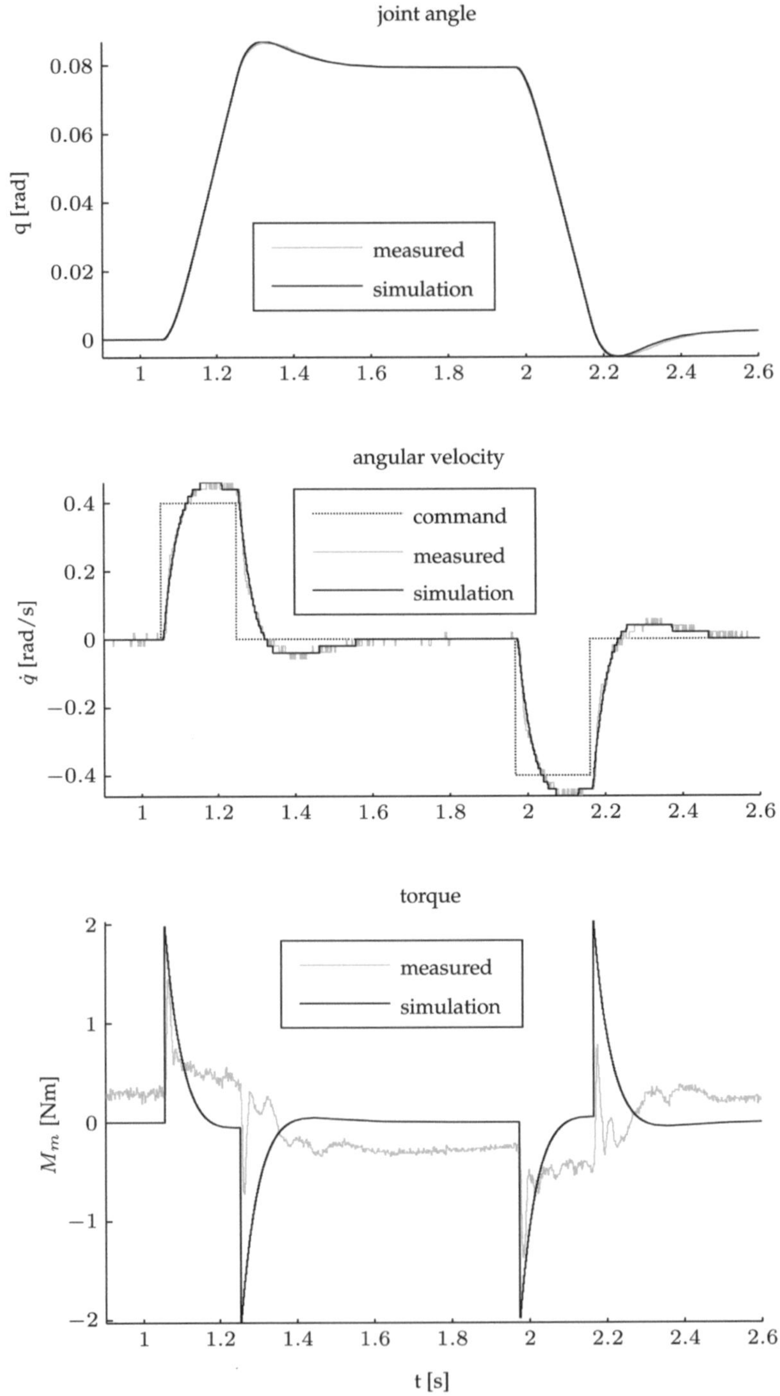

Fig. 6. Simulation results using the identified servo model compared to real measurements for the first shoulder joint ($S1$) in one exemplary scenario different to the identification scenario

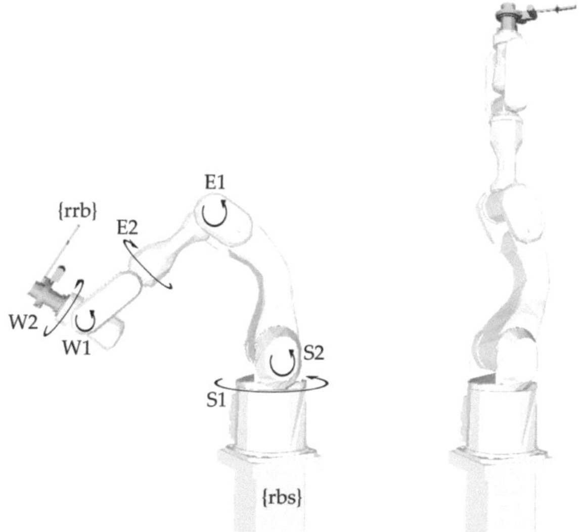

Fig. 7. Differing poses for robot dynamics identification (left) and exemplary verification (right)

be individually manipulated for each simulated reference body. Further, miscalibration between the robot wrist $\{tcp\}$ and its optical reference body $\{rrb\}$ can be simulated through multiplying a corresponding error transformation matrix T_{ϵ}.

The localizer model is actually kept that simple because the current focus lies in exploring how the time performance of any (replaceable) localizer influences the overall tracking behaviour. If a strongly detailed measurement error model of the NDI-POLARIS with its anisotropic measurement characteristics will be desired, mathematical models like e.g. from Wiles *et al.* (2008), an extension of Fitzpatrick *et al.* (1998), can be integrated into the dynamic model of the MODI*CAS* patient tracking procedure in the future.

4.4 Model verification

The full dynamic model that is described above, consisting of the robot model, localizer model, kinematics and tracking algorithms, is verified against measurements from the real MODI*CAS* assistance system while tracking random patient movements. In order to better enable the recognition of dynamic transients in the laboratory, the applied patient motion is much faster than typically expected during any surgical intervention. The results of one verification experiment are presented in Fig. 8 as cartesian trajectories. The corresponding time trajectories of the robot joint angles are further illustrated in Fig. 9. As it can be seen in Fig. 9, especially in the plots for the joints *E*1 and *W*1, there are noticeable differences between the simulated and the measured time trajectories of the joint angles. What firstly seems to be a weak point of modelling, is a valuable feature of the tracking principle from equation (3). Not only does the observed level deviation occur in the joint responses, but it also occurs in the joint angle command trajectories. The reason for that phenomena is that, for the exemplarily presented simulation, no kinematic error has been considered in the model. While the real uncalibrated robot has significant kinematic errors, in the simulation all parameters for link length errors and joint offsets (Fig. 4) were set to zero. Although the real robot has significant kinematic errors, the tracking algorithm within the real system

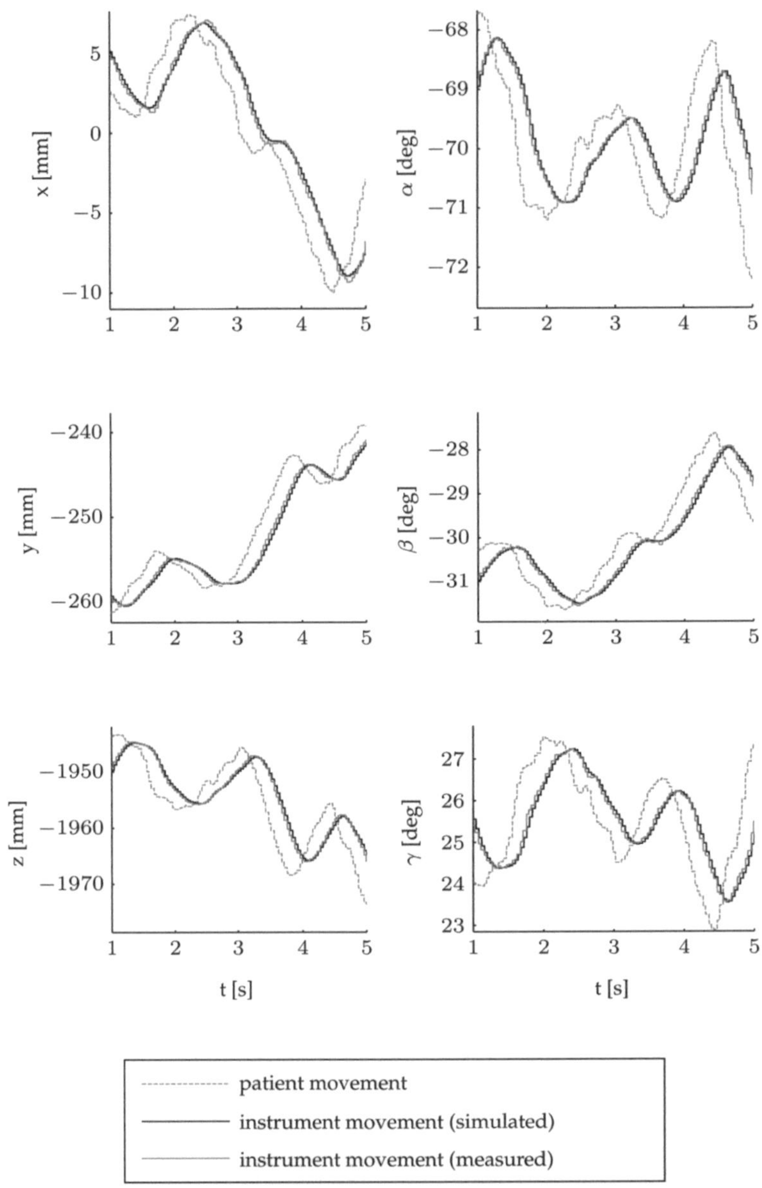

Fig. 8. Verification of the overall tracking procedure model by comparing the model output signals to real measurements (cartesian time trajectories of robot wrist pose)

adjusts the joint angle trajectory commands such that the cartesian trajectories match those of a kinematically precise robot (as simulated in Fig. 8). Accordingly, there will not remain any kinematically caused deviation between the actual and desired pose of the robot wrist in steady state. All in all, Fig. 8 clearly indicates that the simulation of the MODICAS patient tracking function represents the real system behaviour very well and the developed simple model is fully adequate for further investigations, in presence of a joint velocity interfaced robot.

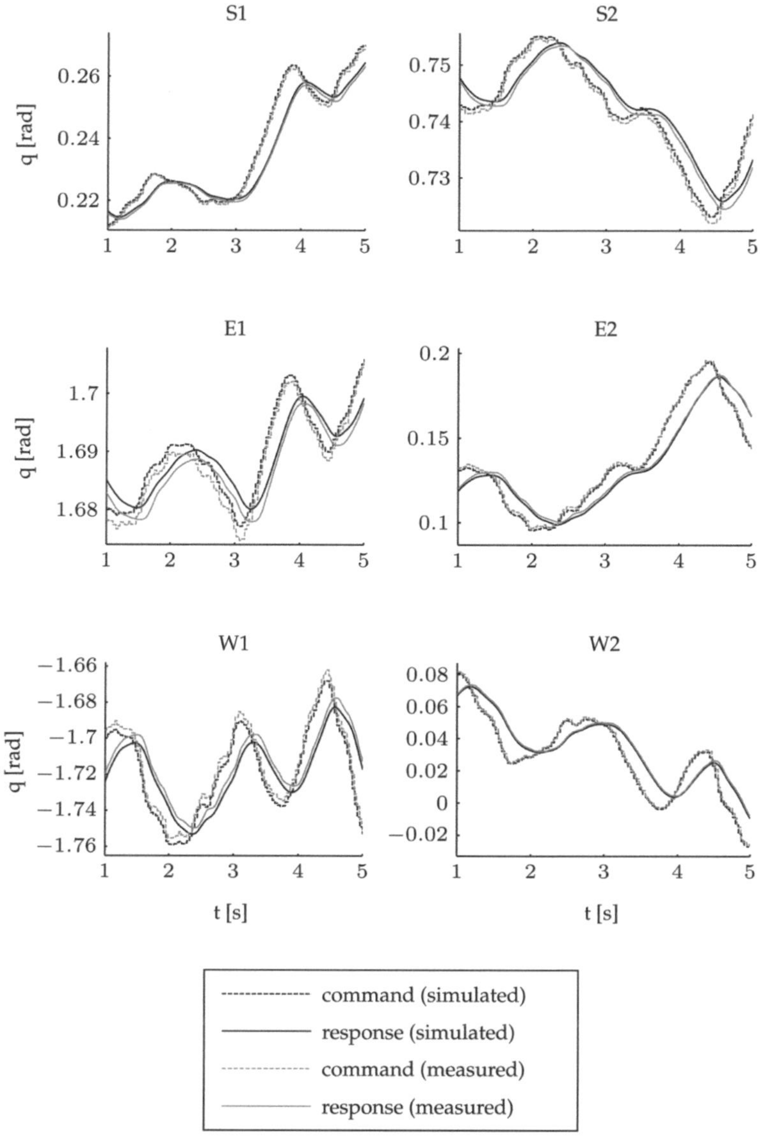

Fig. 9. Verification of the overall tracking procedure model by comparing the model output signals to real measurements (time trajectories of robot joint angles)

5. Application example: model-based controller design

One of the first simulation experiments that have been performed using the novel offline model environment was aimed to compare different control strategies, especially adopted to the time performance of the NDI-POLARIS, at first under the consumption of zero measurement noise. A more general investigation on different control structures within (*image based*) visual closed loop systems has been already presented in Corke & Good (1996). However, our investigation is specially aimed at finding the best possible control strategy

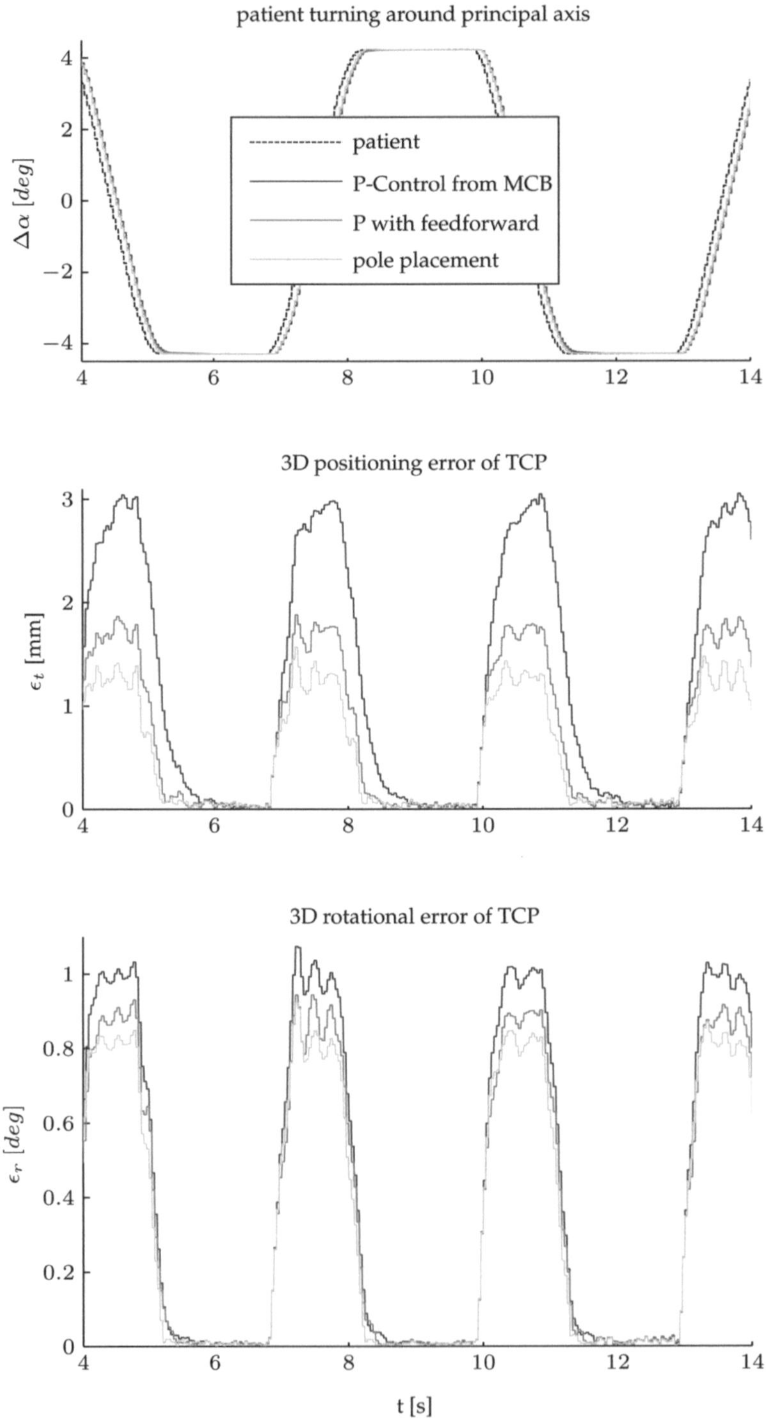

Fig. 10. Comparison of three different control strategies - 1. original proportional controller, 2. proportional with feedforward, 3. pole placement controller

for the MODI*CAS* patient tracking procedure with its functional principle like shown in Fig. 3. As communicated through the manufacturer, only a proportional controller per each joint is generally implemented into the original MHI MCB. With the help of the model-based simulation environment we found out that, regarding the patient tracking function, a specially tuned proportional feedforward controller enhances the overall tracking behaviour, although the feedforward velocity signal, that can be derived from the NDI-POLARIS through a simple differentiation, is poor due to the relatively low sample rate in relation to the time response of the robot.
A further enhancement has been carried out by the use of a pole placement controller, especially developed and adopted to the time performance of the NDI-POLARIS. The results of the two enhanced controllers may be compared to the original one from the MHI MCB by reckoning Fig. 10. In the experiment, a patient dummy is rotated around a defined axis that is assumed to be the principal axis of the patient. The measurement of the patient dummy's reference body is fed into the offline model, where the patient tracking procedure is simulated three times using three different controllers. First, the proportional controller with the original controller gains from the MHI MCB, second the specially tuned proportional feedforward controller and third, the specially developed pole placement controller. As the plots show, in the exemplary tracking experiment, the maximum 3D positioning error is reduced when using the proportional feedforward controller and further reduced when using the pole placement controller. Upcoming experiments will further show how far those controllers can be sufficiently be utilized in the presence of measurement noise or how to then find the best compromise between fast dynamics and high accuracy as well as precision in steady state, respectively.

6. Conclusion

The investigation that is described in this chapter has derived an offline model that simulates the system dynamics of the real MODI*CAS* patient tracking procedure very well, independently from the operating point of the system. The model enables the developer to better understand the functional principle of the tracking procedure and to perform a specific tuning of its parameters in order to increase its overall dynamic performance. One model-based experiment has already delivered an improvement of the tracking control strategy. In the future, further experiments will show how the improvement of the localizer device, especially by means of noise reduction and a faster data aqcuistion, can enhance the overall dynamic performance of the tracking procedure.

7. References

Bompos, N., Artemiadis, P., Oikonomopoulos, A., & Kyriakopoulos, K. (2007). Modeling, full identification and control of the mitsubishi PA-10 robot arm. In *2007 IEEE/ASME International Conference on Advanced Intelligent Mechatronics*. 1–6.

Bruyninckx, H. & Shutter, J. (2001). Introduction to intelligent robotics. Tech. rep., Katholieke Universiteit de Leuven.

Castillo Cruces, R., Schneider, H., & Wahrburg, J. (2008). Cooperative robotic system to support surgical interventions. In *Medical Robotics*, Vienna, Austria: I-Tech Education and Publishing, chap. 35. 481–490.

Corke, P. & Good, M. (1996). Dynamic effects in visual closed-loop systems. *IEEE Transactions on Robotics and Automation*, *12*(5), 671–683.

Fitzpatrick, J., West, J., & Maurer, C. (1998). Predicting error in rigid-body point-based registration. *IEEE Transactions on medical imaging*, *17*(5), 694–702.

Kennedy, C. & Desai, J. (2004). Model-based control of the Mitsubishi PA-10 robot arm: application to robot-assisted surgery. In *Proceedings of the 2004 IEEE International Conference on Robotics and Automation (ICRA'04)*.. New Orleans, LA, USA, vol. 3, 2523–2528.

Kragic, D. & Christensen, H. (2002). Survey on visual servoing for manipulation. Tech. rep., School of Computer Science and Communication, Centre for Autonomous Systems, Numerical Analysis and Computer Science, Stockholm, Sweden.

Schneider, H. & Wahrburg, J. (2008). A Novel Real Time Core for Dynamics and Safety Enhancement of a Navigated Surgical Assistance Robot. *at-Automatisierungstechnik*, *56*(9), 483–493.

Weiss, L., Sanderson, A., & Neuman, C. (1987). Dynamic sensor-based control of robots with visual feedback. *IEEE Journal of Robotics and Automation*, *3*(5), 404–417.

Wiles, A., Likholyot, A., Frantz, D., & Peters, T. (2008). A Statistical Model for Point-Based Target Registration ErrorWith Anisotropic Fiducial Localizer Error. *IEEE TRANSACTIONS ON MEDICAL IMAGING*, *27*(3), 378–390.

SECTION II

5

Robotic Assisted Colorectal Surgery

Seung Hyuk Baik, M.D.
Department of Surgery, Yonsei University College of Medicine, Seoul, Korea

1. Introduction

A robot is generally considered as a physical machine which can move around, operate a mechanical limb and exhibit intelligent and autonomous behavior in public. However, a surgical robot is not like the common robots which have the ability of autonomous action. A surgical robot is a collection of manipulators which just follow the surgeon's hand motions. The manipulators of a surgical robot receive a digitalized signal from the computer which interfaces the surgeon's hand motions with robotic manipulators. These are the important characteristics of a surgical robot, and we can consider it as a developed laparoscopic surgical instrument. Conversely, many patients think that a surgical robot as a robotic surgeon who can perform an operation with its own intelligence. The present surgical robot is just a servant. Thus, we have to understand the surgical robot from this concept. The whole robotic procedure is a robotic assisted procedure and the master surgeon decides the whole surgical procedure and performs the operation. The current surgical robot just helps the surgeon with its advanced technology during the surgical procedure.
The first surgical robot was the Automated Endoscopic System for Optimal Positioning (AESOP) (Computer Motion, Santa Barbara, CA, USA). In 1994, AESOP was approved for clinical use as a robotic camera holder by the Food and Drug Administration (FDA). After that, the Zeus surgical system was invented. However, the Zeus surgical system was approved by the FDA for use only as a surgical assistant. The da Vinci® robotic system (Intuitive Surgical Inc., Sunnyvale, CA, USA) is currently the most popular surgical robotic system. Thus, the manuscript is written based on the da Vinci® robotic system.

2. History of robotic assisted colorectal surgery and technical development

In 2002, Weber et al. used the robotic surgical system to perform a right colectomy and a sigmoid colectomy for benign diseases. Hashizume et al. (2002) reported three cases of robotic assisted colectomies. It is the first trial to apply the robotic assisted colectomy to malignant disease. In 2003, Vibert et al. reported three cases of robotic assisted colectomies and Delaney et al. reported the first comparative study between robotic assisted colectomy and conventional laparoscopic surgery. However, in this study, only six cases of robotic assisted colon surgery were compared. Giulianotti et al. (2003) reported on a series of 16 cases of robotic assisted colorectal surgery and six cases of anterior resection and two cases of abdominoperineal resection. A relatively large comparative study was conducted by D'Annibale et al. (2004). They compared 53 cases of robotic assisted colorectal surgery to 53 cases of conventional laparoscopic colorectal surgery. Twenty two malignant cases were enrolled in the robotic group and forty two malignant cases enrolled in the laparoscopic group. It was the first comparative study with more than 50 cases. In 2005, Brauman et al. reported on robotic assisted cases of four sigmoid colectomies and one right hemicolectomy. Also, Ruurda et al. (2005) and Sebajang et al. (2005) reported twenty three and seven cases of robotic assisted colorectal surgery, respectively. In 2006, Pigazzi et al. compared six cases of robotic assisted low anterior resection to six cases of laparoscopic low anterior resection. They compared not only the short term outcomes but also the surgeon's fatigue level between both groups. They showed that robotic rectal surgery might cause less operator fatigue when compared with standard laparoscopic surgery. In the same year, De Noto et al. (2006) reported eleven cases of robotic assisted sigmoid colectomies. In 2007, Hellan et al. reported on a 39 case series and Rawlings et al. (2007) compared 30 cases of robotic assisted colectomy to laparoscopic colectomy. In 2008, Baik et al. described the robotic technique which used four robotic arms for mid or lower rectal cancer surgery and conducted the first randomized trial. In 2009, Ng et al. reported eight cases of robotic assisted low anterior resection for rectal cancer. A total robotic procedure for rectal cancer was shown by Park et al. (2009) and Hellan et al. (2009). Alberto et al. (2009) reported on laparoscopic and robot-assisted resection of colorectal cancer and of synchronous liver metastasis. Choi et al. (2009) showed the transanal or transvaginal retrieval of the resected specimen in robotic assisted colorectal cancer surgery. Baik et al. (2009) reported that the mesorectal grade in the robotic group was significantly better than the conventional laparoscopic group in the study which compared 56 cases of robotic assisted low anterior resection to 57 cases of laparoscopic low anterior resection.

3. Core technology related to colorectal surgery

3.1 Vision

The robotic surgical system has three components. These components are the surgeon console, the robotic cart (patient-side cart) and the vision system (Fig. 1). The surgeon console is the place where the surgeon can perform the operation. This instrument provides an ergonomic position and three dimensional images. Three dimensional images help the surgeon to overcome visual limitation during the operation and also provide a similar vision like open surgery. The conventional laparoscopic surgery system only provides two dimensional visions. The most recent robotic surgical system is equipped with HD technology also with three dimensional images. Three dimensional HD images are the most optimal imaging technology in laparoscopic surgery and provide a direct hand-eye instrument alignment and a natural depth perception for precise operation near dangerous anatomical structures. In robotic assisted rectal cancer surgery, the surgeon can effectively recognize the hypogastric nerve plexus during dissection around an inferior mesenteric artery. Moreover, the inferior hypogastric nerve can be easily recognized during the pelvic dissection. These nerves are very important in the post operative quality of life. Nerve preservation surgery is essential because it is not necessary to sacrifice the nerve if the tumor did not directly invade the nerve. During laparoscopic surgery, major vessel damage is the common cause of open conversion. Thus, precise dissection is necessary around the major vessels. The three dimensional HD image may help with precise dissection.

Total mesorectal excision (TME) has been the golden standard of rectal cancer surgery (Heald et al., (1982), Enker et al., (1995), Havenga et al., (1996)). The exact recognition of the fascia structure around the rectum is mandatory to perform successful TME. Denonvillier's fascia separates the extraperitotoneal rectum anteriorly from the prostate, the seminal

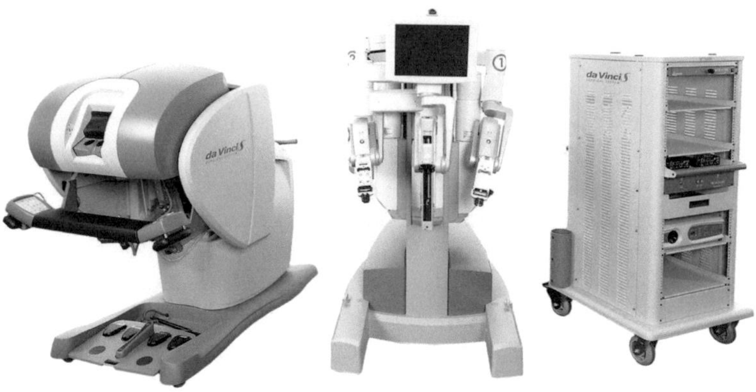

Fig. 1. The robotic surgical system: A) the surgeon console; B) the robotic cart (patient-side cart); C) the vision system

vesicles, or the vagina. A sharp dissection of Denonvillier's fascia is needed for TME. Excision of Denonvillier's fascia means exposure of the prostate and the seminal vesicle, and parasympathetic and sympathetic nerves related to voiding and sexual function are located near the prostate and the seminal vesicle. Thus, improper resection of Denonvillier's fascia is associated with postoperative sexual and voiding dysfunctions. The TME plane of the posterior and lateral side of the rectum is the natural space between the fascia propria of the rectum and the presacral fascia. If the surgeon cannot find the TME plane, the mesorectum or presacral structure may be injured. Mesorectal injury is associated with oncologic outcomes in rectal cancer surgery (Nagtegaal et al., 2002). The presacral fascia encloses the anterior side of the sacrum, the coccyx, the nerves, the middle sacral artery, and the presacral vein. During the dissection of the posterior side of the TME plane, presacral hemorrhage can occur. The reported incidence rate of presacral hemorrhage is from 4.6% to 7.0% during rectal dissection. The presacral vein is drained into the sacral foramen and has a high blood pressure which can reach hydrostatic pressures of 17-23 cm H_20, two to three times the normal pressure of the inferior vena cava (Bruce et al., 2007). Thus, presacral hemorrhage during rectal dissection is a troublesome and life threatening hemorrhage despite venous bleeding. The three dimensional HD image in the robotic system can be beneficial to prevent these critical complications related to the characteristic of the anatomical structure around the rectum.

The robotic surgical system is equipped with four arms. One arm is used for the endoscope holder and the other three arms are used for surgical arms which perform the operation. The robotic arm, which holds the endoscope provide a stable vision without unnecessary movement. If the endoscope is moving unnecessarily, it is like doing an operation in a moving car or train. In conventional laparoscopic surgery, the assistant surgeon holds the endoscope and the vision provided by the assistant surgeon cannot be as stable as like the vision provided by the robotic arm. In the robotic assisted procedure, the master surgeon can move the vision according to their needs. This feature can make the operation run smoothly and the operation time shorter than conventional laparoscopic surgery.

Three dimensional images are created by two lenses (Fig. 2) in one endoscope. A discrepancy of lens focus between the two endoscope lenses can make a visual disturbance and can occur because the three dimensional visual system is so fine and it is a complex instrument. Moreover, the human eye can feel tiny discrepancies and it is uncomfortable to stare into the complex surgical field. This is a disadvantage and malfunction of the robotic surgical system which is equipped with a three dimensional visual system. However, there is no objective data related to the discrepancy of the lens because it is usually detected only by a master surgeon who remembers the most optimal three dimensional views in the complex surgical field. Other assistant staff and engineer may not recognize the tiny discrepancy of the lens focus between the two endoscope lenses.

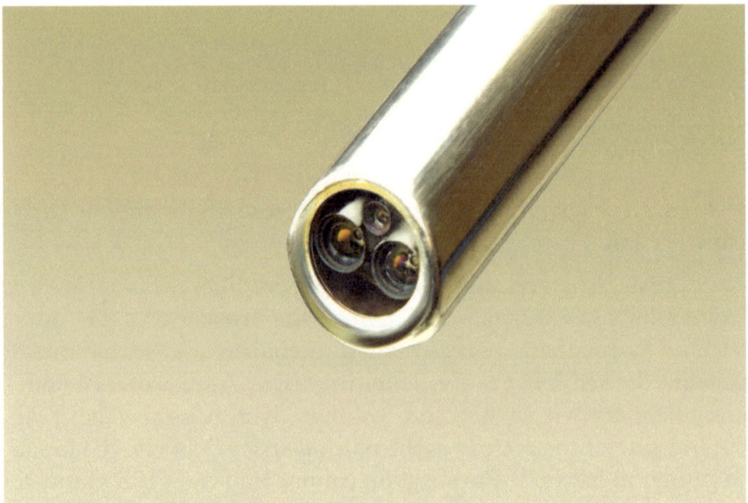

Fig. 2. Endoscope which has two lenses

The robotic surgical system is not equipped with a fumes ventilator. Fumes occur after electric cauterization. Another port site is necessary to vent the fumes effectively. It is a considerable issue in rectal resection because the surgical space of rectal dissection is surrounded by a narrow and deep pelvic cavity. If the surgeon would not like another port for ventilation of the fumes, the valve in the endoscope port or the assistant port can be used to ventilate the fumes. However, this method needs a little time. Conventional laparoscopic instruments have an electric cautery which can perform dissection and ventilation simultaneously. The absence of a ventilation system in the robotic instrument is a drawback compared to the conventional laparoscopic instrument.

Acute and major bleeding can occur during colorectal surgery even though the surgeon performed careful dissection. The arterial bleeding from a major vessel can directly contaminate the endoscope lens. If this situation occurs, the whole surgical field is changed into a red world. This situation is so troublesome and stressful to the surgeon. Rapid separation of the endoscope from the robotic system should be performed and reinserted to control the bleeding after cleaning both lenses. This procedure should be performed as soon as possible. If this procedure is delayed just a few seconds, bleeding control may be impossible due to profound bleeding in the surgical field and then open conversion must be followed as soon as possible. In this situation, the weight of the endoscope can delay the procedure of lens cleaning. Robotic surgery is a highly advanced technological procedure, whereas the cleaning of the lens is performed using water and a towel, and it is not a technological method. It is just time consuming. Thus, a more secure dissection is needed in robotic surgery because more time is needed to control acute bleeding or to convert it into an open procedure.

3.2 Function of articulation of the instrument tips

In the robotic surgical system, the tips of the instruments are designed to mimic the dexterity of the human hand and wrist. It allows seven degrees of freedom and 90 degrees of articulation even though it cannot be exactly similar with the dexterity of the human hand (Fig. 3). This is a very different technology compared with conventional laparoscopic instruments which have five degrees of freedom and is called an endowrist function. The endowrist function allows the surgeon to perform intracorporeal anastomosis such as an ileo-transverse anastomosis after a right hemicolectomy (Rawlings et al. 2006). However, intracorporeal anastomosis is not the commonly used method in colon surgery.

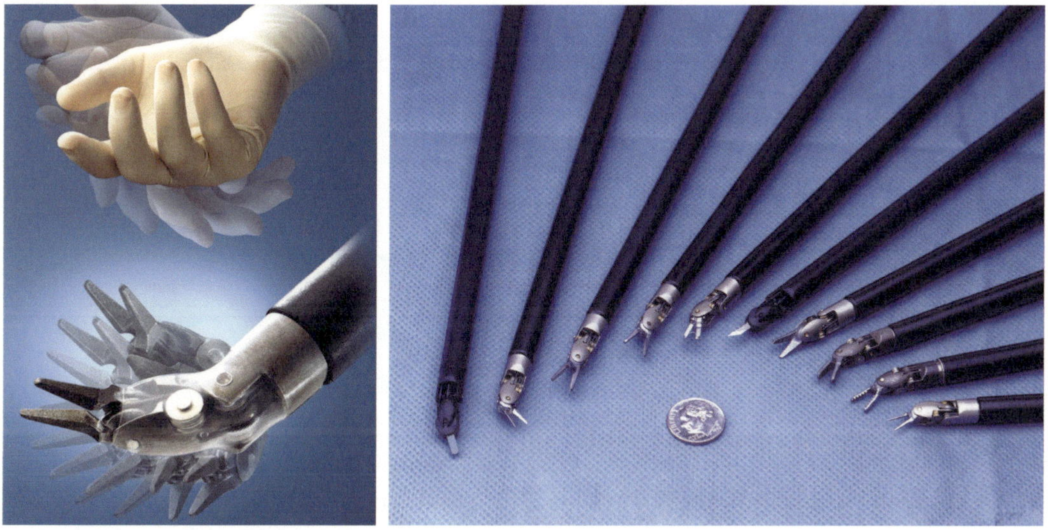

Fig. 3. The tip of the robotic instrument and the surgeon's hand

Extracorporeal anastomosis is commonly used in laparoscopic colon surgery because anastomosis can be easily performed using the specimen extraction site. In laparoscopic rectal surgery, an EEA stapler is used for colorectal anastomosis. Thus, the endowrist function may not often be used for anastomosis in colorectal surgery. However, the endowrist function is useful for posterior dissection of a vessel. The straight instruments of laparoscopic surgery cannot easily reach the posterior side of the vessel, such as the inferior mesenteric artery. The root of the inferior mesenteric artery is fixed on the abdominal aorta. Because of that, it cannot be moved by traction and its posterior side is blocked by itself. Thus, straight conventional instruments of laparoscopic surgery are not appropriate for dissection of the posterior side of the inferior mesenteric artery, whereas angulated tips of

the robotic instrument can reach the posterior side of the vessel of the inferior mesenteric artery. Thus, the dissection of this area can be performed easily and effectively.
Mesorectal transsection is the procedure which is performed in upper rectal cancer surgery. It is a very difficult procedure because the surgical field is usually in the narrow pelvic cavity even though it is performed by the open method. In laparoscopic surgery, the axis of the rectum and the axis of the instrument tip make an acute angle. The instrument tip of conventional laparoscopic surgery can only reach the mesorectum obliquely. Precise dissection of the mesorectum at 4 cm below the tumor is absolutely necessary. However, the oblique approach of the laparoscopic instrument into the mesorectum is a technical demanding procedure to transsect the mesorectum precisely. The surgery can be performed easily when the target organ and the instrument make a right angle. The angulated instrument of the robotic surgical system can make a right angle approach possible during the transsection of the mesorectum. The angulated instrument of the robotic surgical system can also be the L-shape retractor. It can elevate the rectum upward effectively and can move the rectum laterally enclosing the rectum softly. These soft and effective tractions can make a proper surgical space between the fascia propria of the rectum and the presacral fascia. Upward traction of the prostate gland using the straight laparoscopic instrument usually doesn't frequently make a proper surgical space because the instrument can disturb the operation and block the surgical view. Meanwhile, the angulated instrument of the robotic system can make a little larger space, which is the triangle shaped space. The triangle shaped space is helpful to easily dissect in the narrow pelvic space (Fig. 4).

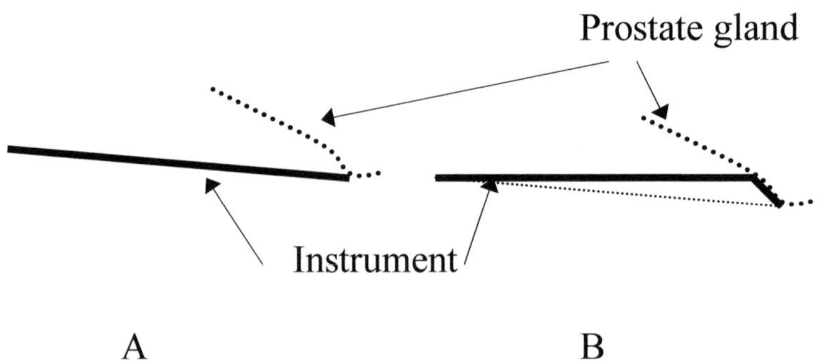

Fig. 4. A. Traction of the prostate using conventional laparoscopic surgery
B. Traction using the robotic surgical system. The angular instrument tip makes a triangular space.

Ultrasonic devices can be used in the robotic surgical system. The major advantage of the ultrasonic devices is the hemostatic effect of a major vessel, and it can be used in a mesorectal transsection. However, it cannot be angulated even though it is equipped in the robotic surgical system. If surgeons choose the ultrasonic device, they may sacrifice the advanced technology of the robotic surgical system because the movements of the ultrasonic device are not different between the robotic surgical system and conventional laparoscopic surgery.

3.3 Motion scaling and tremor elimination

Motion scaling is a characteristic of the robotic surgical system. The computer in the robotic surgical system can scale down a surgeon's hand movements into micromotions. Thus, detailed surgery can be easily performed using the robotic surgical system. However, motion scaling is generally not proper for colorectal surgery because the surgical field and target organs are too large to scale down. But tremor reduction is one of the advanced technologies of the robotic surgical system. It may be helpful for the surgeon who has a hand tremor.

3.4 Ergonomic position

The surgeon performs the operation in an ergonomic position in the robotic surgical system. The most important ergonomic posture is the sitting position. The surgeon sits in the chair and grasps the master controls with the hands and wrists naturally positioned during the robotic assisted procedure. Pigazzi et al. (2006) reported that robotic rectal surgery might cause less operator fatigue when compared with conventional laparoscopic surgery and explained that the ergonomic position for the surgeon sitting at the console might be the important reason.

4. Surgical technique

4.1 General considerations

Robotic assisted surgery is the operation method of which the essential step is performed using the robotic surgical system. The following concepts are the general considerable issues related to robotic assisted surgery. A successful robotic assisted surgery is determined by the harmonious application of the specific standard procedures for each disease and the following considerations.

1. The robotic cart is located at the same side of the target organ.
2. The surgeon's right hand is the left arm of the robotic system. The signals of the surgeon's hand are conversely interfaced to the robotic arms.
3. The robotic endoscope arm should be aligned with the robotic cart and the endoscope port in a straight line (Fig. 5).

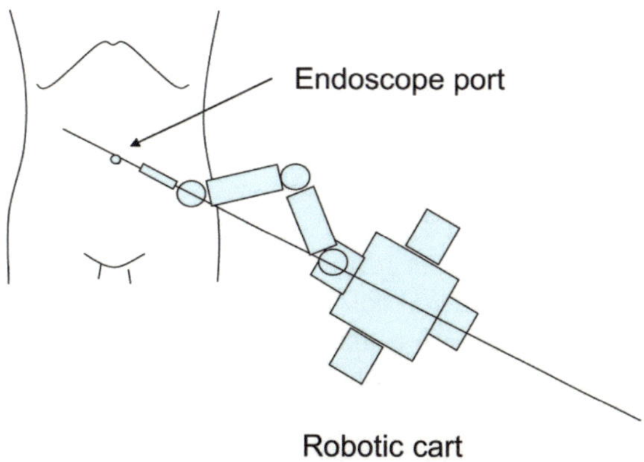

Fig. 5. Alignment between the patient's cart and the endoscope port

4. The distance between the ports should be larger than 7 cm.
5. All ports should be located as close as possible on the concentric circle which has an axis on the robotic cart.

6. The angle between the robotic arms should be as wide as possible. If the angle between the robotic arms become narrower, the chance of extracorporeal collision between the robotic arms are increased (Fig. 6).

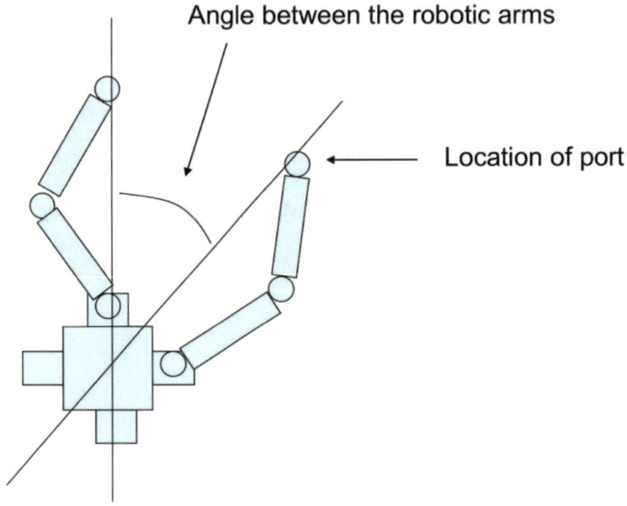

Fig. 6. Angle between the robotic arms

7. The robotic arms cannot cross each other.
8. The position of the patient cannot be changed after docking of the robotic cart.
9. The procedure is easy when the target organ is on a straight line from the robotic cart to the endoscope port.
10. If the target site of the operation becomes further from the straight line from the robotic cart to the endoscope port into both lateral sides, the chance of extracorporeal collision is increased.
11. The robotic arms don't interface the tactile sense and the tensile strength from the patient to the surgeon's hand. The surgeon has to recognize the tactile sense and the tensile strength by visual cue.
12. No. 1 arm is the right first arm which receives a signal from the surgeon's right hand. No. 2 arm is the left second arm which receives a signal from the surgeon's left hand. No. 3 arm is the left or right arm which can be switched with No. 1 or No. 2 arm (Fig. 7).
13. The procedures of robotic assisted colorectal surgery basically follow the procedures of standard laparoscopic colorectal surgery.

Until now, all published robotic assisted colorectal procedures needed an assistant surgeon. Hellan et al. (2009) insisted that the assistant surgeon plays an important role in providing additional countertraction and stapling of the inferior mesenteric vein and artery. It is difficult to understand because people expect the robotic surgical system to operate by itself without human assistance. Hellan et al.'s opinion (2009) implies that robotic assisted surgery of the present generation needs more technological developments.

The most important step in robotic assisted colorectal surgery is the design of the trocar position. Dislocation of the trocar is the main reason of extracorporeal collision between the robotic arms and if a collision occurs, further operation is not possible. In this situation, open or laparoscopic conversion is needed.

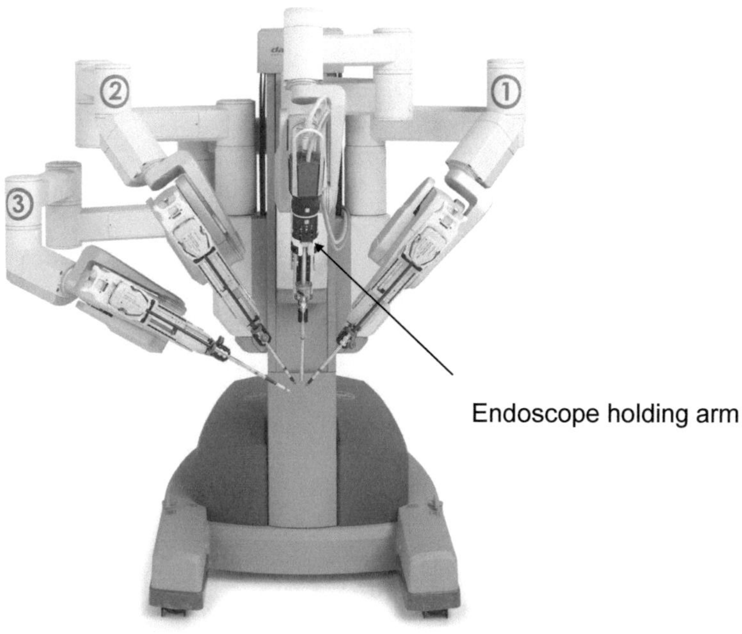

Fig. 7. Robotic cart has one endoscope holding arm and three surgical arms.

There are several trocar positions according to the surgeon's preference and another new design of the trocar position will be developed due to an increase of robotic assisted colorectal surgery. Thus, this description will provide a general technical method with several examples.
The endoscope trocar and the trocar for the endovascular stapler or endo-GIA are 12 mm in size. The robotic arm trocar is 8 mm or 5 mm. The assistant trocar is usually 5 mm. If the assistant trocar is used for endoclipping, a 10 mm size trocar should be used and for an endo-GIA, a 12 mm size trocar should be used.

4.2 Right colectomy

The patient is placed supine on the surgical table. Both of the patient's arms are secured at the sides of the patient's trunk. Pneumoperitoneum was established using a Veress needle through the umbilicus. The endoscope trocar is inserted at the periumbilical area. Other robotic arms and assistant trocars are placed properly according to the general considerations. In the procedure which was reported by Rawlings et al. (2006), the robotic cart is located at the upper right side of the patient. The endoscope port is placed in the periumbilical area. The lower right and upper left quadrant ports are placed. These three trocars are occupied by the robotic arms. Additional upper left and lower left trocars are placed (Fig. 8A).
The author prefers that the robotic cart is located at the right side of the patient, which is the same level as the location of the endoscope port. The endoscope port is located at the supraumblical area and the robotic cart. The upper left, lower left and suprapubic ports are used for the robotic arms. The left lateral port is used for the assistant surgeon (Fig. 8B).

After the placement of the trocars, the surgical table is tilted to the left to allow the small intestine to fall off from the surgical field. Then, the robotic cart is docked.

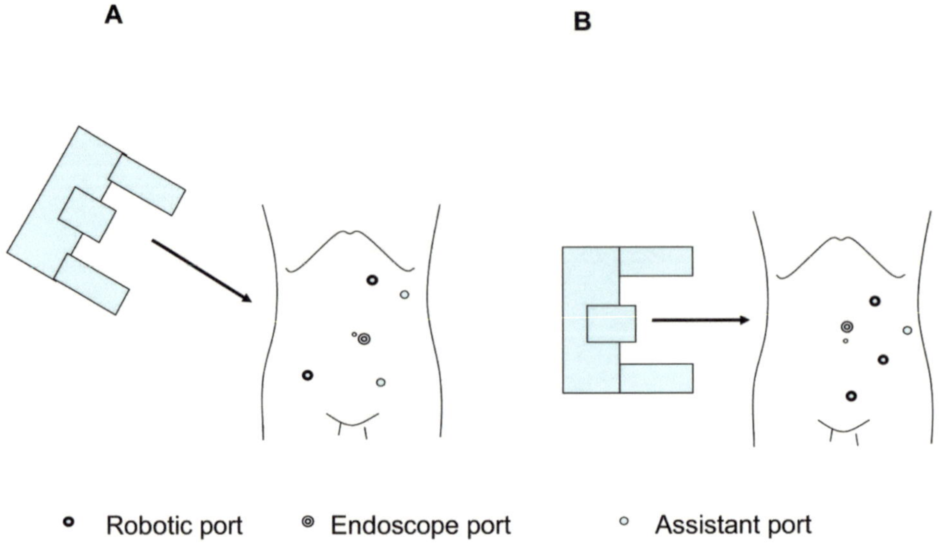

Fig. 8. The location of the ports and robotic cart for robotic assisted right colectomy: A) The right upper oblique location of the robotic cart; B) The right vertical location of the robotic cart

Careful examination of the abdomen and pelvic contents is performed. This examination can be performed before docking by manual manipulation of the robotic endoscope. The first right robotic arm uses the instrument which will dissect. The electric cautery, hook, scissors and ultrasonic device can be used at this step. The second left robotic arm uses the grasper. The bipolar grasper can also be used. The usual manner is the medial to lateral approach.

The ileocolic vasculatures are dissected at the root level and ligated by an endoclip or a vascular stapler. This allows identification of the right colic artery and the dissection plane between the right colon mesentery and Gerota's fascia. The right colic artery and vein and the hepatic branch of the middle colic artery and vein are ligated.

The ileal mesentery is divided with an ultrasonic device or a vascular stapler. The hepatic flexure suspensory ligaments and the transverse mesocolon are divided with the same instruments. Then, the attached paracolic gutter is divided. Both intracorporeal and extracorporeal can be performed on the specimen resection. Intracorporeal resection and anastomosis can be performed using the robotic system. However, the author prefers extracorporeal resection of the specimen and anastomosis because it can shorten the total operation time and needs no additional wound extension compared to the method of intracorporeal anastomosis using the robotic system. In colon cancer surgery, oncologic principles should be followed.

4.3 Sigmoid colectomy

The patient is placed supine in a modified lithotomy position with legs in adjustable stirrups. Both shoulder supporters are applied to prevent accidental movement of the patient on the surgical table. Both of the patient's arms are attached to both sides of the trunk. The pneumoperitoneum is established using the Veress needle. The endoscope port is located at the periumbilical area. The first right robotic arm trocar is inserted at the lower right abdominal area and the second left robotic arm trocar is inserted at the upper right abdominal area. The third robotic arm trocar is inserted at upper left area and the assistant trocar is inserted at the right lateral area at the level of the umbilicus. A careful examination of the abdomen and pelvic contents is performed. The patient is tilted to the right in a Trendelenburg position. Then, the robotic cart is docked (Fig. 9B). The sigmoid mesocolon is divided from the right iliac crest area. The prominence of the right iliac artery is a good landmark to dissect. The inferior mesenteric artery (IMA) is carefully skeletonized at the origin without injuring the hypogastric nerve flexus by electric cautery or hook. Then, IMA is ligated by an endoclip or a vascular stapler. Medial to lateral dissection is performed in the left gutter. The remaining attachment between the left gutter and colon are divided by an electric cautery or hook. The splenic flexure is completely mobilized. Then, the upper rectal area is dissected in the same manner. The upper mesorectum is divided by the ultrasonic device or the electric cautery using an endoclip. The robot is disengaged, and the upper rectum is divided using an endo-GIA. Then, the specimen is externalized through the vertically extended endoscope port, which is protected with a polyurethane retrieval bag. The specimen is resected at the proximal part, and the EEA stapler anvil is introduced.

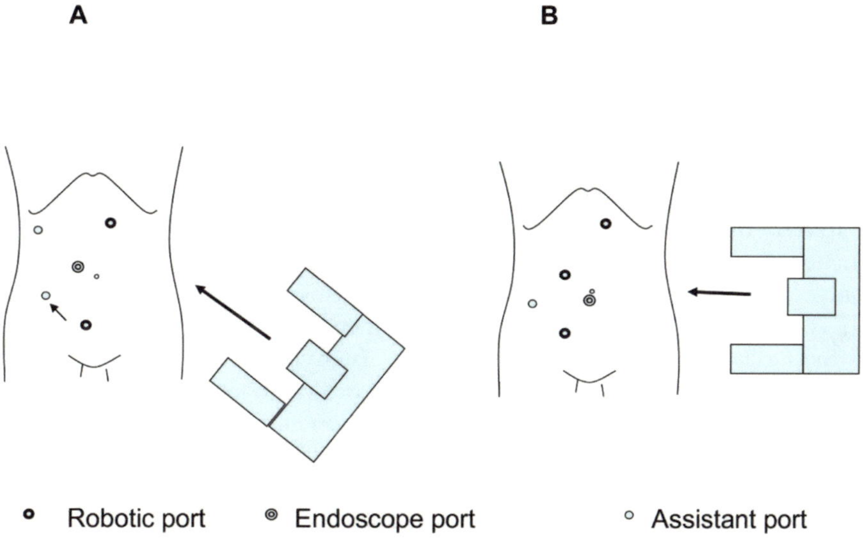

Fig. 9. The location of the ports and robotic cart for the robotic assisted sigmoid colectomy: A) The lower left oblique location of the robotic cart; B) The left vertical location of the robotic cart.

Then, the proximal colon is dropped back in the abdomen. The specimen extracted site is closed and the pneumoperitoneum is established again. The endoscope is introduced through the previous assistant trocar and a standard end to end anastomosis is performed using the EEA stapler.

In the robotic assisted sigmoid colectomy, the robotic cart can be brought from the lower left area (Fig. 9A). The procedure can be divided into two steps (Rawlings et al., 2006). At the first step, the endoscope port is located at the periumbilical area and the right robotic port and left robotic port are located at the suprapubic area and the upper left abdominal area.

The patient is tilted to the right and the reverse Trendelenburg position is added. It is better to perform the splenic flexure and upper left colon mobilization with a right tilt and the reverse Trendelenburg position. In this step, the splenic flexure is fully mobilized. Then, all the robotic arms are disengaged. The position of the patient is changed to the right tilt and the Trendelenbrug position. Then, the robotic cart is docked again. However, the suprapubic robotic arm moves to the lower right abdominal trocar to prepare for an effective operation of the IMA area and the upper part of the rectum. A change in the robotic cart position is not needed in this situation. Only three robotic arms are adjusted as the patient is placed in a Trendelenburg position.

4.4 Low anterior resection

The low anterior resection is a technically demanding procedure in robotic assisted colorectal surgery because it needs not only the upper left quadrant approach for splenic flexure mobilization but also the lower left quadrant approach for total mesorectal excision in rectal cancer patients. However, the robotic surgical system is not appropriate for the multi quadrant approach because of its technological limitation. Thus, the robotic cart should be placed at the upper left side of the patient for splenic flexure mobilization, and it should be placed in front of the perineum between both legs for rectal dissection. However, the movement of the robotic cart is so complicated because of its large size and heavy weight. Moreover, more robotic arm ports are needed for two step robotic operations. Because of this reason, the hybrid method was developed. Left colon mobilization, splenic flexure mobilization and IMA ligation are performed using conventional laparoscopic instruments, and rectal dissection is performed using the robotic surgical system in the hybrid method. In the hybrid method, the technological advantage can concentrate on the total mesorectal excision, which is the golden standard procedure in rectal cancer surgery. In fact, splenic flexure mobilization and left colon mobilization is the procedure for reconstruction. Proper mobilization is necessary for tension free colorectal anastomosis. In rectal cancer surgery, the most important issue is how we can obtain a complete TME specimen. A complete TME specimen can be obtained from a secure dissection without any injury to the fascia propria of the rectum. Thus, the hybrid method, which mostly uses a robotic system for TME is reasonable. However, according to the development of the robotic surgical system, the range of the robotic arm motion is increasing and the instruments become longer. Also, the robotic arms are smaller. Thus, several authors reported on the full robotic procedure for rectal cancer surgery (Park et al., 2009, Luca et al., 2009, Hellan et al., 2009). In this chapter, both methods will be described.

4.4.1 Hybrid method

The patient is placed supine in a modified lithotomy position with legs in adjustable stirrups. Shoulder supporters are applied to both sides to prevent accidental movement of the patient on the surgical table. Both of the patient's arms are attached to both sides of the trunk. The pneumoperitoneum is established using the Veress needle. The endoscope port is located at the supraumbilical area. The first right robotic arm trocar is inserted at the lower right abdominal area which is at the midpoint on the line between the supraumbilical trocar and the right anterior superior iliac spine. The second and third robotic arm trocars are inserted in the one-third and two-thirds points on the line between the supraumbilical trocar and the left anterior iliac spine. The assistant trocar is inserted in the upper right abdominal area on the midaxillary line to allow the surgeon access for mobilization of the left colon and the splenic flexure (Fig. 10A). A careful examination of the abdomen and pelvic contents are performed using an endoscope. Then, the patient is tilted to the right in a Trendelenburg position. The sigmoid mesocolon is divided from the right ileac crest area using conventional laparoscopic instruments. The surgeon stands on the right side of the patient. The main trocars in which the surgeon uses are the lower right and upper right trocars. IMA ligation, left colon mobilization and splenic flexure mobilization are performed in the same manner as the sigmoid colectomy using conventional laparoscopic instruments. Left colon mobilization is performed until the rectosigmoid junction. Then the robotic cart is brought from below. The robotic cart is placed in front of the perineal area between both legs. The first right robotic arm is inserted into the right robotic trocar. The second left robotic arm is inserted into the left robotic trocar near the endoscope trocar and the third robotic arm is inserted into the left lateral robotic trocar near the left anterior superior iliac spine. Rectal dissection is performed by the TME principle. If the mesorectum needs to be transected, it is performed using a bipolar grasper and an electric cautery. An ultrasonic device can be used at this step. However, the author does not prefer the ultrasonic device because it doesn't have an articulation function which is the core technology of the robotic surgical system. After full dissection of the rectum, the robotic cart is disengaged. Then, the lower right robotic trocar is changed to a 12 mm trocar to introduce the endo-GIA. The rectum is transected using an endo-GIA. Then, the left lateral robotic trocar extended 4 cm into the direction of the suprapubic area. This location of the wound is located below the patient's underpants. The following methods are the same with a sigmoid colectomy. According to the tumor location, coloanal anastomosis and abdominoperineal resection can be applied.

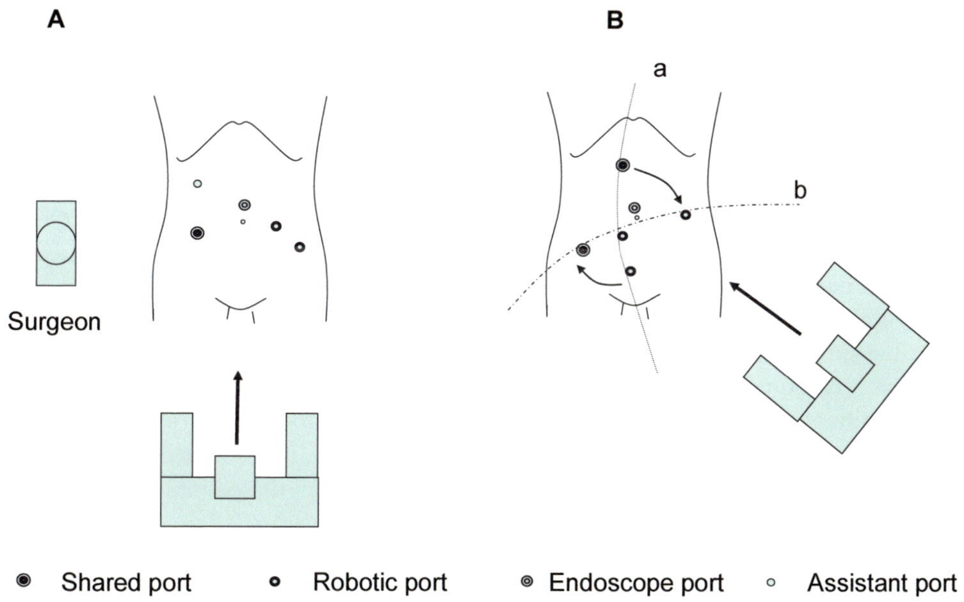

Fig. 10. The set up of the robotic cart and the location of the ports for low anterior resection: A) Hybrid method; B) Full robotic method.

4.4.2 Full robotic method

The full robotic method of low anterior resection for rectal cancer surgery is composed of two steps. The first step is for IMA and IMV ligation, left and sigmoid colon mobilization and splenic flexure mobilization. The second step is for rectal dissection. In the first step, the whole robotic ports are in line a. The endoscope port is located at the supraumbilical area. The right first robotic arm is placed 7-8 cm apart between the endoscope port on the imaginary line between the endoscope port and the anterior superior iliac spine. The second robotic left arm is placed at the upper abdomen which is 1cm right lateral from the midline. The third robotic arm is at the right supra pubic area. These four robotic ports are used for the first step. In this step, the assistant port is placed at the lower right area on line b, and it is used for the third right robotic port in the second step. After the first step, the second left robotic arm is disengaged and moves to the left robotic port on line b. The third right robotic arm moves to the lower right robotic port on line b, which is used for the assistant port in the first step (Fig. 10B). Then, the specimen is externalized through the horizontally extended suprapubic port, which is protected with a polyurethane retrieval bag. The following procedure is similar with the hybrid method.

5. Outcomes of robotic assisted colorectal surgery

Laparoscopic colorectal surgery is increased due to several benefits such as reduced post operative pain, shorter hospital stay and better cosmetics compared to open surgery. A lot of single center studies (Hoffman et al., 1994, Liang et al., 2007) support these results and the COST trial (Nelson et al., 2004) confirmed not only the benefits of the short term outcomes but also the long term outcomes in laparoscopic colon surgery. However, laparoscopic rectal surgery has been apprehended in that inadequate laparoscopic resection of the rectum may influence poor oncologic outcomes. The CLASICC trial (Guillou et al., 2005) and several single center studies (Feliciotti et al., 2003, Morino et al., 2003) reported the safety and the feasibility of laparoscopic rectal surgery.

However, the CLASICC trial (Guillou et al., 2005) insisted that the laparoscopic approach should be set against the slightly raised risk of a positive circumferential resection margin (CRM). This is a really important issue in rectal cancer surgery even though the CLASICC trial (Jayne et al., 2007) reported a higher positivity of CRM seen after laparoscopic anterior resection had not resulted in an increased incidence of local recurrence.

Most surgeons agree that there is a risk of an increasing rate of CRM involvement rate in laparoscopic surgery because rectal dissection is a technically demanding procedure and the laparoscopic procedure is a minimal invasive surgery which means that there are several technical limitations to perform the surgery compared to open surgery. Thus, until now there is no definite evidence of oncologic safety, which is confirmed by large scale prospective randomized multicenter trials, in laparoscopic dissection for rectal cancer patients.

Robotic assisted colorectal surgery can be considered as laparoscopic surgery. Their clinical application can be justified by the evidence of conventional laparoscopic colorectal surgery. Robotic assisted colorectal surgery has been performed continuously since Weber et al. (2002) performed the first two cases of robotic assisted colectomies. However, the majority of published papers are technical notes and comparative studies with a small number of patients. Systemic analysis is limited.

5.1 Operation time

Robotic assisted colorectal surgery needs a set up time for the robotic system. The time was reported from 15 min to 50 min (Rawlings et al., 2006, D'Annibale et al., 2004). It makes the total operation time longer than the conventional laparoscopic operation. The robotic system set up time is especially longer in the first few cases in the learning period and decreases according to accumulation of operating experiences. It also can be decreased by a developed robotic system model. The operation time of the robotic system is the summation of the set up time, robotic time and non robotic time.

Authors	No. of patients	Procedures (No.)	Mean Op time (min)	Malignancy (No.)
Giulianotti et al., (2003)	16	RHC(5) / ICR(2) / SC(1) / LAR(6) / APR(2)	172 / 150 / 240 / 270 / 180	14
Ruurda et al., (2005)	23	RP(16) / ICR(5) / SCS(2)	150 / 95 / 75	-
DeNoto et al., (2006)	11	SC (11)	196.7	-
Hellan et al., (2007)	39	LAR(33) / APR (6)	285	39
Park et al., (2009)	45	LAR(42) / APR (3)	293.8	45
Luca et al., (2009)	55	LAR(21) / APR (7) LHC(27)	290	55
Choi et al., (2009)	13	LAR(11) / SC(2)	260.8	13

RHC; Right hemicolectomy, ICR; Ileocecal resection, LHC; Left hemicolectomy, LAR; Low anterior resection, APR; Abdominoperineal resection. RP; Rectopexy, SCS; Sigmoid colostomy, SC; Sigmoid colectomy

Table 1. Case series of robotic assisted colorectal surgery with at least 10 patients.

Rawlings et al. (2006) reported that total operation time of a robotic assisted right hemicolectomy was 218.9 ± 44.6 min (range, 167 - 340 min). The total operation time of a robotic assisted sigmoid colectomy was 225.2 ± 37.1 min (range, 147 - 283 min).

D'Annibale et al. (2004) did not differentiate the operation time according to the type of operation. Then the overall robotic assisted colorectal operation time was 222 ±77 min. Park et al. (2009) reported the operation time of the total robotic assisted low anterior resection for rectal cancer as 293.8 ± 79.7 min. Luca et al.(2009) reported the operation of the total robotic assisted colorectal resection as 290 ± 69 min (range 164 - 487 min). In this study, the operation time was the mean of the operation time of robotic assisted abdominoperineal resection, anterior resection of the rectum and left hemicolectomy. Hellan et al. (2007) reported that the operation time of a robotic assisted low anterior resection was 285 min (range 180 - 540 min) in a 39 case series.

In comparative studies, the robotic assisted operation time was longer than conventional laparoscopic surgery. Spinoglio et al. (2008) reported that the operation time was 383.8 min in robotic assisted colorectal resections (n=50) and 266.3 min in conventional laparoscopic colorectal resections (n=161). The operation time in the robotic group was significantly longer than the conventional laparoscopic group (P< 0.001). Rawlings et al. (2007) also reported the operation time of a robotic assisted right hemicolectomy was significantly longer than a conventional laparoscopic right hemicolectomy. The operation time of the robotic group was 218.9 ± 44.6 min and the operation time of the laparoscopic group was 169.2 ± 37.5 min (P=0.002). In the same study, the operation time of a robotic assisted sigmoid colectomy was 225.2 ± 37.1 min and it was also longer than the operation time of a laparoscopic sigmoid colectomy (199.4 ± 44.5 min) even though it did not reach a significant difference (P=0.128). Woeste et al. (2005) compared 4 cases of the robotic assisted sigmoid colectomy to 23 cases of the conventional laparoscopic colectomy for diverticulitis. The operation time was 236.7 ± 5.8 min and 172.4 ±38 min, respectively. The operation time of the robotic group was significantly longer than the laparoscopic group (P=0.05). However, Baik et al. (2009) reported a similar operation time in the study which compared the robotic assisted low anterior resection to the conventional laparoscopic low anterior resection for rectal cancer patients. The operation time was 190 ± 45 min (range 120 min - 315 min) in the robotic group and 191.1 ± 65.3 min (range 100 min - 360 min) in the laparoscopic group and there was no statistical difference between the groups (P=0.924).

Rawlings et al. (2007) commented on the etiology of the longer operation time of robotic assisted right hemicolectomy was due to intracorporeal anastomosis instead of extracorporeal anastomosis. However, they did not show the exact robotic intracorporeal anastomosis time. The reason of the longer operation time of robotic assisted colorectal surgery has not been defined until now. The absence of tactile sense may be a reason. The surgeon can feel the tactile sense from the instrument tips during laparoscopic surgery even though it was remarkably decreased than open surgery. The tactile sense allows little movement of the instrument tips outside of the laparoscopic view area because the surgeon can immediately stop when resistance is felt from something outside of the laparoscopic view. However, the surgeon cannot absolutely feel tactile sense in robotic assisted surgery. Thus, the instrument cannot be manipulated outside the laparoscopic view. The endoscope must always be moved appropriately to see the instrument. Then the instrument can be manipulated. These consecutive movements are a time consuming procedure. Also, the robotic arm movements cannot follow the speed of experienced surgeon's hands in the abdominal operative field until now.

However, in Baik et al.'s (2009) study, there was no difference in the operation time between the robotic and conventional laparoscopic surgeries. The operation method in the robotic group was the hybrid method. Left colon mobilization and ligation of the inferior mesenteric artery and vein were performed using conventional laparoscopic instruments. The rectal dissection procedures were performed by the robotic surgical system. During pelvic dissection, the necessity of the movement of the endoscope is needed less than colon surgery because the surgical space is confined by the narrow pelvic cavity. The advanced technology in the robotic surgical system may shorten the time of rectal dissection. Also, the surgeon's experience may influence and shorten the operation time because the present generation robotic surgical system just follows the surgeon's hand motions and decisions. The robotic surgical system is upgrading rapidly and continuously. Thus, it cannot be declared that the operation time of robotic colorectal surgery is longer than the operation time of conventional laparoscopic procedure.

5.2 Short term outcomes

D'Annibale et al. (2004) compared the first day to diet, the first day to bowel function recovery and the period of hospital stay of 53 cases of robotic assisted colorectal surgery to the results of 53 cases of conventional laparoscopic colorectal surgery. The first day to diet was 3 ± 2 in the robotic group and 3 ± 1 in the laparoscopic group. The first day to bowel function recovery was the same as 4 ± 2 in both groups. The period of hospital stay was 10 ± 4 days and 10 ± 6 days, respectively. These parameters were not significantly different between the groups. Blood loss was 21 ± 80 ml and 37 ± 102 ml, respectively. It also was not significantly different between the groups. The complications were intestinal obstruction, bowel injury, cerebrovascular accident and wound infection in the robotic group.

Authors	First flatus/ Length of stay (day)	Blood loss (ml)	Conversion No. (%)	Complication No. (%)
DeNoto et al., (2006)	- / 3.4	-	1 (9.1)	0 (0.0)
Hellan et al., (2007)	- / 4	200	1 (2.6)	15 (38.5)
Park et al., (2009)	- / 9.8	-	1 (2.2)	5 (11.1)
Luca et al., (2009)	2.02 / 7.5	68	0 (0.0)	12 (21.8)
Choi et al., (2009)	- / 7	-	0 (0.0)	3 (23.1)

Table 2. Short term outcomes of case series studies with at least 10 patients

Rawlings et al. (2007) reported the comparison results between 30 cases of robotic assisted colectomies and 27 cases of laparoscopic assisted colectomies. They compared the length of hospital stay, estimated blood loss and conversion rate. The cases of the robotic group were divided into 17 cases of robotic assisted right hemicolectomy and 13 cases of robotic assisted sigmoid colectomy. In the subgroup analysis of the right hemicolectomy, the length of hospital stay was 5.2 ± 5.8 days in the robotic group and 5.5 ± 3.4 days in the laparoscopic group (P=0.862). Estimated blood loss was 40.4 ± 24.9 ml, 66.3 ± 50.7 ml, respectively (P=0.067). In the subgroup analysis of the sigmoid colectomy, the length of hospital stay was 6.0 ± 7.3 days in the robotic group and 6.6 ± 8.3 days in the laparoscopic group (0.854). The estimated blood loss was 90.4 ± 60.0 ml and 65.4 ± 52.1 ml, respectively (P=0.280). Conversion occurred in two cases of the laparoscopic right hemicolectomies and in two cases of robotic assisted sigmoid colectomies. In these analyses, there were no significant differences of short term clinical outcomes between the robotic assisted colectomy and the laparoscopic colectomy.

Spinoglio et al. (2008) compared the first 50 consecutive cases of robotic assisted colorectal surgery to 161 cases of laparoscopic colorectal surgery. The first day to diet was 1.04 day in the robotic group and 1.08 day in the laparoscopic group (P=0.603). The first day to passing flatus was 1.48 day and 1.67 day, respectively (P=0.704). The length of hospital stay was 8.31 days and 7.74 days, respectively (P=0.928). Complications occurred in 7 cases (14%) of the robotic group and in 27 cases (17%) in the laparoscopic group (P=0.489). The conversion rate also was not different between group (P=0.603). Two cases (4%) were converted in the robotic group and 4 cases (4%) were converted in the laparoscopic group. In the conversion cases of the robotic group, one case was converted to standard laparoscopic procedure and the other case was converted to the open procedure.

Baik et al. (2009) analyzed 56 homogenous cases of robotic assisted low anterior resection for rectal cancer. They showed a significant shorter length of hospital stay of the robotic group than the laparoscopic group. The length of hospital stay was 5.7 ± 1.1 days in the robotic group and 7.6 ± 3.0 days in the laparoscopic group (P=0.001). Also, the serious complication rate was 5.4% in the robotic group and 19.3% in the laparoscopic group, and it reached a statistical significance (P=0.025). They postulated that the technical advantage of the robotic surgical system might decrease the serious complication rate and it was related to the shorter length of hospital stay.

	D'Annibale (2004)	Rawlings (2007)	Spinoglio (2008)	Baik (2009)
	Robotic assisted surgery / Laparoscopic surgery			
No. of patients	53 / 53	30 / 27	50 / 161	56 / 57
Malignancy (No.)	22 / 42	5 / 8	44 / 128	56 / 57
Procedure (No.)				
RHC	10 / 13	17 / 15	18 / 50	0 / 0
LHC	17 / 17	0 / 0	10 / 73	0 / 0
SC	11 / 4	13 / 12	0 / 0	0 / 0
LAR	10 / 15	0 / 0	19 / 26	56 / 57
APR	1 / 0	0 / 0	1 / 7	0 / 0
Others	4 / 6	0 / 0	2 / 5	0 / 0
Conversion (No.) (%)	6(11.3)/ 3(5.6)	2(6.6)/2(7.4)	2(4) / 4(4)	0(0.0) / 6(10.5)*
Mean Op time (min)	240 / 222	†218.9/169.2* ‡225.2/199.4	383.8/ 266.3*	190.1 / 191.1
Length of stay (day)	NA	†5.2/5.5 ‡6.0/6.6	7.7 / 8.3	5.7 / 7.6*
First flatus (day)		NA	1.67 / 1.48	1.9 / 2.1
Blood loss (ml)	21 / 37	†40.0/66.3 ‡90.4/65.4	NA	NA
Complication(No.)(%)	4(7.5)/ 9(17.0)	5(16.7)/4(14.8)	7(14.0) / -	6(10.7)/11(19.3)
Mortality (No.)	0 / 0	0 / 0	0 / 0	0 / 0
DRM (cm)	NA	NA	7.3 / 7.9	4.0 / 3.6
CRM positivity (No.)	NA	NA	NA	4 / 5
No.of Harvested LN	17 / 16	NA	22.03 / 22.85	18.4 /18.7

RHC; Right hemicolectomy, LHC; Left hemicolectomy, SC; Sigmoid colectomy, LAR; Low anterior resection, APR; Abdominoperineal resection, PRM; Proximal resection margin, DRM; Distal resection margin, CRM; Circumferential resection margin, LN; Lymph node, NA; not available, † Cases of right hemicolectomy, ‡ Cases of sigmoid colectomy,
* Statistically significant parameter

Table 3. Comparative studies comparing robotic assisted to laparoscopic colorectal surgery with at least 10 patients

There were no conversion cases in the robotic group and six conversion cases in the laparoscopic group. The reasons for the conversions in the laparoscopic group were severe hemorrhage from the lateral pelvic wall, severe narrow pelvic cavity, and rectal perforation. They thought that these reasons for conversion could be overcome by the advanced technology of the robotic surgical system such as the ability for fine dissection in a narrow surgical field. This study showed firstly the better short term outcomes of robotic colorectal surgery than laparoscopic colorectal surgery. However, it was a single surgeon's experience and a comparative study with a small number of cases.

In 2009, several authors reported cases of a series of robotic assisted colorectal surgery with new technical procedures (Park et al. (2009), Patriti et al. (2009), Choi et al. (2009), Ng et al. (2009)). The common results of these studies were the safety and feasibility of robotic assisted colorectal surgery.

5.3 Oncologic outcomes

Robotic colorectal surgery has not only been used in benign diseases but also in malignant diseases. Spinoglio et al. (2008) reported that there was no significant difference of the number of harvested lymph nodes between robotic assisted and laparoscopic colorectal surgery in the study which contained 44 malignant cases in the robotic group and 128 malignant cases in the laparoscopic group.

The important issue for better oncologic outcomes in colorectal cancer is a curative resection which means proper lymph node dissection. In rectal cancer surgery, the golden standard procedure is total mesorectal excision (TME) (Heald et al., 1982, Enker et al., 1995, Havenga et al., 1996). A complete TME procedure requires a precise dissection of loose avascular areola tissue between the fascia propria of the rectum and the presacral fascia without any injury to the fascia propria of the rectum. The macroscopic completeness of the fascia propria of the rectum is scored into three grades (complete, nearly complete, incomplete) and is a predictive factor of the patient's prognosis (Nagtegaal et al., 2002). In Baik et al.'s study (2007), the pathologic results with macroscopic grades were excellent. These results could be the reason for decreasing the local recurrence rate and improving long term survival rates in rectal cancer patients. The technological advantages of the surgical system may influence the results of the excellent mesorectal grade of robotic assisted TME. In 2009, Baik et al. reported that the mesorectal grade after robotic assisted low anterior resection was significantly better than the mesorectal grade after conventional laparoscopic low anterior resection in their comparative study. This data supports that robotic assisted low anterior resection may be better than laparoscopic assisted low anterior resection for rectal cancer patients in terms of oncologic outcomes. However, the circumferential resection margin (CRM) involvement rate was not different between the robotic assisted low anterior resection group and the laparoscopic low anterior resection group. Involvement of CRM is influenced by the tumor location from the fascia propria of the rectum and the quality of rectal dissection. The advanced robotic technology influences the quality of rectal dissection and did not influence the location of the tumor. The different results between the CRM involvement rate and mesorectal grade could be explained by the above reason.

In colon cancer surgery, the laparoscopic procedure has been increased because it improves the quality of life and there are no adverse effects of laparoscopic surgery in survival (COST trial, 2004). These results mean that laparoscopic colon resection fulfills the concept of oncologic resection with a proper resection margin and lymph node dissection similar to the open procedure. Thus, there is no further prospect to improve survival in minimally invasive procedures such as laparoscopic or robotic assisted colon cancer surgeries.

Until now, there is no comparable oncologic data between robotic assisted colorectal surgery and laparoscopic or open colorectal surgery. Future large scale prospective randomized trials are necessary.

6. Conclusions

Improvements of the robotic surgical system are continuously being made to overcome the technical limitations and disadvantages found during the surgeries. So detailed operation methods are newly designed to adapt to the upgraded model of the robotic surgical system. The major core technologies of the robotic surgical system are a three dimensional image of the surgical field and a function of articulation of the instruments tips compared to conventional laparoscopic instruments. With the help of these technologies, the incidence of robotic assisted colorectal surgery is somewhat increased for the cure of not only benign diseases but also malignant diseases with the rapidly developing technology of the robotic surgical system. However, most studies have reported only on the feasibility and the safety of the robotic assisted colorectal surgery. Moreover, oncologic outcomes have not been reported until now even though the robotic surgical system has been used for colorectal cancer. Thus, future studies should be performed not only to find the validity to use the robotic surgical system but also to establish the benefits of its use.

7. Acknowledgement

The author would like to acknowledge Mrs. MiSun Park for her dedicated assistance of manuscript editing and English revision.

8. References

Anvari M., Birch D.W., Bamehriz F., Gryfe R., Chapman T. (2004). Robotic-assisted laparoscopic colorectal surgery. Surg Laparosc Endosc Percutan Tech, 14, 311-315.

Baik S.H., Lee W.J., Rha K.H., et al. (2007). Robotic total mesorectal excision for rectal cancer using four robotic arms. Surg Endosc, 22, 792-797.

Baik S.H., Ko Y.T., Kang C.M., et al. (2008). Robotic tumor-specific mesorectal excision of rectal cancer: short-term outcome of a pilot randomized trial. Surg Endosc, 22, 1601-1608.

Baik S.H., Kwon H.Y., Kim J.S., et al. (2009). Robotic verus laparoscopic low anterior resection of rectal cancer: short-term outcome of a prospective comparative study. Ann Surg Oncol, 16, 1480-1487.

Braumann C., Jacobi C.A., Menenakos C., et al. (2005). Computer-assisted laparoscopic colon resection with the da Vinci system: our first experiences. Dis Colon Rectum, 48, 1820-1827.

Bruce G.W., Fleshman J.W., Beck D.E., et al. (2007), The ASCRS textbook of colon and rectal surgery, NY, USA, Springer.

D'Annibale A., Morpurgo E., Fiscon V., et al. (2004). Robotic and laparoscopic surgery for treatment of colorectal disease. Dis Colon Rectum, 47, 2162-2168.

Delaney C.P., Lynch A.C., Senagore A.J., Fazio V.W. (2003). Comparison of robotically performed and traditional laparoscopic colorectal surgery. Dis Colon Rectum, 46, 1633-1639.

DeNoto G., Rubach E., Ravikumar T.S. (2006). A standardized technique for robotically performed sigmoid colectomy. J Laparoendosc Adv Surg Tech A, 16, 551-556.

Enker W., Thaler H.T., Cranor M.L., Polyak T. (1995). Total mesorectal excision in the operative treatment of carcinoma of the rectum. J Am Coll Surg, 181, 335-346.

Feliciotti F., Guerrieri M., Paganini A.M., DeSanctis A., et al. (2003). Long term results of laparoscopic vs open resections for rectal cancer for 124 unselected patients. Surg Endosc, 17, 1530-1535.

Giulianotti P.C., Coratti A., Angelini M., et al. (2003). Robotics in general surgery: personal experience in a large community hospital. Arch Surg, 138, 777-784.

Guillou P.J., Quirke P., Thorpe H., et al. (2005). Short-term endpoint of conventional versus laparoscopic-assisted surgery in patients with colorectal cancer (MRC CLASICC trial): multicenter, randomized controlled trial. Lancet, 365, 1718-1726.

Hashizume M., Shimada M., Tomikawa M., et al. (2002). Early experiences of endoscopic procedrues in general surgery assisted by a computer-enhanced surgical system. Surg Endosc, 16, 1187-1191.

Havenga K., DeRuiter M.D., Enker W.E., Welvarrt K. (1996). Anatomic basis of autonomic nerve preserving total mesorecal excision for rectal cancer. Br J Surg, 83, 384-388.

Heald R.J., Husband E.M., Ryall R.D. (1982). The mesorectum in rectal cancer surgery - clue to pelvic recurrence? Br J Surg, 69, 613-616.

Hellan M., Anderson C., Ellenhorn J.D.I., Paz B., Pigazzi A. (2007). Short-term outcomes after robotic-assisted total mesorectal excision for rectal cancer. Ann Surg Oncol, 14, 3168-3173.

Hoffman GC, Baker JW, Fitchett CW, Vansant JH. (1994). Laparoscopic-assisted colectomy: initial experience. Ann Surg, 219, 732-740.

Jayne D.G., Guillou P.J., Thorpe H., et al. (2007). Randomized trial of laparoscopic-assisted resection of colorectal carcinoma: 3-year results of the UK MRC CLASICC trial group, J Clin Oncol, 25, 3061-3068.

Liang JT, Lai HS, Lee PH. (2007). Laparoscopic medial to lateral approach for the curative resection of right sided colon cancer. Ann Surg Oncol, 14, 1878-1879.

Liang JT, Huang KC, Lai HS, Lee PH, Sun CT. (2007). Oncologic results of laparoscopic D3 lymphadenectomy for male sigmoid and upper rectal cancer with clinically positive lymph nodes. Ann Surg Oncol, 14, 1980-1990.

Morino M., Parini U., Giraudo G., et al. (2003). Laparoscopic total mesorectal excision: a consecutive series of 100 patients. Ann of Surg, 237, 335-342.

Nagtegaal I.D., Van de Velde C.J., Van der Worp E., Kapiteijn E., Quirke P., Van Krieken J.H. Cooperative Clinical Investigators of the Dutch Colorectal Cancer Group (2002). Macroscopic evaluation of rectal cancer resection specimen: clinical significance of the pathologist in quality control. J Clin Oncol, 20, 1729-1734.

Nelson H., Sargent D.J., Wienad H.S., et al. (2004), A comparison of laparoscopically assisted and open colectomy for colon cancer. N Engl J Med, 350, 2050-2059.

Pigazzi A., Ellenhorn J.D.I., Ballantyne G.H., Paz I.B. (2006). Robotic-assisted laparoscopic low anterior resection with total mesorectal excision for rectal cancer. Surg Endosc, 20, 1521-1525.

Rawlings A.L., Woodland J.H., Vegunta R.K., Crawford D.L. (2007). Robotic versus laparoscopic colectomy. Surg Endosc, 21, 1701-1708.

Rawlings A.L., Woodland J.H., Crawford D.L. (2006). Telerobotic surgery for right and sigmoid colectomies: 30 consecutive cases. Surg Endosc, 20, 1713-1718.

Ruurda J.P., Draaisma W.A., Van Hillegesberg R., et al. (2005). Robot-assisted endoscopic surgery: a four-year single-centre experience. Dig Surg, 22, 313-320.

Sebajang H., Trudeau P., Dougall A., Hegge S., Mckinley C., Anvari M. (2006). The role of telementoring and telerobotic assistance in the provision of laparoscopic colorectal surgery in rural areas. Surg Endosc, 20, 1389-1393.

Spinoglio G., Summa M., Priora F., et al. (2008). Robotic colorectal surgery: first 50 cases experience. Dis Colon Rectum, 51, 1627-1632.

Vibert E., Denet C., Gayet B. (2003). Major digestive surgery using a remote-controlled robot: the next revolution. Arch Surg, 138, 1002-1006.

Weber P.A., Merola S., Wasieleswski A, Ballantyne G.H. (2002). Telerobotic-assisted laparoscopic right and sigmoid colectomies for benign disease. Dis Colon Rectum, 45, 1689-1694.

Woeste G., Bechstein W.O., Wullstein C. (2005). Does telerobotic assistance improve laparoscopic colorectal surgery? Int J Colorectal Dis, 20, 253-257.

6

Robotic Surgery of the Colon: The Peoria Experience

Steven S Tsoraides, M.D., M.P.H., Franziska Huettner, M.D., P.h.D., Arthur L Rawlings M.D., M.Div. and David L Crawford, M.D.
Department of Surgery, University of Illinois College of Medicine at Peoria, Illinois USA

1. Introduction

The application of robotics in surgery has expanded since its introduction not so long ago. Robotic surgery is promoted by hospitals and sought out by patients. Residency programs are including training in robotics and the next generation of surgeons is becoming more facile with robotic procedures. Use of robotics in surgery has been applied to general surgical, gynecologic, urologic, and cardiac procedures.

As this technology expands, many questions arise. Cost is a major concern, as are the resources and staffing necessary for robotic procedures. Although these debates are ongoing, it is clear that the technology is expanding and robotics will continue to be promoted and applied. Here we present our experience with robotic colectomy and discuss some of the pertinent issues related to this topic.

2. Background and history

Robotic surgery developed as a project of the Department of Defense with the goal of enabling a surgeon to operate remotely from a patient. Although its application in this aspect has not been realized, robotic systems have advanced, and it is now the private sector which has taken on this technology. The Automated Endoscopic System for Optimal Position (AESOP) was the first robotic system approved for intraabdominal surgery by the Food and Drug Administration (FDA) in 1993 (Computer Motion, Goleta, California) (Oddsdottir et al., 2004). This computerized robotic camera assistant is used in laparoscopic surgery. The voice-activated system allows a surgeon to control the visual field while keeping his/her hands free for operating.

The da Vinci system (Intuitive Surgical, Inc., Sunnyvale, California) was introduced in 1997 and approved by the FDA in 2000. This system allows for direct manipulation and dissection capabilities and has become the only available "robotic" system. The first robotic procedure using the da Vinci system was a cholecystectomy performed in Brussels in 1997 (Kelley, 2002).

The da Vinci system includes a surgeon's console, a surgical cart, and the vision tower. Although newer generations are available, the basic concepts are similar. The surgeon's console includes binocular monitors, foot pedals, and hand-held masters for manipulation of the surgical instruments and camera. The robot is draped into the field and includes up to four surgical arms, one for the camera, two for the operating surgeon's hands, and a fourth as an assistant arm. The vision tower includes similar equipment to a laparoscopic tower: an insufflator, light source, camera, and printer, as well as the 3-D image synchronizing hardware.

Participating as a university-affiliated, community training program at the University of Illinois College of Medicine at Peoria, The Peoria Surgical Group became the first private practice owner of the da Vinci system in 2002. The system has since been purchased by the local hospital, and a second hospital in our community also has a da Vinci system. More recently, one of our hospitals has purchased a recent generation da Vinci Si HD system. Robotic procedures are performed by general and cardiac surgeons, urologists, and gynecologists. A wide variety of general surgical procedures have been performed, including foregut and colon operations. We will focus our discussion on a single-surgeon (DLC) experience with robotic colectomy.

Right colectomy was the first laparoscopic procedure performed on the colon by Moises Jacobs in 1990 in Miami (Jacobs et al., 1991). Robotic-assisted colectomy was reported eleven years later in 2001 (Ballantyne et al., 2001). Multiple reports have since been published on robotic colectomy, including our own results. The benefits of cosmesis and recovery translate similarly to both techniques. Robotic surgery can be applied in both benign and malignant disease as long as appropriate principles are adhered to. Although controversy still exists as to the application of minimally invasive techniques in the treatment of rectal malignancies, multiple reports in the recent literature describe the use of the robot in performing pelvic dissection. It seems the benefits of using the robot in colorectal surgery are most appreciated in performing a total mesorectal excision, where the constraints of the pelvis limit maneuverability with common laparoscopic instruments. Although this area will likely receive more attention in the near future, it is not part of the senior author's practice currently.

3. Procedures

The decision to proceed with a robotic colectomy is made after discussion between the operating surgeon and the patient. Of the three hospitals in our community, two have a da Vinci system available. If the patient is a candidate for minimally invasive surgery and has been scheduled at one of these two hospitals, they are offered the option of robotic surgery. These cases are typically scheduled as the first case of the day to allow for adequate staffing and preparation. Indications for surgery are similar to those for laparscopic colectomy. Procedures performed include Robotic Right Colectomy and Robotic Sigmoid Colectomy.

3.1 Robotic right colectomy

Robotic Right Colectomy is performed with the patient in the supine position. The patient is placed on a bean bag and the bag wraps the left arm. The chest and legs are secured to the table with conventional straps on the legs and heavy tape at the level of the clavicles (Image 1). These measures are essential given the degree and variation of positioning necessary to carry out the procedure. Once pneumoperitoneum is established, trocars are placed as depicted in Figure 1. The camera is placed through the 12mm periumbilical trocar. With the omentum retracted cranially, the planned point of division of the transverse colon and mesocolon are marked with endoclips based on the right branch of the middle colic artery. The terminal ileum is also run for 20-30cm to ensure it is not fixed in the pelvis, as it must reach the transverse colon for anastomosis. The table is then tilted to the left and slightly head down to allow the small bowel to retract out of the visual field and to encourage the omentum to stay above the transverse colon. The robot is positioned over the right upper quadrant and the camera and instruments are docked. The robot's right/green arm is placed through the 5mm epigastric trocar and the left/yellow arm is placed through the 5mm right lower quadrant trocar. A five millimeter trocar is inserted in the left lower quadrant for use by an assistant in retracting and exposing the ileocolic vascular pedicle. A grasper placed through the 12mm left lateral abdominal wall port can be used to hold the transverse mesocolon up and out of the way.

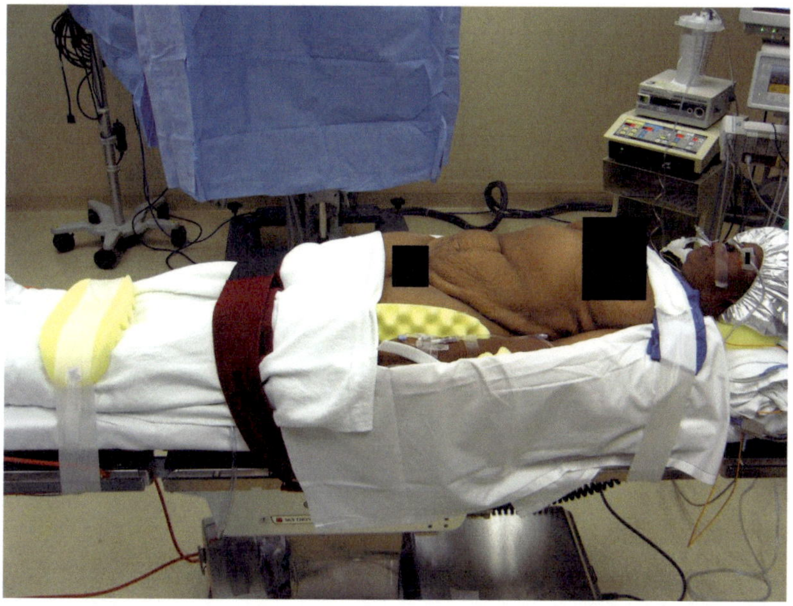

Image 1. Patient Positioning

We proceed with a medial to lateral dissection by dividing the ileocolic vascular pedicle with a vascular load laparoscopic stapler at the level of the duodenum. The right mesocolon is then mobilized from Gerota's fascia. After identification of the ureter, the ileal mesentery is divided using a harmonic energy device to a point ten centimeters proximal to the ileocecal valve. Once the entire right colon is mobilized out to the abdominal wall and around to the duodenal sweep, attention is directed to the transverse mesocolon. The previously incised or clipped line on the mesocolon is found and the right branch of the middle colic artery is identified. Clips and vascular staplers are used as needed to control this at its base. The mesocolon is then divided with a harmonic device up to the colon. The transverse colon and ileum are then divided intracorporeally with a laparoscopic stapler, however the right colon remains attached to its lateral peritoneal attachments to keep it retracted laterally. Once the transverse colon is divided, we improve the view in the area of the final attachments of the colon to the head of the pancreas as well as the distal stomach and duodenum. These final attachments are taken down with harmonic energy or clips until the specimen is free.

An intracorporeal anastomosis is then created in an isoperistaltic side-to-side fashion between the ileum and transverse colon. The ileum is adjoined to the transverse colon 6cm from the end of the ileum using a 30cm 2-0 silk suture on a Keith needle. This needle is then externalized in the right upper quadrant and clamped externally for retraction (Image 2). A harmonic energy device is then used to create enterotomies, through which the ends of an

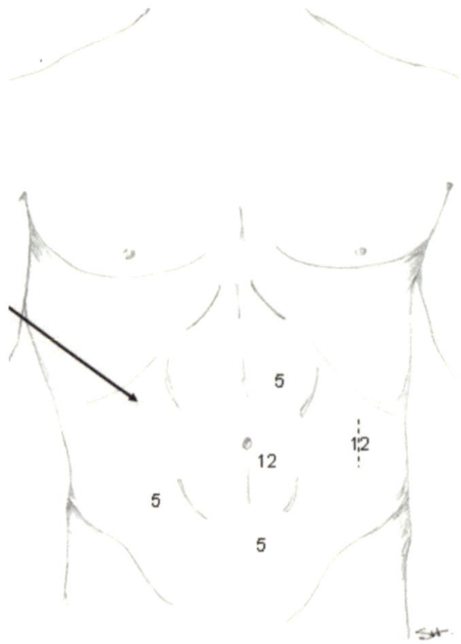

Fig. 1. Trocar Placement for Robotic Right Colectomy.

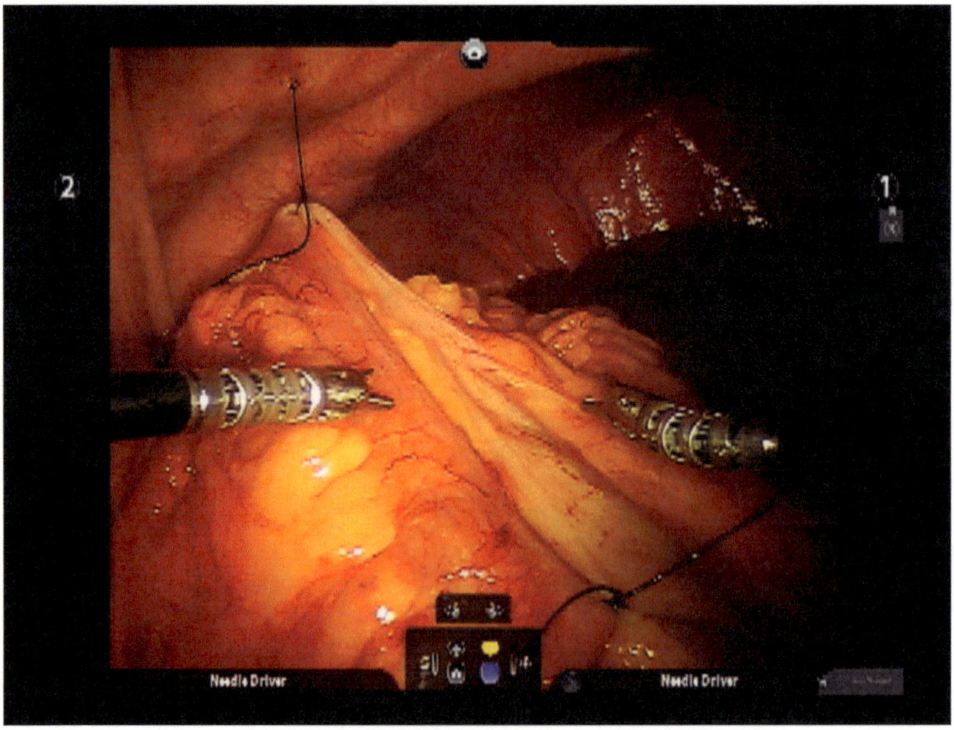

Image 2. Bowel Alignment for Intracorporeal Ileocolic Anastomosis

endoscopic linear cutting stapler are inserted through the left lateral 12mm trocar and the stapler is fired. The defect is closed with a running 2-0 absorbable braided suture. The mesenteric defect is then closed with absorbable suture. The retracting 2-0 silk suture is divided and the lateral attachments of the right colon are taken down with a harmonic device or cautery. The specimen is extracted through the left lateral 12mm trocar site, which is extended to approximately four centimeters to accommodate extraction. The wound is protected with a bag to prevent contact with the specimen. Standard closure techniques are then followed.

3.2 Robotic Sigmoid Colectomy

Robotic Sigmoid Colectomy is performed with the patient in a supine modified lithotomy position, in which the anterior thighs are in the same plane as the abdominal wall. The patient is placed on a bean bag so that the bag can wrap the right arm and the chest is secured to the table with heavy tape at the clavicles. Trocars are placed as seen in Figure 2 after pneumoperitoneum is obtained. The procedure is begun with the patient in a steep right sided tilt and reverse Trendelenburg position. The robot is brought in from the left side of the patient (see arrow a, Figure2). The right/green arm and its trocar are slipped through the suprapubic 12mm port or the arm can be docked to the left lateral abdominal wall 5mm robot port. The left/yellow arm is docked to the epigastric port. A harmonic energy device is used in the left arm and a grasper in the right. The splenic flexure is taken down by dividing the gastrocolic ligament then elevating the mesocolon off of Gerota's fascia. Downward and medial retraction by the assistant from the right sided trocars is invaluable. Electrocautery can be used for the latter portion of this mobilization over Gerota's fascia but harmonic energy is particularly helpful with the thick and often vascular gastrocolic ligament. Visualization of the ligament of Treitz through the mesentery marks the medial extent of proximal mobilization. The inferior mesenteric vein is selectively taken for benign diagnoses and routinely taken for malignant. Because left ureter visualization medially is

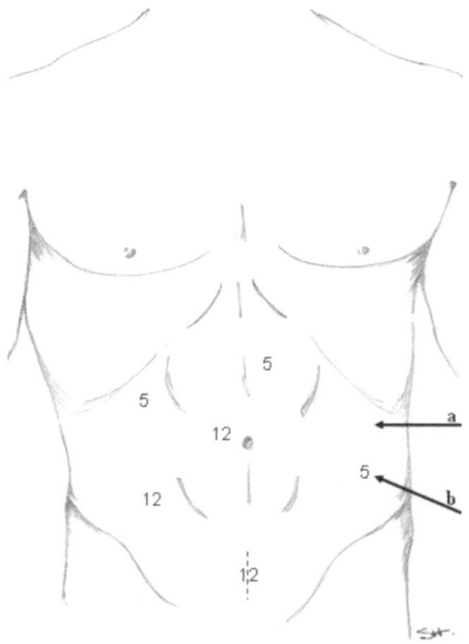

Fig. 2. Trocar Placement for Robotic Sigmoid Colectomy.

the goal all the way to the pelvic brim, changing table position is required. The robot is disengaged and drawn back from the table. The patient is placed in Trendelenberg position and the robot is brought in from the left hip (see arrow b, Figure 2). The right/green arm and its trocar are slipped through the right lower quadrant 12mm port and cautery or harmonic energy device is attached. The left/yellow arm is connected to the left lateral abdominal wall robot trocar and a grasper is inserted. The sigmoid colon is elevated and the inferior mesenteric vascular pedicle is demonstrated. The peritoneum on the right side of the rectosigomid colon is scored at its base and the inferior mesenteric artery is isolated. The rectosigmoid colon is then mobilized circumferentially down to the desired level on the rectum while visualizing both ureters.

At this point the robot is disengaged and endoscopic staplers are used to divide the inferior mesenteric artery and the rectum. The suprapubic port is extended to accommodate externalization of the specimen through a protecting bag. After proximal division of the colon and resection of the specimen, the anvil of an end-to-end anastomotic stapler is secured into the end of the colon. The colon is returned to the abdomen and the fascia is closed to allow for reestablishment of the pneumoperitoneum. The stapler is then inserted transanally through the rectum and attached to the anvil and fired. We routinely test our anastomoses with insufflation. Standard closure techniques are then followed.

Post operative care is similar to that in patients undergoing laparoscopic colectomy, with an emphasis on quicker recovery times. Clear liquids are offered the day of surgery and early ambulation is encouraged. Patient controlled analgesia is employed until patients are tolerating diet and oral medicines. Epidurals are not used. Criteria for discharge include tolerance of liquids, ability to void, adequate pain control with oral analgesics and evidence of bowel function. Follow up visits are scheduled within one to two weeks from the day of discharge.

4. Methods

Institutional Review Board (IRB) approval was obtained. From 2002 to 2009 a total of 102 consecutive robotic colectomies were performed by a single surgeon (DLC) at two institutions with varying amounts of resident participation. Data was recorded in a Statistical Package for the Social Services (SPSS) database prospectively and a retrospective review of this data was performed.

5. Results

One-hundred and two robotic colectomies were performed. Procedures included 59 right colectomies and 43 sigmoid colectomies. For all colectomies, average patient age was 63.5 years (22-86). Forty-nine patients were male and 53 were female. Preoperative indications included polyps in 53 patients, diverticular disease in 27 patients, cancer in 19 patients, and carcinoid in 3 patients.

Total operative time for all cases averaged 219.6 minutes ± 45.1, with an average robot time of 126.6 minutes ± 41.6. For right colectomies port time averaged 32.4 minutes ± 10.5, robot time 145.2 minutes ± 39.6, and total case time 212.3 minutes ± 46.4. For the sigmoid colectomies port time averaged 31.2 minutes ± 9.6, robot time 101.2 minutes ± 29.2, and total case time 229.7 minutes ± 41.6.

Average blood loss was 66.6 milliliters. Four procedures were converted to laparoscopy and five to an open approach, with an overall conversion rate of 8.8%. Complications occurred in

19 patients with an overall complication rate of 18.6%. Anastomotic leak occurred in one patient (0.98%). Median length of stay for all patients was 3 days with a range of 2 to 27 days.

6. Discussion

The advance of technology in the recent era of surgery has outpaced the ability of the medical community to adequately interrogate the true utility of certain techniques prior to their widespread adoption. Often hospitals and patients within a community seeking the latest technology become a driving force for surgeons to adopt new techniques. Ideally, the benefit of these measures are examined and discussed within the surgical community prior to their establishment as "common practice." Many surgeons would argue that the true role for robotics in surgery is yet to be properly defined. Certainly there is an appeal for hospitals in marketing themselves as centers offering robotic surgery, and for surgeons to be promoted as regional experts in robotics and minimally invasive surgery. Although they may not know why, patients request robotic surgery in the hopes that they are receiving the most advanced care possible. We as surgeons, however, must decide when the application of robotics is truly advantageous.

There is no doubt that the robot enhances the technical ability of the surgeon in ways that common laparoscopic techniques currently do not. The wristed instruments increase the maneuverability of the operating instruments with two more degrees of freedom than traditional laparoscopic instruments. The robot adds internal pitch and yaw to the pitch, yaw, grasp, rotation, and in-and-out motions of the laparoscopic instruments. The end result is that the instruments mimic the motion of a surgeon's hands with the added benefits of tremor reduction and motion scaling. Confined spaces such as the pelvis and mediastinum provide arenas where these benefits are best realized.

The visualization offered by the da Vinci system also serves as an enhancement to traditional laparoscopy. A stereoscopic camera allows for representation in both two-dimensional and three-dimensional views. The three-dimensional view provides a clarity and depth of field which further improves the surgeon's ability to discriminate among tissue planes. Furthermore, the surgeon has the added benefit of control over the camera with one of the robot arms. This eliminates the frustration that can be met with inexperienced or fatigued camera operators and enhances the ability of the surgeon to complete difficult maneuvers in an efficient fashion.

Another benefit of robotics not to be overlooked is the reduction of surgeon fatigue. The long term toll of laparoscopy on an individual surgeon may still not be fully realized given the fairly recent adoption of laparoscopy into the every day practice of many surgeons. Over the course of a twenty to thirty year career, the stresses of awkward positioning and maneuvering may prove to be detrimental to the health of many operating surgeons. During a robotic procedure, the surgeon is sitting comfortably with arms and head resting against padded surfaces. Recentering of hand controls eliminates the cumbersome task of maintaining positions beyond the normal range of comfort and convenience. Control of the visual field with the head comfortably supported reduces the neck strain often encountered during many laparoscopic procedures. Although the immediate benefit to any given patient is difficult to demonstrate, the pending dilemma of physician shortage reminds us that physician longevity is perhaps more important than previously thought. The robotic model presents an opportunity to minimize surgeon fatigue that may warrant further investigation.

These advantages must be weighed against the disadvantages of using the robot for any given procedure. System-based considerations include staffing and accessibility. Staff must be properly educated on setup and troubleshooting to ensure that robotic procedures can be completed without undue delay. Often, an increased number of skilled staff is required to execute a robotic procedure. Operative suites must be of adequate size to accommodate the robot while at the same time ensure procedures not requiring the robot be unhindered by its presence. Rooms must be fashioned in a way that allows for effective surgeon to staff communication, as the traditional prominence of the surgeon standing over the patient is altered in robotic surgery.

Technically, the loss of tactile sensation and the ability to accurately gauge "strength" presents a challenge to the operating surgeon. The risk of patient injury is increased if the surgeon is unfamiliar with these limitations and visual clues become very important to the surgeon when handling tissue. Also limiting is the difficulty in operating in the far lateral extensions of the operative field, where robot arms are restricted from operating beyond a certain distance. Robot arms can interfere with each other outside the patient as well, creating an added challenge not encountered in traditional laparoscopy. Port placement, experience, and planning are critical in minimizing the incidence of this problem. Unlike traditional laparoscopy, instruments and camera are not conveniently interchanged to accommodate the various fields encountered in a given procedure. The robot must be moved in and out of the docked position to accomplish significant alterations in port, camera, and instrument positions. This is often timely and cumbersome. An important goal with any robotic procedure is to minimize time wasted with repositioning of the robot. Positioning of the patient too is important. Laparoscopy often requires frequent and exaggerated position changes to assist in retraction and accessibility of tissues. This must be anticipated in any robotic case, as most patient position changes require repositioning of the robot as well.

The largest concern, of course, is cost. The system itself is expensive to acquire, as are instruments and the disposable equipment required for robotic cases. Often, increased time and staffing are required to accommodate robotic procedures. No specific reimbursement pattern exists to recuperate these costs. Whether private or nationally supported, a payer source must be able to justify the cost of the technology for it to survive in modern health care. This is an ongoing debate, and the outcome of this debate may determine what role robotics plays in the future.

In our previous review, adjusted to 2005 US dollars, robotic colectomy carried a 15% greater total hospital cost compared to laparoscopic colectomy, although there was not statistical significance. In 17 robotic right colectomy cases, average total hospital cost was $9,255 compared to $8,073 for laparoscopic cases (Rawlings et al., 2007). Little else has been published regarding cost data, despite the fact that this is often a matter of debate. Delaney et al. also showed a higher total hospital cost for robotic procedures, with a $350 difference in operating room and equipment costs (Delaney et al., 2003). These costs have to be taken on by the operating institution. Interestingly, it is often these same institutions pushing surgeons to utilize the technology, despite the lack of avenues to directly regain the difference in cost. This cost, in some ways, can be considered a "marketing" expense that institutions assume when purchasing the da Vinci system. Any surgeon considering performing robotic surgery must also consider the local financial and institutional environment and should have support from their institution prior to employing robotics within their practice. Surgeons should be open about cost issues with both their patients and their institutions to avoid misconceptions about this significant matter.

Taking the above issues into consideration, one must ask "why robotics?" Certainly there are advantages and disadvantages, as there are many proponents and perhaps even more opponents to robotic surgery. When looking at the literature, we find that it is difficult to show a clear outcomes benefit to patients when comparing laparoscopy to robotic surgery of the colon. Multiple authors have reported their experiences and common points of discussion typically include operative time, cost, length of stay and complications. From 2004, we have identified five papers reporting experience with robotic surgery of at least 30 patients, as well as our own (Table 1). Here we discuss these papers.

Author	Year	n	Total Case Time (min)	Conversion	Complications
Luca	2009	55	290	0	12
Baik	2009	56	190.1	0	6
Spinoglio	2008	50	383.8	2	7
Crawford	2008	70	225	8	8
Hellan	2007	39	285	1	5
Crawford	2006	30	226	2	6
D'Annibale	2004	53	240	6	4

Table 1. Publications of Robotic Colon Surgery with at least 30 patients

When looking at the literature, operative time for robotic surgery of the colon typically ranges from 200 to 300 minutes, however some reach almost 400 minutes. In the papers we have focused on, average reported total procedure time is 262.8 minutes in 353 robotic colon cases. This includes all types of cases, from right colectomy to intersphincteric resection and APR. Conversion occurred in 19 (5.4%) cases with 9 to laparoscopic and 9 to open. Outcomes from robotic colectomy reflect those of laparoscopic colectomy. Complications were reported in 48 (13.6%) of the 353 patients with 14 (4.0%) representing anastomotic leak. Our low anastomotic leak rate and operative time compare favorably to these results. Our conversion rate was slightly higher, but similar to these results.

In considering available series discussing robotic surgery of the colon, we find a good deal of inconsistency in the data collected. Conversion tends to be a rather infrequent occurrence, with conversion to both conventional laparoscopy and laparotomy (Table 2). Operative times vary, and no clear trend can be identified between operative experience and total case time. Outcomes also vary, but here too it seems results are comparable to those in conventional laparoscopic surgery. Certainly it can be argued that robotic surgery is safe and feasible for surgery of the colon when considering patient outcomes. The increase in operative time may be a concern when dealing with patients of increased preoperative morbidity, and we advocate surgeon discretion in these scenarios.

					Conversion Type	
Author	Year	n	Total Case Time (min)	Conversion	Laparotomy	Laparoscopy
Crawford	2009	102	219.6 (50-380)	9	5	4
Luca	2009	55	290 (164-487)	0		
Baik	2009	56	190.1 (120.0-315.0)	0		
Choi	2009	13	260.8 (210-390)	0		
Spinoglio	2008	50	383.8	2	1	1
Baik	2008	18	217.1 (149-315)	0		
Crawford	2008	70	225 (147-380)	8	5	3
Baik	2007	9	220.8 (153-315)	0		
Hellan	2007	39	285 (180-540)	1	1	0
DeNoto	2006	11	197 (145-345)	1	0	1
Crawford	2006	30	226 (90-340)	2	2	0
Ayav	2005	6	172 (45 - 280)	1	1	0
Braumann	2005	5	201 (80-300)	2	2	0
Anvari	2005	6	109 (90 - 160)	0		
Woeste	2004	4	236.7	1	1	
D'Annibale	2004	53	240	5	0	5
Anvari	2004	10	155.3	0		
Ayav	2004	5	265 (180 - 240)	1	1	
Hanly	2004	35	177	5	5	0
Hubens	2004	7	NA	0		
Ewing	2004	12	248 (180-350)	0		
Delaney	2003	6	216.5 (170 - 274)	1	0	1
Giulianotti	2003	16	211 (90 - 360)	0		
Vibert	2003	3	380 (330 - 450)	0		
Weber	2002	2	284 (228 - 340)	0		
Hashizume	2002	3	260 (180 - 335)	0		

Table 2. Series of Robotic Surgery of the Colon

Also deserving mention is the role robotic technology plays in surgical training programs. Graduating surgeons must be familiar with modern techniques in order to remain relevant to contemporary practice. Although robotic surgery is not considered mainstream at the current time, being familiar with the technology and the opportunities it presents are important assets to have. Resident involvement in robotic surgery plays an important role at our institution. The residents participate in robotic cases starting their first year of training.

During the first and second years of training the residents attend a half day course that includes didactic lectures on the history and development of robotic surgery. They also receive hands on instruction with the device regarding setup, instrument exchanges, robot positioning and troubleshooting. They then receive individual instruction while sitting at the surgeon's console with dexterity exercises and suturing. During this early stage the resident assists the surgeon while standing at the operating table. Over time, according to training level, interest, and operative talent, the residents become more involved in performing more integral portions of the procedure from the surgeon's console. Senior residents often do more than 90% of the case, while the attending surgeon remains as assistant and instructor at the operating table.

When looking at our data, we find that resident involvement in robotic cases increases throughout training (Table 3). The exception to this is the fourth year of training due to the increased time spent on trauma and night float rotations. As the resident advances, we also see that the number of cases in which he or she performs >90% of the procedure also increases, along with the total cases participated in. It has been the senior author's observation that the formal incorporation of robotic training in the curriculum has allowed residents to learn robotic techniques in an effective manner. Most residents are able to adapt to the technology quickly, often with less difficulty than in traditional laparoscopic surgery. This involvement has an added benefit in the recruitment of future residents. Allowing significant resident involvement in robotic surgery reassures applicants that they are pursuing a program which will not only expose them to, but train them in cutting edge techniques with cutting edge technology. We see this technology, therefore, advancing within academic training centers, where new applications and adaptations to robotics can be developed and applied.

Table 3. Resident Involvement in Robotic Cases According to Training Level

6.1 Conclusion

Robotic technology has presented many opportunities and controversies for surgeons. Many are quick to adopt new technology, while others remain skeptical of the true benefits of robotics in abdominal surgery. We have presented our experience with robotic surgery in order to further the discussion of this matter in regards to surgery of the colon. How robotics will continue to be employed in colonic procedures remains to be settled. Certainly, the technology will continue to evolve, and perhaps be adapted to take on different forms and purposes. As attention turns to natural orifice surgery and single incision laparoscopic procedures, robotic technology may provide solutions for limitations in these areas. Regardless of outcome, it is essential as surgeons and academicians, that we continue this debate for the purpose of enhancement of our profession and improvement in patient outcomes.

Illustrations by Steven Henriques, M.D.

7. References

Anavari M, Birch, D, Bamehriz F, Gryfe R, Chapman T (2004) Robotic-assited laparoscopic colorectal surgery. *Surgical Laparoscopy, Endoscopy and Percutaneous Techniques* 14(6): 311-15

Anavari M, McKinley C, Stein H (2005) Establishment of the world's first telerobotic remote rurgical service for provision of advanced laparoscopic surgery in a rural sommunity. *Annals of Surgery* 241(3): 460-64

Ayav A, Bresler L, Brunaud L, Boissel P (2004) Early results of one-year robotic surgery using the da vinci system to perform advance laparoscopic procedures. *Jounal of Gastrointestinal Surgery* 8(6): 720-26

Ayav A, Bresler L, Hubert J, Brunaud L, Boissel P (2005) Robotic-assisted pelvic organ prolaps surgery. *Surgical Endoscopy* 19(9): 1200-03

Baik SH, Ko YT, Kang CM, Lee WJ, Kim NK, Sohn SK, Chi HS, Cho CH (2008) Robotic tumor-specific mesorectal excision of rectal cancer: short-term outcome of a pilot randomized trial. *Surg Endosc* 22:1601-1608

Baik SH, Kwon HY, Kim JS, Hur H, Sohn SK, Cho CH, Kim H (2009) Robotic versus laparoscopic low anterior resection of rectal cancer: short-term outcome of a prospective comparativesStudy. *Ann Surg Oncol* 16:1480-1487

Baik SH, Lee WJL, Rha KH, Kim NK, Sohn SK, Chi HS, Cho CH, Lee SK, Cheon JH, Ahn JB, Kim WH (2007) Robotic total mesorectal excision for rectal cancer using four robotic arms. *Surg Endosc* 22:792-797

Ballantyne G, Merola S, Weger P, Wasielewski A (2001) Robotic solutions to the pitfalls of laparoscopic colectomy. *Osp Ital Chir* 7: 405-12

Braumann, C, Jacobi C, Menenakos C, Borchert U, Rueckert J, Mueller J (2005) Computer-assisted laparoscopic colon resection with the davinci system: our first experiences. *Diseases of the Colon and Rectum* 48(9): 1820–27

Choi GS, Park IJ, Kang BM, Lim KH, Jun SH (2009) A noval approach of robotic-assisted anterior resection with transanal or transvaginal retrieval of the specimen for colorectal cancer. *Surg Endosc* 2009 May 14. (Epub ahead of print)

D'Annibale A, Morpurgo E, Fiscon V, Trevisan P, Sovernigo G, Orsini C, Guidolin D (2004) Robotic and laparoscopic surgery for treatment of colorectal diseases. *Diseases of the Colon and Rectum* 47(12): 2162-68

Delaney C, Lynch A, Senagore A, Fazio V (2003) Comparison of robotically performed and traditional laparoscopic colorectal surgery. *Dis Colon Rectum* 46: 1633-39

DeNoto G, Rubach E, Ravikumar TS (2006) A standardized technique for robotically performed sigmoid colectomy. *J Laparoendosc Adv Surg Tech A* 16(6): 551-6

Ewing DR, Pigazzi A, D'Annibale A, Morpurgo E, Fiscon V, Haag BL, Ballantyne GH (2004) Telerobotic laparoscopic colorectal surgery. In: Ballantyne GH, Marescaux J, Giulianotti P (eds) *Primer of robotic and telerobotic surgery.* Lippincott Williams and Wilkins, Philadelphia, pp 171-180

Giulianotti P, Coratti A, Angelini M, Sbrana F, Cecconi S, Balestracci T, Caravaglois G (2003) Robotics in general surgery: personal experience in a large community hospital. *Archives of Surgery* 138(7): 777-84

Hanly E, Talamini M (2004) Robotic abdominal surgery. *The American Journal of Surgery* 188(4A): 19S-26S

Hashizume M, Shimada M, Tomikawa M, Ikeda Y, Takahashi I, Abe R, Foga F, Gotoh N, Konishi K, Maehara S, Sugimachi K (2002) Early experience of endoscopic procedures in general surgery assisted by a computer-enhanced surgical system. *Surgical Endoscopy* 16(8): 1187-91

Hellan M, Anderson C, Ellenhorn JDI, Paz B, Pigazzi A (2007) Short-term outcomes after robotic-assisted total mesorectal excision for rectal cancer. *Annals of Surgical Oncology* 14(11): 3168-73

Hubens G, Ruppert M, Balliu L, Vaneerdeweg W (2004) What have we learnt after two years working with the da vinci robot system in digestive surgery? *Acta chirurgica Belgica* 104(6): 609–14

Huettner F, Rawlings AL, McVay WB, Crawford DL (2008) Robot-assisted laparoscopic colectomy: 70 cases - one surgeon. *J Robotic Surg* 2: 227-34

Jacobs M, Verdeja J, Goldstein H (1991) Minimally invasive colon resection (laparoscopic colectomy). *Surg Laparosc Endosc* 1(3): 144-50

Kelley W (2002) Robotic surgery: The promise and early development. *Laparoscopy* 1:6-10

Luca F, Cenciarelli S, Valvo M, Pozzi S, Faso FL, Ravizza D, Zampino G, Sonzogni A, Biffi R (2009) Full robotic left colon and rectal cancer resection: technique and early outcome. *Ann Surg Oncol* 16:1274-78

Oddsdottir M, Birgisson G (2004) AESOP: A voice-controlled camera holder, In: *Primer of Robotic & Telerobotic Surgery,* Ballantyne G, Marescaux J, Gulianotti P. (Ed.), pp. 35-41, Lippincott Williams & Wilkins, ISBN 0-7817-4844-5, Philadelphia

Rawlings AL, Woodland JH, Crawford DL (2006) Telerobotic surgery for right and sigmoid colectomies: 30 consecutive cases. *Surg Endosc* 20: 1713-18

Rawlings AL, Woodland JH, Vegunta RK, Crawford DL (2007) Robotic versus laparoscopic colectomy. *Surgical Endoscopy 21: 1701-08*

Spinoglio G, Summa M, Priora F, Quarati R, Testa S (2008) Robotic colorectal surgery: first 50 cases experience. *Dis Colon Rectum* 51: 1627-32

Vibert E, Denet C, Gayet B (2003) Major digestive surgery using a remote-controlled robot: the next revolution. *Archives of Surgery* 138(9): 1002-06

Weber P, Merola S, Wasielewski A, Ballantyne G (2002) Telerobotic-assisted laparoscopic right and sigmoid colectomies for benign disease. *Dis Colon Rectum* 45: 1689-1696

Woeste G, Bechstein W, Wullstein C (2005) Does telerobotic assistance improve laparoscopic colorectal surgery? *Int J Colorectal Dis* 20(3):253-7

7

Robotic Sacrocolpopexy and Sacrocervicopexy for the Correction of Pelvic Organ Prolapse

James C Brien[1], Michael D Fabrizio[1] and James C Lukban[2]
[1]Department of Urology, Eastern Virginia Medical School, Norfolk, Virginia,
[2]Division of Urogynecology, Eastern Virgina Medical School, Norfolk, Virginia, USA

1. Introduction

The lifetime risk for undergoing a single operation for prolapse (or incontinence) is 11%, with the National Center for Health Statistics reporting 400,000 procedures for these conditions performed annually.[1] Swift et al. described the epidemiologic distribution of pelvic organ prolapse (POP) in a sample of 1004 women presenting for an annual gynecologic exam, evaluated with a validated staging system (Pelvic Organ Prolapse Quantification System or POP-Q).[2,3] Despite a relatively young mean age of 42.7 years, clinically significant (Stage II or greater) vaginal wall descensus was identified in 37% of subjects. In a larger study as part of the Women's Health Initiative, those between the ages of 50 and 79 were screened for POP through a non-validated system.[4] Of 16,616 subjects with no previous hysterectomy, 41.1% had some form of prolapse, while 38% of 10,727 hysterectomized women exhibited POP. The true incidence of POP is likely higher, as many women may not report their condition due to embarrassment, or they may feel that such changes are a normal part of aging.

2. Anatomy of the pelvic floor

The pelvic floor is comprised of layers of connective tissue and muscle that provide support to the pelvic viscera. The urethra, vagina and rectum are attached to the pelvic sidewalls by the endopelvic fascia, which in turn is supported by the pelvic floor musculature (PFM).[5] The PFM consists of the levator ani (pubococcygeus and iliococcygeus) and coccygeus muscles, providing tonic support to the endoplvic fascia and viscera through a preponderance of type I (slow twitch) fibers.[6] Thus, a robust PFM is essential in maintaining the position of the viscera within the pelvis.

3. Etiology of pelvic organ prolapse

Pelvic organ prolpase represents an attenuation or disruption of the connective tissue comprising the pubocervical endopelvic "fascia" anteriorly or rectovaginal endopelvic "fascia" posteriorly, manifesting as anterior or posterior vaginal wall prolapse, respectively. Additionally, a weak or torn cardinal - uterosacral ligament complex may lead to vaginal apex (cuff post hysterectomy or cervix) descent. Predominant risk factors for POP include age and parity, with partial denervation of the PFM proven to be the result of parturition, senescence, or some combination.[7,8] As the PFM becomes weak, support to the endopelvic fascia and viscera is lost, placing the connective tissue at risk for attenuation and/or discrete breaks with resultant POP. When encountered in a younger subject, POP may reasonably be the sequela of acute obstetric trauma, or the result of a genetic alteration in the proportion of fascial collagen subtypes.[9]

4. Considerations prior to surgical correction of pelvic organ prolapse

The goal of POP repair is to restore pelvic anatomy, and facilitate normal visceral and sexual function. To this end, the surgeon must consider, first and foremost, the integrity of the vaginal apex. The Surgery for Pelvic Organ Prolapse Committee of the 3rd International Consultation on Incontinence noted, "...the apex is the keystone of pelvic organ support". [10] Additionally, they concluded that anterior and posterior repairs are doomed to fail unless the apex is adequately supported. While multiple approaches exist to address vaginal apical prolapse, choosing the optimal repair is critical to a successful outcome.

In the following text, we will discuss several methods for the repair of apical descensus, examine the surgical evolution from vaginal and abdominal surgery to laparoscopic and robotic approaches, and describe our technique of robot assisted laparoscopic sacrocolpopexy and sacrocervicopexy.

5. Transvaginal surgery for apical prolapse

Uterosacral ligament suspension is an intraperitoneal technique in which the remnants of the ureterosacral ligaments are brought together with permanent suture, and subsequently attached to the vaginal apices bilaterally employing delayed absorbable stitch. Recurrent apical prolapse following this procedure has been reported between 1% and 18%, with the anterior segment found to be the most common site of persistent prolapse.[11,12] Overall, reported patient satisfaction is high, with a re-operation rate of 5.5% in one series.[13] Although bowel injury and bleeding complications are relatively infrequent, ureteral injury or kinking has been reported to be as high as 11%, emphasizing the importance of interrogating the ureters endoscopically after suspension.[12,13]

Sacrospinous ligament fixation involves an extraperitoneal rectovaginal dissection with support of the vaginal apex through attachment to the sacrospinous ligament either unilaterally or bilaterally. Exposing the ischial spine and ligament may, at times, be a challenge, with the attendant risk of neurovascular trauma. The surgeon must avoid the hypogastic plexus, the inferior gluteal and internal pudendal vessels, and the pudendal and sciatic nerves. Outcomes are variable, with recurrence ranging from 3-30%. [14-16] Additional potential complications include gluteal pain and rectal injury.

Iliococcygeus fascial suspension is also an extraperitoneal technique performed through a posterior vaginal incision. Dissection is carried out laterally and cephalad until the iliococcygeus musculature is identified, at which point an absorbable suture is placed through the fascia and ipsilateral vaginal apex bilaterally. While Shull and colleagues reported recurrence as low as 5% with low complication rates compared to other transvaginal approaches, the potential for hemorrhagic morbidity exists, with one author reporting an average estimated blood loss (EBL) of 358 mL.[17,18]

6. Transvaginal mesh repairs

The introduction of a variety of mesh products has been implemented for the repair of stress urinary incontinence as well as POP. Although a thorough review of this modality is beyond the scope of this chapter, a brief account of contemporary outcomes will be discussed.

Several synthetic graft materials have been used historically including expanded PTFE and polyester, with polypropylene being the dominant synthetic used in contemporary kits due its macroporous nature, allowing for tissue in-growth and minimal inflammatory response.[19,20] Commercial kits, designed to allow for minimally invasive mesh insertion, include Elevate (American Medical Systems, Minnetonka, MN, USA) and Gynecare Prolift System (Ethicon Women's Health and Urology, Somerville, NJ, USA), along with several other products and approaches for mesh support of the vaginal apex.

In a review of clinical trials and observational studies addressing apical prolapse repair, Diwadkar and colleagues included 3,425 patients from 24 studies employing vaginal mesh kits, reporting a low rate of reoperation for recurrent POP (1.3 % at 17 months), with an overall complication rate (14.5 %) similar to traditional vaginal (15.3 %) and abdominal (17.1%) approaches.[21] However, the majority of complications associated with mesh kits required surgical intervention under general anesthesia (8.5 %), due in part to mesh erosion (vaginal exposure of synthetic material). In a retrospective review comparing outcomes following Prolift mesh repair, uterosacral ligament suspension and abdominal sacrocolpopexy, no difference in operative success (% with Stage 0 or I at follow-up) was observed between the three groups; however, mean change in apical support was significantly better after abdominal sacrocolpopexy compared to transvaginal mesh repair and uterosacral ligament suspension.[22]

7. Abdominal surgery for apical prolapse

High uterosacral ligament suspension, similar to its vaginal counterpart, involves suspension of the vaginal apex to plicated ureterosacral ligaments. After entrance into the abdomen, the cul-de-sac is obliterated to address any co-existing enterocele. Subsequently, the apex of the vagina is exposed and reapproximated to the plicated uterosacral ligaments.

Abdominal sacral colpopexy (ASC) involves securing the apex of the vagina to the sacral promonatory with intervening mesh. After a laparotomy incision is made and hysterectomy performed (if uterus present), the vagina is elevated with an end-to-end anastomosis (EEA) sizer followed by dissection of the vesicovaginal and rectovaginal spaces. The anterior and posterior leafs of a Y-shaped polypropylene mesh are sutured to the anterior and posterior vaginal walls, respectively. After opening the peritoneum over the sacral promontory, multiple nonabsorbable sutures are placed through the anterior longitudinal ligament, and secured to the single tail of the "Y". Lastly, the peritoneum over the sacrum and vaginal apex is closed.

Several studies document durable success following ASC, with recurrent prolapse ranging from 1 - 7% at long term follow up.[23,24] A recent Cochrane Review of the Surgical Management of Pelvic Organ Prolapse concluded that ASC was superior to sacrospinous fixation, exhibiting a lower rate of recurrent prolapse and less postoperative dyspareunia.[25] Abdominal sacrocolpopexy, however, was associated with longer operative time, longer recovery time and higher costs. Complications are infrequent, and include injury to bowel and bladder, with the potential for significant hemorrhage from presacral vessels. While mesh erosion has historically been higher with ASC employing small pore multifilament material, rates of apical exposure of graft have been 5% or less with the use of polypropylene.[26]

Given the durability of ASC, such an approach is considered by many to represent the "gold standard" in the treatment of apical prolapse. In considering the attendant risks of open abdominal procedures and the availability of burgeoning technology, practitioners have made the logical progression to a less invasive approach using minimally invasive instrumentation in the performance of sacrocolpopexy.

8. Laparoscopic sacrocolpopexy (LSC)

The concept and surgical technique of LSC is similar to that of its open counterpart. With the introduction of laparoscopy to vaginal reconstruction, many studies have been published evaluating the efficacy and safety of LSC as compared to ASC. Overall, LSC appears to be durable, with a low rate of recurrence (0-4%),[28-30] exhibiting favorable quality of life outcomes[28] and high patient satisfaction (96%).[30] Complications are overall infrequent, and include erosions (0-9%), dysparunia (1%), spondylitis (<1%), partial small bowel obstruction (0-4%) and a low conversion to open rate of 2.2%.[28-31] Reported operative times have ranged from 97 min to 219 minutes depending on surgeon experience.[29-30] In two retrospective comparative trials, LSC was associated with lower EBL, shorter hospital stay and increased time in the operating room (OR) as compared to ASC.[27,29] From this data, we may conclude LSC to be non-inferior to it's open counterpart with a low incidence of adverse events.

9. Robot assisted laparoscopic sacral colpopexy and cervicopexy (RALSC)

The da Vinci surgical system (Intuitive Surgical, Sunnyvale, CA, USA) has augmented traditional laparoscopy adding three-dimensional vision, wristed instrumentation with seven degrees of freedom (versus 3 degrees with laparoscopy) and improved surgical ergonomics. Specific to sacrocolpopexy, the addition of the 4th arm adds facilitation of sigmoid colon reflection.

Robot assist laparoscopic sacrocolpopexy (RALSC) has been found to have similar outcomes to its pure laparoscopic predecessor. Efficacy appears durable with one non-comparative study of 30 patients reporting 6% recurrence at 24 months,[32] and surgical failure in two additional studies ranging from 0 - 4.7% at shorter follow up.[33,34] Such data are comparable to the 7% rate of recurrence reported in a large series of open sacralcolpopexy by Snyder and Krantz.[24] Daneshgardi and colleagues evaluated preoperative and postoperative POP-Q values in patients undergoing RALSC, reporting not only an overall improvement in global POP-Q scores, but statistically significant improvement of anterior, posterior and apical POP-Q scores separately.

Mesh erosion rates are comparable to an open incidence of 7% reported by Kohli and colleagues.[37] Length of hospital stay in 4 series ranges from 1 - 2.4 days[32,33,35,38] with operative times ranging 186 – 328 minutes.[32,34-36,38] One series reported a 25% decrease in procedure time after the initial 10 cases, suggesting a steep, but short learning curve.[36] Complications of RALSC are comparable to LSC. Ureteral injury, enterotomy and cystotomy are infrequent (0 - 1.2%) as is post op small bowel obstruction (4.7%).[32,34,36] While no randomized-controlled trials comparing RALSC to LSC have been published to our knowledge, a retrospective comparison of RALSC with ASC by Geller et al.found the former to be associated with slightly better postoperative POP-Q "C" (apex) improvement, less EBL and shorter hospital stay. While RALSC was observed to have longer operative times, there was no significant difference with respect to intraoperative or postoperative complications between the two groups.[38]

10. Description of RALSC

The patient is given appropriate antibiotic prophylaxis in the preoperative area and sequential pneumatic compression devices are applied for deep venous thrombosis prophylaxis. After intubation, the patient is placed in low - lithotomy position and straps are placed across the shoulders and chest in a criss - cross pattern to secure the patient on the table. The arms are padded and tucked. See Figure 1 for operating room configuration.

After prepping and draping of the abdomen, perineum and vagina, a foley catheter is placed. A Veress needle may be inserted through the umbilicus (or just cephalad) to facilitate insufflation of the abdomen, or the initial trocar may be introduced under direct vision employing a clear blunt-tipped device with lens inside prior to introduction of gas. In patients suspected of having significant midline abdominal adhesions, one may enter the abdomen with a 5 mm laparoscope loaded into a 5 mm clear blunt-tipped trocar at Palmer's point (3 cm below the left costal margin in the mid-clavicular line) to visualize subsequent midline trocar placement.[39]

The initial 12 mm camera port is inserted no less than 15 cm and no greater than 22 cm from the pubic symphysis in the midline. Prior to placement of lateral trocars, the patient is placed in a steep Trendelenburg tilt. With full insufflation (not to exceed 15 mm Hg), measurements are made on the anterior abdomen to ensure appropriate placement of subsequent trocars, and avoid collision of the robotic arms (Fig. 2). Two lateral 8 mm ports are then placed 10 cm inferolateral to the camera port in the direction of the ipsilateral anterior superior iliac spine (ports 1 and 2). A 3rd 8 mm port is placed 8 - 10 cm superolateral to port 2 (port 3) and a 12 mm assistant port is placed 8 cm lateral to port 1. The robot is docked and ports secured (Fig. 3).

The sigmoid is reflected with the fourth arm employing a non-fenestrated grasper in the open position, facilitatating visualization of the sacrum. If the sigmoid shows significant redundancy, additional retraction may be provided by the introduction of a 0 - polypropylene suture on a straight needle passed percutaneously through the left lower abdomen to tether the sigmoid. Several passes are made through the appendices epiploicae and the needle re-passed to exit the abdomen at a point 1 cm lateral to its site of entry. The sigmoid is placed on gentle traction to complete exposure. The peritoneum over the promontory is then incised, with dissection carried out distally to the pelvis in between the right ureter and rectosigmoid. The pre-sacral fat is cleared and the anterior longitudinal ligament exposed (Fig. 4). This area should be well inspected for presacral vessels, the inadvertent injury to which may lead to troublesome bleeding. Should this occur we prefer the use of bipolar cautery or Ligasure® (Covidien, Norwalk, CT, USA) to control hemorrhage.

Using an EEA placed transvaginally, the apex is identified and peritoneum over the cuff incised, allowing for dissection of the vesicovaginal and rectovaginal spaces (Fig. 5). A polypropylene Y- shaped mesh is then passed through the assistant port. The mesh is tailored to ensure coverage of the anterior vaginal wall to a point just above the trigone, and the posterior wall to the level of the perineal body. The anterior limb is secured to the anterior vagina with 6 interrupted sutures of expanded PTFE or braided polyester suture (Fig. 6). Similarly, the posterior limb of the mesh is sutured to the posterior vagina, employing 8 sutures of the same (Fig. 7). Care is taken not to pass the stitch through full thickness vagina.

Next, the single arm of the Y- mesh is brought to the sacral promontory. Excess mesh is trimmed to the appropriate length (Fig. 8). Once the appropriate tension is set the, the mesh may be held with fixed tension with the fourth arm and sutured to the promontory with 2 to 4 interrupted sutures of expanded PTFE or braided polyester (Fig. 9).

Finally, the peritoneum is closed over the mesh to avoid bowel adhesions, potential erosion or small bowel obstruction (Fig. 10). This is accomplished with a running absorbable suture with a Lapra-Ty® (Ethicon Endo-Surgery, Albuquerque, NM, USA) fixed to the end (we prefer 2-0 piloglecaprone 25 stitch due to its relatively short persistence and ability to slide). The abdomen is inspected for bleeding or any unrecognized visceral injury. The vagina is inspected to confirm the apex is well supported.

The camera and robotic ports are subsequently decoupled from robotic arms and all ports removed under direct endoscopic visualization. We close both 12 mm ports with an interrupted suture of 0 polyglactin suture using the Carter-Thomason CloseSure System (Inlet Medical, Eden Prarie, MN, USA).

Patients are evaluated for ureteral patency postoperatively with cystoscopy following the intravenous administration of indigo carmine. An anti-incontinence procedure may also be performed at this time if stress urinary incontinence has been diagnosed preoperatively on urodynamic testing with prolapse reduction.

11. Innovations in robotic surgical techniques for apex suspension

Traditional docking of the robot patient cart often restricts access to the patient's perineum, a potential problem in those patients requiring concomitant vaginal and intracorporeal approaches. In this situation, side docking should be considered. Proper docking requires the patient cart to be aligned with the ipsilateral anterior superior iliac spine and midline camera port. Additionally, this technique may require lateral displacement of the 3rd robotic port, with the 4th port placed in the horizontal plane slightly above the camera site, bisecting the camera and 3rd ports (Fig. 11). We have recently adopted this technique for cases requiring simultaneous perineal and intraabdominal access, including robotic assisted laparoscopic creation of an ileal neovagina, finding overall good range of motion and relative ease of set up.

12. Conclusion

While level 1 evidence favors outcomes of abdominal sacrocolpopexy over sacrospinous ligament repairs, this comes with the attendant morbidity of a traditional open abdominal procedure. Robot assisted laparoscopic sacrocolpopexy offers the ability to support the apex in a fashion similar to the open approach with equal efficacy. This technique offers the advantages of a minimally invasive option using a modality the traditional open surgeon can adopt with a demonstrated steep but short learning curve.

13. References

[1] Olsen AL, Smith VJ, Bergsrom JO et al. Epidemiology of surgically managed pelvic organ prolpase and urinary incontinence. Obstet Gynecol 1997; 89:501

[2] Swift S, Woodman R, O'Boyle A et al. Pelvic Organ Support Study (POSST): the distribution, clinical definition, and epidemiologic condition of pelvic organ support defects. Am J Obstet Gynecol 2005; 192:795

[3] Bump RC, Mattiasson A, Bo K et al. The standardization of terminology of female pelvic organ prolapse and pelvic floor dysfunction. Am J Obstet Gynecol 1996; 175:10

[4] Hendrix SL, Clark A, Nygaard I et al. Pelvic organ prolapse in the Women's Heath Initiative: gravity and gravidity. Am J Obstet Gynecol 2002; 186:1160

[5] Delancey JOL. Surgical anatomy of the female pelvis, In: Rock JA, Thompson JD, eds. TeLinde's Operative Gynecology, ed 8. Philadelphia: Lippincott-Raven; 1997:63-93

[6] Gosling JA, Dixon JS, Critchley HOD et al. A comparative study of the human external sphincter and periurethral levator ani muscles. Br J Urol 1981;53:35-41

[7] Allen RE, Hosker GL, Smith ARB et al. Pelvic floor damage and childbirth: a neurophysiological study. Br J Obstet Gynaecol 1990;97: 770-779

[8] Smith ARB, Hosker GL, Warrell DW. The role of partial denervation of the pelvic floor in the etiology of genitourinary prolapse and stress incontinence of urine. A neurophysiological study. Br J Obstet Gynaecol 1989;96:24-28

[9] Chen HY, Chung YW, Lin WY et al. Collagen type 3 alpha 1 polymorphism and risk of pelvic organ prolapse. Int J Gynecol Obstet 2008;103:55-58

[10] Brubaker L, Bump R, Fynes M et al. Surgery for Pelvic Organ Prolapse, In: Abrams P, Cardozo L, Khoury S et al. editors. Incontinence, Management. Third International Consultation on Incontinence. Vol. 2, Monaco: International Continence Society 2005. pp 1371-402, chapter 21

[11] Shull BL, Bachofen C, Coats KW, et al. A transvaginal approach to repair of apical and other associated sites of pelvic organ prolapse with uterosacral ligaments. Am J Obstet Gynecol 2000;183:1365

[12] Barber MD, Visco AG, Weidner AC et al. Bilateral uterosacral ligament vaginal vault suspension with site-specific endopelvic fascia defect repair for treatment of pelvic organ prolapse. Am J Obstet Gynecol 2000;183: 1402

[13] Karram M, Goldwasser S, Kleeman S et al. High uterosacral vaginal vault suspension with fascial reconstruction for vaginal repair of enterocele and vaginal vault prolapse. Am J Obstet Gynecol 2001;185:1339

[14] Richter K, Albright W. Long-term results following fixation of the vagina on the sacrospinous ligament by the vaginal route. Am J Obstet Gynecol 1981; 151: 811

[15] Nichols DH. Sacrospinous fixation for massive eversion of the vagina. Am J Obstet Gynecol 1982; 142:901

[16] Sze E, Miklos J, Patroll L, et al. Sacrospinous ligament fixation with transvaginal needle suspension for advanced pelvic organ prolapse and stress incontinence. Obstet Gynecol 1997; 98: 94

[17] Shull BL, Capen CV, Riggs MW, et al. Bilateral attachment of the vaginal cuff to iliococcygeus fascia: an effective method of cuff suspension. Am J Obstet Gynecol.1993; 168:1669

[18] Meeks GR, Washburne JF, McGehee RP, et al.. Repair of vaginal vault prolapse by suspension of the vagina to the iliococcygeus (prespinous) fascia. Am J Obstet Gynecol 1994; 171:1444-54

[19] Amid PK. Classification of biomaterials and their complications in abdominal wall hernia surgery. Hernia 1997;1: 15
[20] Cosson M, Debodinance P, Boukerrou M, et al. Mechanical properties of synthetic implants used in the repair of prolapse and urinary incontinence in women: which is the ideal material? Int Urogynecol J Pelvic Floor Dysfunct. 2003; 14:169
[21] Diwadkar GB, Barber MD, Feiner B, et al. Complication and reoperation rates after apical vaginal prolapse surgical repair: a systematic review. Obstet Gynecol 2009; 113: 367
[22] Sanses TVD, Shahryarinejad A, Molden S, et al. Anatomic outcomes of vaginal mesh procedure (Prolift) compared with uterosacral ligament suspension and abdominal sacrocolpopexy for pelvic organ prolapse: a Fellow's Pelvic Research Network study. Am J Obstet Gynecol 2009
[23] Timmons MC, Addison WA, Addison SB, et al. Abdominal sacral colpopexy in 163 women with post hysterectomy vaginal vault prolapse and enterocele. Evolution of operative techniques. J Reprod Med 1992; 37: 323
[24] Snyder TE, Krantz KE. Abdominal-retroperitoneal sacral colpopexy for the correction of vaginal prolpase. Obstet Gynecol 1991; 77:944
[25] Maher C, Baessler K, Glazener CMA et al. Surgical management of pelvic organ prolapse in women (Review). The Cochrane Collaboration. The Cochrane Library 2007, Issue 2
[26] Cundiff GW, Varner E, Visco AG, Zyczynski HM, Nager CW, Norton PA, Schaffer J, Brown MB, Brubaker L; Pelvic Floor Disorders Network. Am J Obstet Gynecol 2008; 199:e1-5.
[27] Paraiso MFR, Walters MD, Rackley RR et al. Laparoscopic and abdominal sacral colpopexy: A comparative cohort study. Am J Obstet Gynecol 2005; 192:1752
[28] Sarlos D, Brandner S, Kots L et al. Laparoscopic sacrocolpopexy for uterine and post-hysterectomy prolapse: anatomical results, quality of life and perioperative outcome - a prospective study with 101 cases. Int Urogynecol J Pelvic Floor Dysfunct 2008; 19:1415
[29] Hsiao KC, Latchamsetty K, Govier FE et al. Comparison of laparoscopic and abdominal sacrocolpopexy for the treatment of vaginal vault prolapse. J Endourol 2007;21:926
[30] Rozet F, Mandron E, Arroyo C et al. Laparoscopic sacral colpopexy approach for gentio-urinary prolapse: experience with 363 cases. Eur Urol 2005;47:230
[31] Ross JW, Preston M. Laparoscopic sacrocolpopexy for severe vaginal vault prolapse: five-year outcome. J Minim Invasive Gynecol 2005;12:221
[32] Elliott DS, Krambeck AE, Chow GK. Long-term results of robotic assisted laparoscopic sacrocolpopexy for the treatment of high grade vaginal vault prolpase. J Urol 2006;176:655
[33] Di Marco DS, Chow GK, Gettman MT et al. Robotic-assisted laparoscopic sacrocolpopexy for treatment of vaginal vault prolapse. Urology 2004;63:373
[34] Kramer BA, Whelan CM, Powell TM et al. Robotic-assisted laparoscopic sacrocolpopexy as management for pelvic organ prolpase. J Endourol 2009;23:655
[35] Daneshgari F, Kefer JC, Moore C et al. Robotic abdominal sacrocolpopexy/ sacrouteropexy repair of advanced female pelvic organ prolapse (POP): utilizing POP-quantification-based staging and outcomes. BJU Int. 2007; 100: 875

[36] Akl MN, Long JB, Giles DL et al. Robotic - assisted sacrocolpopexy: technique and learning curve. Surg Endosc 2009 (27)
[37] Kohli N, Walsh PM, Roat TW et al. Mesh erosion after abdominal sacrocolpopexy. Obstet Gynecol 1998;92:999
[38] Geller EJ, Siddiqui NY, Wu JM et al. Soft-term outcomes of robotic sacrocolpopexy compared with abdominal sacrocolpopexy. Obstet Gynecol 2008;112:1198
[39] Chang FH, Lee CL, Soong YK. Use of Palmer's Point for Insertion of the Operative Laparoscope in Patients with Severe Pelvic Adhesions: Experience of Seventeen Cases. J Am Assoc Gynecol Laparosc 1994;1:S7

Figures

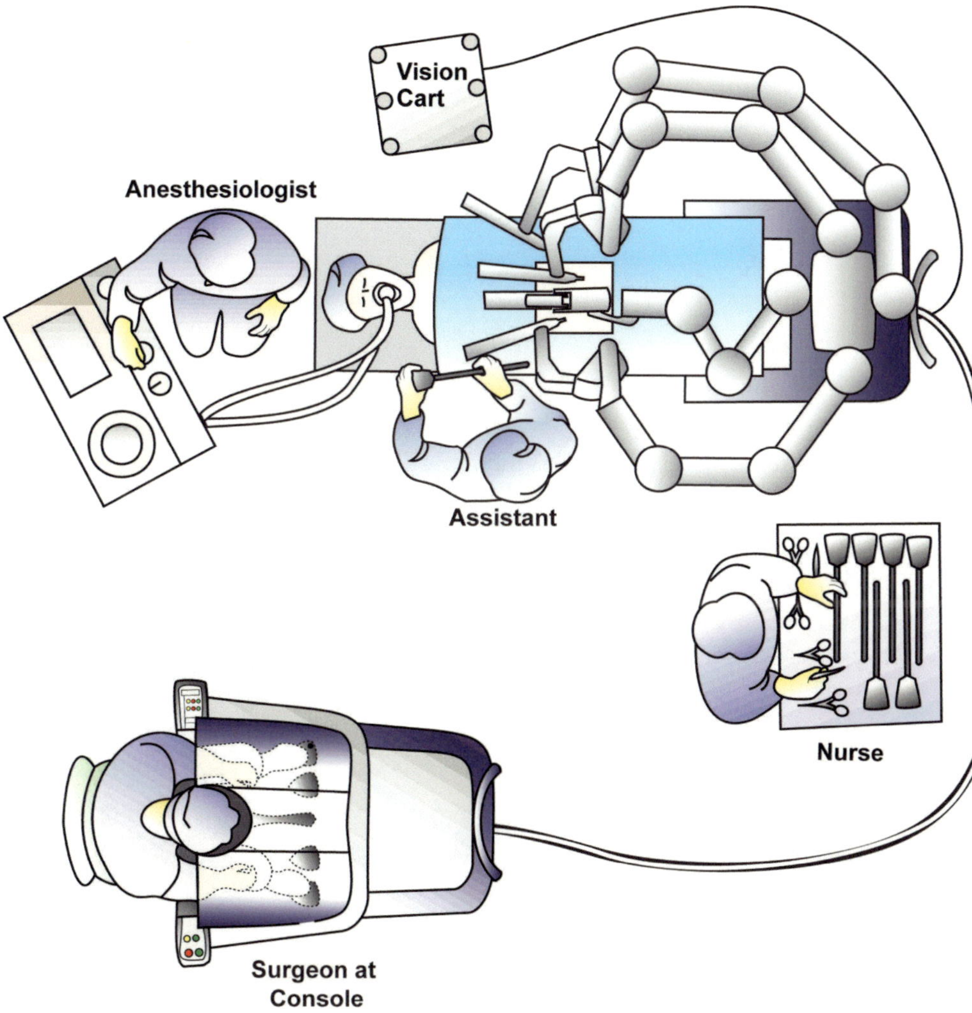

Fig. 1. Operating room configuration

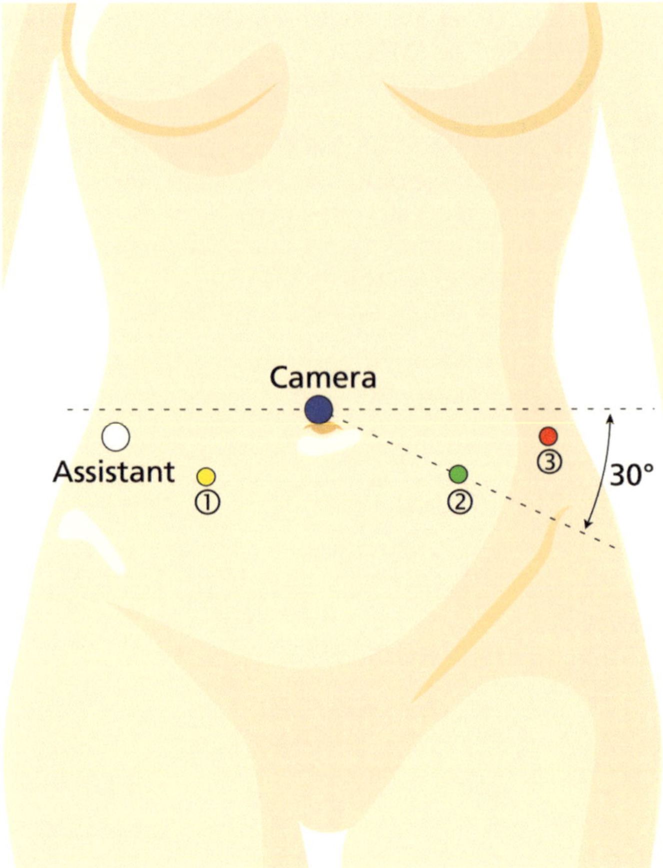

Fig. 2. Port placement for RALSC (4-arm DaVinci)

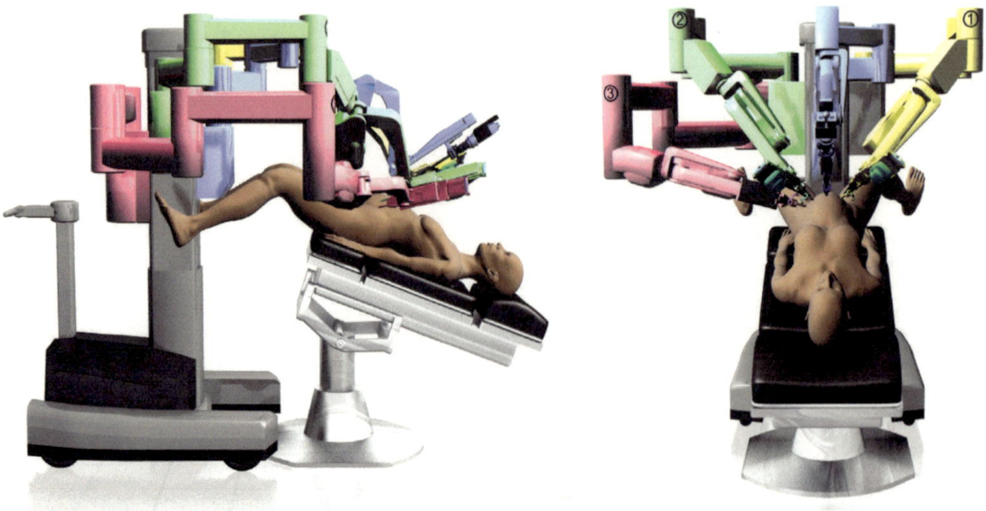

Fig. 3. Patient positioning and patient cart docking of 4-arm DaVinci

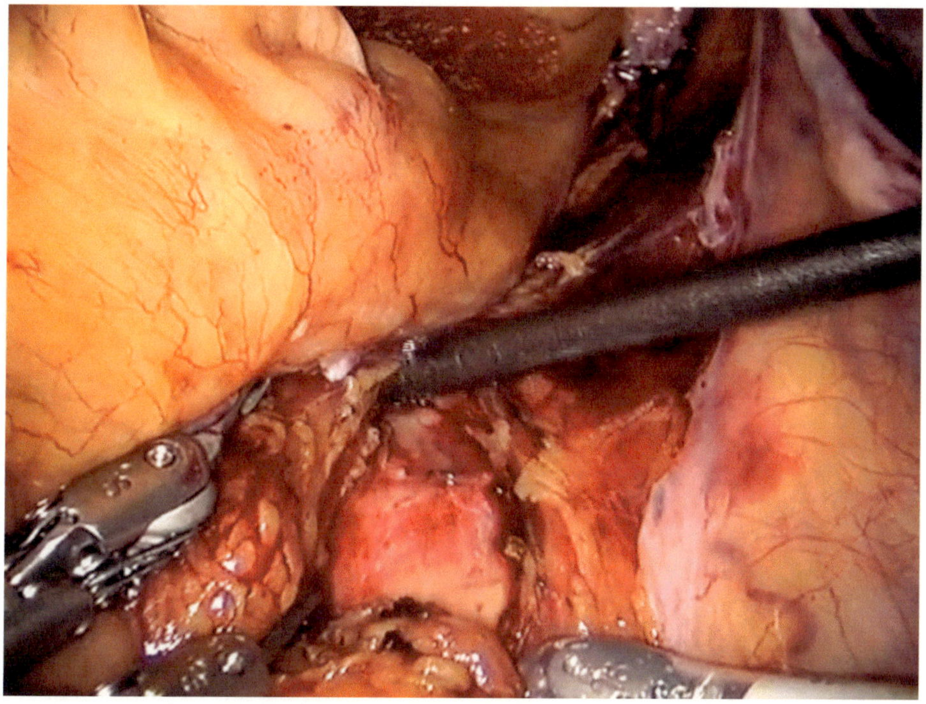

Fig. 4. Exposed anterior longitudinal ligament over sacral promontory

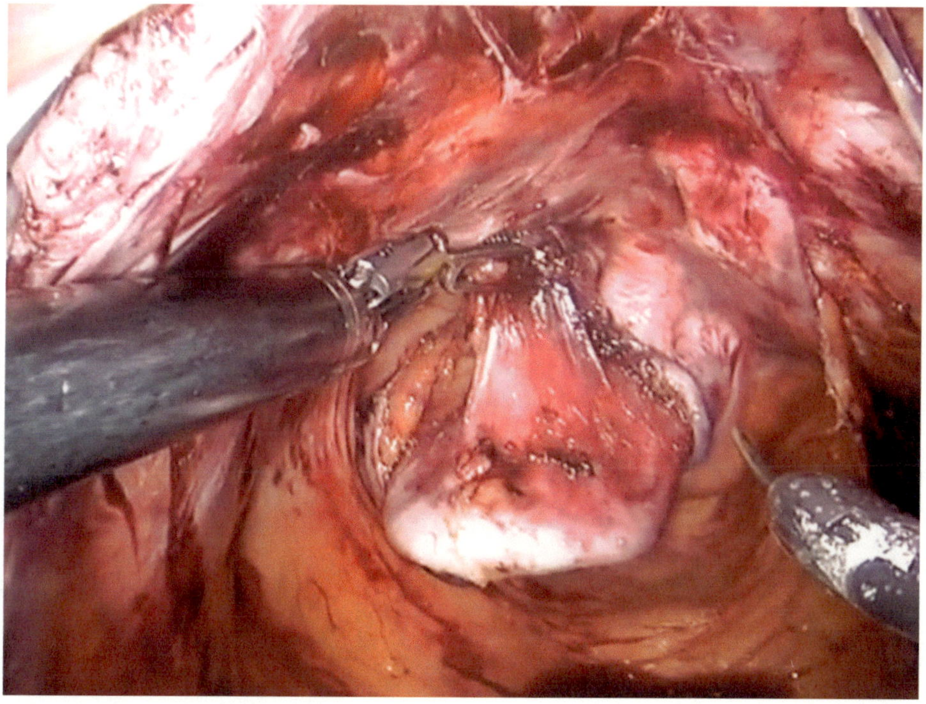

Fig. 5. Dissecting peritoneum from vaginal cuff

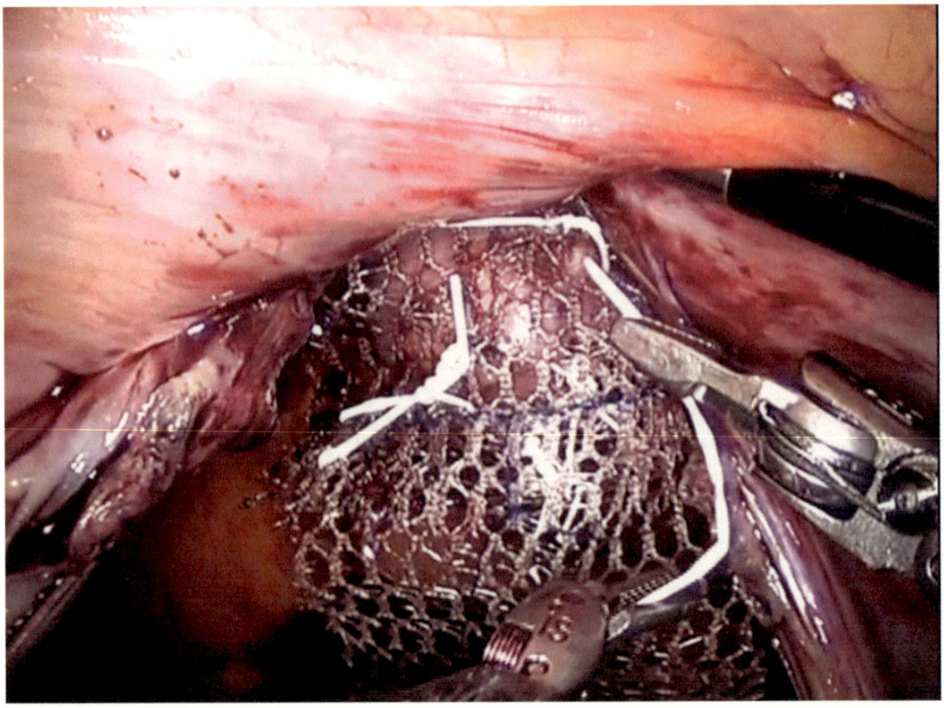

Fig. 6. Securing mesh to anterior vaginal wall

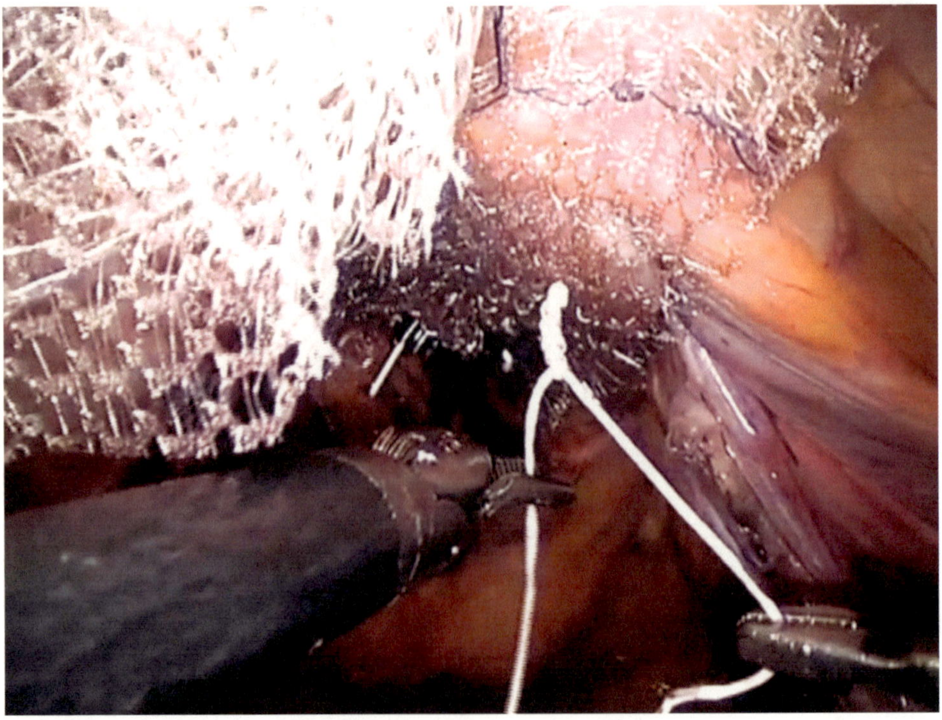

Fig. 7. Securing mesh to posterior vaginal wall

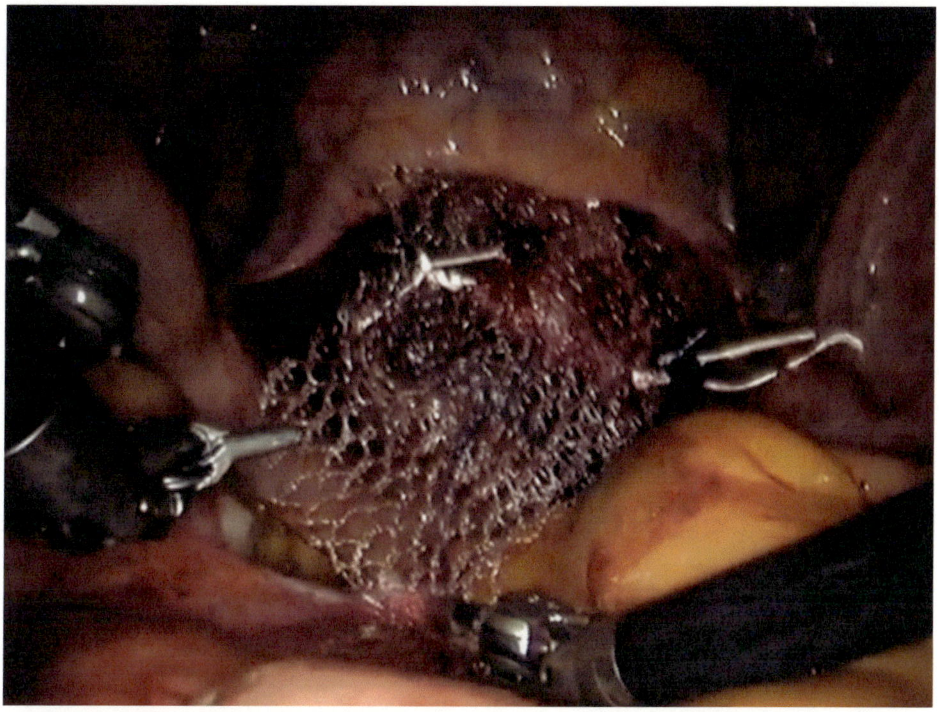

Fig. 8. Mesh trimmed to appropriate size

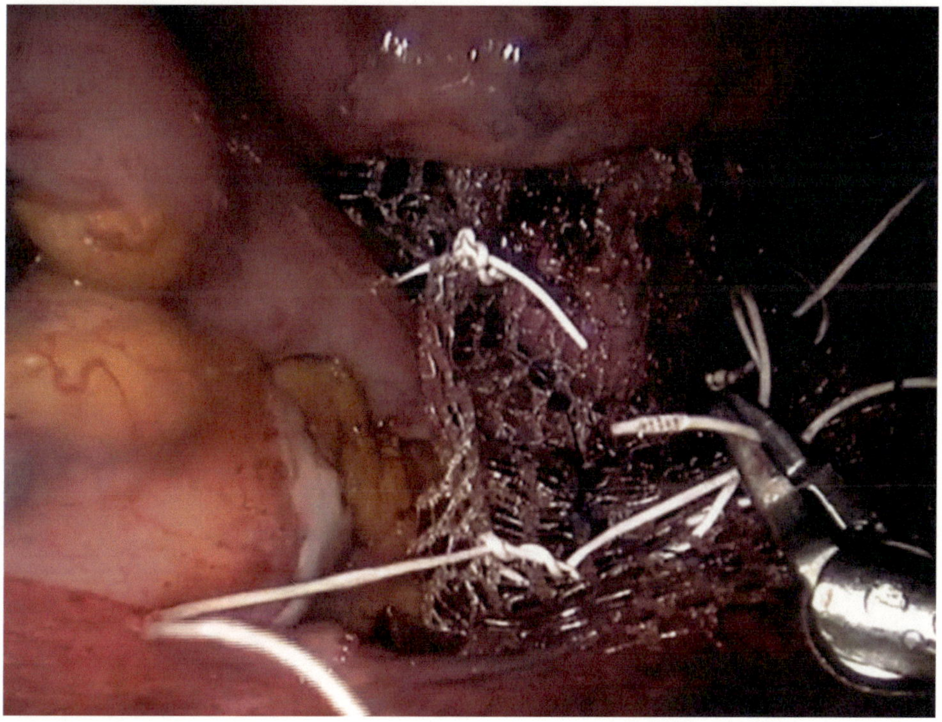

Fig. 9. Securing mesh to sacral promontory

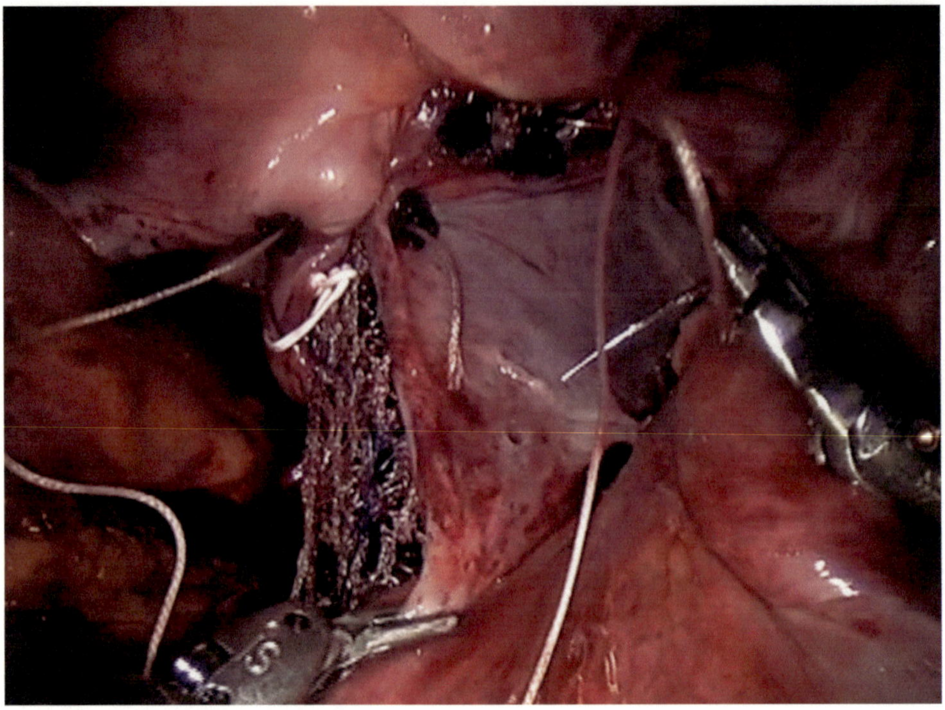

Fig. 10. Closure of peritoneum over mesh

Fig. 11. Alternative side-docking 4-arm DaVinci for pelvic surgery

8

Robotic Assisted Laparoscopic Hysterectomy

Khaled Sakhel
Eastern Virginia Medical School,
USA

1. Introduction

In 1495 Leonardo Da Vinci designed what was to be the first automated humanoid and it is speculated that this was to be for the entertainment of royalty. It is not known whether an actual prototype was ever built. The word robot was first introduced by the Czech writer Karel Capek in his play *Rossum's Universal Robots* (R.U.R) in 1920. The Czech word *robota* means labor or servitude. The play takes place on an island where the robot factory is producing robots to be sold to the world as cheap labor. The robots turn around and try to take over the world and end the human race. Isaac Asimov wrote a sequence of short stories in 1940 on the difficulties that would be faced if autonomous robots populated the Earth. He laid 3 laws of robotics which state "(the first law) A robot may not injure a human being, or through inaction allow a human being to come to harm, (the second law) A robot must obey the orders given it by human beings except where such orders would conflict with First Law and (the third law) A robot must protect its own existence as long as such protection does not conflict with the First and Second Law". As his writings became more intricate and complex, so did the relationship between man and robot. He then felt the need to add another law which was more basic and more important than the first three which he then called the zeroth law "A robot may not injure humanity, or through inaction, allow humanity to come to harm". This gave a broader picture of the laws governing robots.
Robotic technology is now incorporated into our everyday life which can range from the large manufacturing assembly lines to everyday household chores. The field of Medicine is no exception where robotic applications are gaining momentum.
One of the first robotic applications came from the Stanford Artificial Intelligence Lab (SAIL) in 1969. They designed a robotic arm with 6 degrees of freedom (6-dof) all-electric mechanical manipulator exclusively for computer control. The Stanford Arm and SAIL helped to develop the knowledge base which has been applied in essentially all the industrial robots.
The first commercially available robotic system was the ROBODOC which was used for orthopedic surgery. AESOP was designed to allow the surgeon greater control over visualization and to eliminate the need for an assistant holding the scope. The ZEUS robot was then developed which had a two-dimensional imaging system. Intuitive Surgical Inc (Intuitive Surgical Inc, Moutain View, CA) developed the Da Vinci robotic system and the first successful surgery was performed in 1997 in Belgium.
The Da Vinci Robotic system is now also utilized by gynecologists to perform a number of procedures including hysterectomy myomectomy, tubal reversal and sacrocolpopexy as

well as cancer surgeries. This chapter will discuss the use of robotic technology during hysterectomy procedures for benign conditions.

2. Why laparoscopic hysterectomy?

With more than 600,000 procedures performed annually in the US, hysterectomy is by far one of the most common procedures in women's health and the most common in the non-pregnant women. [1] Traditionally this procedure is performed through 3 routes which include abdominal, vaginal and laparoscopic. The abdominal route is considered to be the most invasive while the vaginal route is the least invasive. The laparoscopic approach is considered minimally invasive and sort of in between those two ends of the spectrum.

Even though the vaginal route is considered the least invasive on the patients, still around 65-70% of hysterectomy procedures are performed via the abdominal route.[1] The decision on the route is multifaceted. It includes the anticipated complexity of the surgery, size of the uterus, presence of adhesions, vaginal exposure, concomitant procedures such as oophorectomy and the surgeon's skill level. In addition, vaginal hysterectomy does not allow adequate inspection of the pelvis and abdomen.

It has been over 20 years since Reich performed the first laparoscopic hysterectomy. [2] Since then laparoscopic hysterectomy has undergone many changes and tools have been developed to assist with this procedure. This procedure has gained much attention and popularity. A trend toward higher rate of laparoscopic hysterectomy was observed in the 1990s with an increase from 0.3% to 9.9% and a drop in abdominal hysterectomy rates from 73.6% to 63.0% over a period of 7 years.[1] Vaginal hysterectomy remained stable at around 23-24%. Some of the reasons behind the added interest in the laparoscopic approach include the ability to survey the pelvis and easy access to the infundibulo-pelvic ligaments as compared to the vaginal route, and the potential for benefits of a minimally invasive procedure as compared to the abdominal route. Especially considering that the ovaries are concomitantly removed in 73% of these procedures. [3] When compared to abdominal hysterectomy, the laparoscopic route results in a shorter hospital stay, less abdominal wound morbidity, quicker return to normal daily activity and decreased blood loss, however at the cost of increased surgical time and urinary tract injuries. [4, 5] Similar to Vaginal hysterectomy, this procedure is highly dependent on the skill and experience of the surgeon.

3. Why robotic hysterectomy?

The straight laparoscopic hysterectomy is limited by the 2-dimensional view and four degrees of freedom and the most significant recent addition to the laparoscopic armamentarium is the robotic assistance. The Da Vinci Robotic System has three main components: the robotic cart (actual robot with arms), the operating console (which contains the surgeon's hand controls and foot pedals) and the endoscopic stack (or tower). With multiple arms, seven degrees of freedom and 3-dimension high definition magnified image inside the peritoneal cavity, the potential is there to complete the most daunting procedure with ease and precision. The robot will also automatically filter out any tremors in the hand of the surgeon and scale the movements to a smooth single motion. The lack of tactile feedback which the surgeon would have otherwise obtained from the laparoscopic instruments is replaced by visual feedback. Finally the surgeon is seated in an ergonomically comfortable console which makes the prolonged cases more tolerable.

Robot assisted laparoscopic hysterectomy (RALH) has been shown to be safe and effective. [6-11] A recent study by Payne et al comparing straight laparoscopic hysterectomy to RALH, noted that the robotic cohort was associated with significantly less blood loss, decreased hospital stay, but longer operative time. The intra-operative conversion rate to abdominal route from laparoscopic dropped from 9% to 4% when the robot assistance was introduced and there were no post-operative exploratory laparatomy in the robotic cohort as compared to 11% in the straight laparoscopic. [12] In another similar study by Sakhel et al, RALH was associated with less total operative room time, less blood loss and no conversion to laparatomy as compared to 11% conversion rate with straight laparoscopic hysterectomy. [13]

3. Preoperative preparations

As with any procedure, the preoperative preparations are of utmost importance and can help make it a success. Some form of mechanical bowel preparation should be used the day before surgery while the patient is on clear liquid diet. Even though strong data to support the practice of mechanical bowel preparation does not exist, [14] we believe this helps to deflate the bowels for visualization and also decrease the risk of contamination should the bowel be injured accidentally. On the other hand, it may be advisable to discuss this with the team who would be performing any bowel repair should you encounter bowel injury.
The patients should also be instructed to refrain from taking anything by mouth past midnight. All patients should be screened for blood thinners and medical conditions that require further workup and management. The need for pneumo-peritoneum and steep Trendelenburg may make some patients poor candidates for laparoscopic procedures. In the preoperative holding area the patients are given antibiotic prophylaxis (2 grams of cefazolin intravenously) and some form of an anti-emetic regimen especially if the patient is to be discharged the same day.

4. Patient positioning

After general endotracheal anesthesia is induced, the patient is positioned in the dorsal lithotomy position with the buttock just off the table. The patient must be securely positioned on the OR table with the use of shoulder braces, chest straps, underbody foam "egg-crate" mattress or a combination of those. It is advisable to use stirrups that allow for leg repositioning as this will facilitate adequate visualization of the cervix for the insertion of the uterine manipulator. The arms are padded and tucked in on the side of the patient in the neutral position with the thumb pointing up. Some form of protection of the face may be utilized and this can be in the form of a foam or gel pad. An Oro-gastric tube may be inserted to deflate the stomach especially if a left upper quadrant trocar insertion is contemplated.

5. Uterine manipulator

The patient may be placed in some Trendelenburg and the legs may be elevated with the use of the stirrups. An examination under anesthesia is performed to estimate the size and position of the uterus. A speculum is inserted, the cervix is held using a single tooth tenaculum and the uterus is sounded. If the cervix is to be excised with the uterus then a uterine manipulator is a must for successful colpotomy and completion of the surgery. Currently there are 3 commonly used uterine manipulators which have a colpotomy ring. They are the Vcare Uterine

Manipulator (ConMed Corporation, Utica, N.Y.), the Rumi and the Zumi Uterine Manipulators (Cooper Surgical, Trumbull, CT) with a Koh ring and balloon pneumo-occluder attached. The uterine manipulator of choice is inserted into the uterus and the uterine balloon is insufflated. The single tooth tenaculum is removed. The colpotomy ring is placed ensuring that is fits well all around the cervix by a sweep of the index and middle fingers (Fig. 1). The speculum is removed. A Foley catheter is then inserted into the bladder.

6. Trocars placement and docking

At this point the Trendelenburg is reversed, the patient is placed in the neutral position and the legs are put down. A pneumo-peritoneum is secured in the usual manner. This can be achieved with a Veress needle, direct umbilical trocar insertion or left upper quadrant trocar insertion. Alternatively an open technique with a Hasson trocar may be used. We prefer the direct insertion with a bladeless trocar that allows visualization of the tip. The first trocar to be inserted is the umbilical trocar. This is a 12mm bladeless to be used for the camera arm and may be placed higher in the midline abdomen to ensure a distance of 10 cm from the fundus of the uterus. The patient is then placed in maximal Trendelenburg. This is a must for procedures that involve the pelvis as this will allow the bowels to migrate into the abdomen for visualization. This should not increase the risk of the patient sliding back down the OR table nor affect oxygenation even in the morbidly obese, if the patient is securely positioned. The left and right 8mm robotic arm trocars are placed 10cm lateral and 3cm inferior to the umbilical trocar under direct laparoscopic visualization. This ensures an arc across the fundus of the uterus. If the 4th arm is needed, it is placed 10cm lateral and 3cm inferior to the left robotic trocar. A 10-12mm bladeless surgeon's assistant trocar is placed about 5-7cm superior and midway between the umbilical trocar and the right or left upper robotic trocar (Fig. 2). The robot is then docked (Fig. 3).

7. Operative technique

After the docking of the robot is completed, the surgeon may then leave the sterile field and move over to the surgeon console. The surgeon's assistant will then insert the camera and Endowrist instruments of choice into the robotic ports. This is performed under direct vision of the trocar by the robotic camera. Our preferred instruments include the monopolar Hot Shears on the right, the fenestrated bipolar on the left and if the 4th arm is needed a Cobra Grasper or a Tenaculum is inserted. A common variation to this set up is to use the PK Dissecting Forceps in place of the bipolar fenestrated while that is used for retraction.
The hysterectomy described is the AAGL type IVE which is defined as a totally laparoscopic removal of the uterus and cervix including vaginal cuff closure. [15]

Step 1. Survey of the Pelvis
A comprehensive survey of the pelvic and lower abdominal structures is performed. The ureters and identified on either side.

Step 2. Opening of the broad ligament.
The round ligament is identified, cauterized using the fenestrated bipolar and cut using the monopolar Hot shears. The anterior leaf of the broad ligament is then incised towards the bladder and the vesicouterine reflection (bladder flap) is started. The surgical assistant will either be retracting from above with a tenaculum or using the suction irrigation to provide adequate exposure and removing excess surgical smoke (Fig. 4).

Step 3. The ovaries
If the ovaries are to be removed, the infundibulopelvic ligament is then cauterized with bipolar and cut with shears ensuring the safety of the ureter. If the ovaries are to be conserved then the utero-ovarian ligament is cauterized and cut (Fig.5).

Step 4. The contra lateral side
In a similar fashion the contra lateral side is secured.

Step 5. The Vesico-uterine reflection
At this point a 30° down camera may be used for adequate visualization anteriorly especially if the uterus is enlarged. The anterior leaf of the broad ligament is completely incised creating the vesicouterine reflection anteriorly. The vesicouterine reflection is tented up using the fenestrated bipolar and the bladder is gently dissected off the uterus and cervix using mostly sharp dissection with the shears. This will ensure adequate visualization of the colpotomy ring (Fig. 6).
A few common variations to the above noted steps include starting with the Infundibulopelvic or Utero-ovarian ligament and working caudal toward the round ligament. This ensures adequate visualization of the broad ligament. In addition, other vessel occluding devices may be inserted from the surgeon assistant port for securing pedicles.

Step 6. Uterine Vessels
Once the vesico-uterine reflection is completed, the uterine arteries can be skeletonized adequately. This will ensure that the ureters are sufficiently lateral and out of harms way. The uterine arteries can then be coagulated using the bipolar and cut with the shears. It is advisable to begin coagulation at the ascending branch of the uterine artery and move caudal along the cardinal ligaments (Fig. 7).

Step 7. Colpotomy
The colpotomy is performed using the monopolar Hot Shears and taken all around. At one point the uterine manipulator will no longer suffice for retraction as the colpotomy progresses. At that point either the 4th arm or the surgeon assistant may grasp the uterus and provide tension for completion of the colpotomy. The specimen can be pulled through the incision if it is small enough to pass through vaginal cuff or it can be divided or morcellated first. The uterus can serve as a pneumo-occluder in the vagina or the balloon occluder can be replaced into the vagina (Fig. 8).

Step 8. Vaginal cuff closure
Irrigation is performed and any significant bleeding is controlled. Minimal oozing from the vaginal cuff can be controlled with the closure. Excessive cautery should be avoided at the vaginal cuff as this may predispose the patient to cuff dehiscence. The bipolar fenestrated and shears are replaced with needle holders. The vaginal cuff can then be closed with interrupted figure of eight stitches using 2-0 Vicryl incorporating the uterosacral ligaments. The needle is passed in and out of the abdomen by the surgeon assistant. Alternatively, the vaginal cuff can be closed with a running stitch and the use of Lapra-ty clips (Ethicon Endosurgery, Cincinnati, OH) (Fig. 9, 10).

Step 9. Repair of the trocar sites
Once the vaginal cuff repair is completed, the pelvis is irrigated and inspected for hemostasis. The instruments are then removed under vision, the robot is undocked, the trocars are removed and the abdomen is deflated. The sites of the trocars are repaired in the usual manner as per the surgeon's preference. The rate of bowel herniation at the 12mm bladeless trocar sites has been reported to be 0.7% [16] and

therefore we prefer to re-approximate the fascia of those sites separately using the Carter-Thomason Closure system XL (Inlet Medical, Eden Prairie, Minnesota) or the EndoClose (Tyco International, Inc. Norwalk, CT).

Step 10. Cystoscopy

While the repair of the skin incisions is being performed, the patient is given indigo carmine intravenously. Cystoscopy is then performed to ensure patency of the uteters and the integrity of the bladder. The rate of bladder and ureteral injury during laparoscopic has been reported to be 2.9% and 1.7% respectively. [17] Only one fourth of injuries to the urinary tract are detected by visual inspection. For this purpose a 30° or 70° scope can be used with saline for distention medium.

8. Postoperative care

Postoperatively the patient may be placed on a diet of her choice and this can be started immediately after surgery. The Foley catheter may be removed immediately especially if the patient is to be discharged. Even though abdominal trocar wound site infections are rare the patients are advised to keep them clean. The rate of vaginal cuff evisceration is 2.9% for RALH. [18] For this reason we recommend that they refrain from vaginal intercourse for 6-8 weeks. We have found that patients can be discharged the day of the procedure if she is noted to be stable 4-6 hours later or early the next day.

9. References:

[1] Farquhar CM, Steiner CA. Hysterectomy rates in the United States 1990-1997. Obstet Gynecol 2002; 99:229.

[2] Reich H, Decaprio J, McGlynn F. Laparoscopic hysterectomy. *J Gynecol Surg*. 1989; 5:213-216.

[3] "Hysterectomy". National Women's Health Information Center. 2006-07-01

[4] Nieboer TE, Johnson N, Lethaby A, Tavender E, Curr E, Garry R, van Voorst S, Mol BW, Kluivers KB. Surgical approach to hysterectomy for benign gynaecologic disease. Cochrane Database Syst Rev. 2009 Jul 8;(3):CD003677

[5] Manolitsas TP, Copeland LJ, Cohn DE, Eaton LA, Fowler JM. Ureteroileoneocystostomy: the use of an ileal segment for ureteral substitution in gynecologic oncology. Gynecol Oncol. 2002 Jan; 84(1):110-4.

[6] Margossian H, Falcone T. Robotically assisted laparoscopic hysterectomy and adnexal surgery. J Laparpemdpsc Adv Surg Tech A. 2001;11:161-165

[7] Diaz-Arrastia C, Jurnalov C, Gomez G, Townsend C Jr. Laparoscopic hysterectomy using a computer-enhanced surgical robot. Surg Endosc. 2002; 16:1271-1273

[8] Advincula AP, reynolds RK. The use of robot-assisted laparoscopic hysterectomy in the patient with a scarred or obliterated anterior cul-de-sac. JSLS. 2005;9:287-291

[9] Beste TM, Nelson KH, Daucher JA. Total laparoscopic hysterectomy utilizing a robotic surgical system. JSLS. 2005;9:13-15

[10] Marchal F, Rauch P, Vandromme J, Laurent I, Lobontiu A, Ahcel B et al. Telerobotic-assisted laparoscopic hysterectomy for benign and oncologic pathologies: initial clinical experience with 30 patients. Surg endosc. 2005;19:826-31.

[11] Fiorentino RP, Zepeda MA, Goldstein BH, John CR, Rettenmaier MA. Pilot study assessing robotic laparoscopic hysterectomy and patient outcomes. J Minim Invasive Gynecol. 2006; 13:60-63.

[12] Payne TN, Dauterive FR. A comparison of total laparoscopic hysterectomy to robotically assisted hysterectomy: surgical outcomes in a community practice. J Minim Invasive Gynecol. 2008 May-Jun; 15 (3):286-91.
[13] Sakhel K, Kirakosyan A, Lukban J, Hines J. Comparison between Robot-Assisted Laparoscopic Hysterectomy and Total Laparoscopic Hysterectomy - A Cohort Study. Presented at the AAGL annual meeting, 38th Global Congress, Orlando, November 17th 2009.
[14] Guenaga KF, Matos D, Castro AA, Atallah AN, Wille-Jorgensen P. Mechanical bowel preparation for elective colorectal surgery. Cochrane Database Syst Rev 2005 Jan 25;(1):CD001544.
[15] Olive DL, Parker WH, Cooper JM, Levine RL. The AAGL classification system for laparoscopic hysterectomy. J Am Assoc Gynecol Laparosc. 2000;7:9-15
[16] Chiong E, Hegarty PK, Davis JW, Kamat AM, Pisters LL , Matin SF. Port-site Hernias Occurring After the Use of Bladeless Radially Expanding Trocars. Urology October 2009
[17] Gilmour DT, Das S, Flowerdew G. Rates of urinary tract injury from gynecologic surgery and the role of intraoperative cystoscopy. Obstet Gynecol. 2006; 107(6):1366-72.
[18] Robinson BL, Liao JB, Adams SF, Randall TC. Vaginal Cuff Dehiscence After Robotic Total Laparoscopic Hysterectomy Obstet Gynecol 2009;114(2):369-371.

Figures

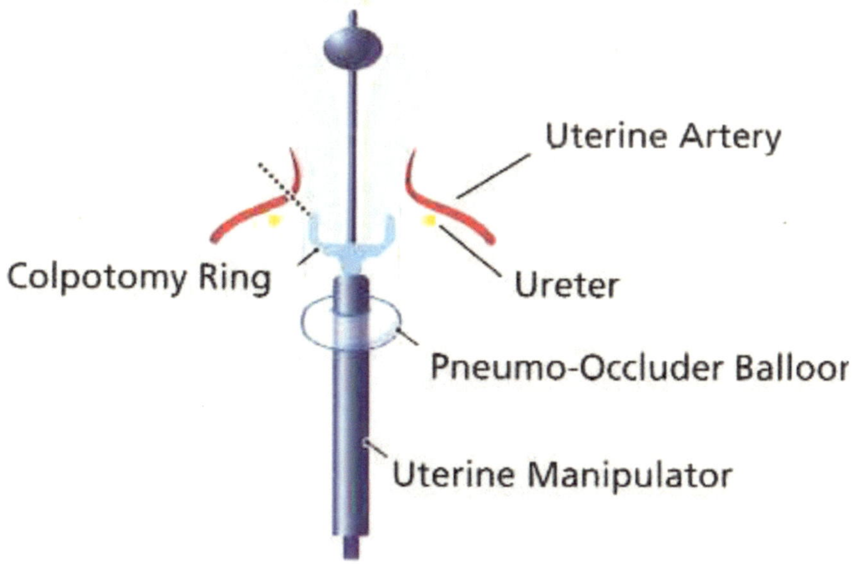

Fig. 1. Uterine Manipulator (Courtesy of Intuitive Surgical)

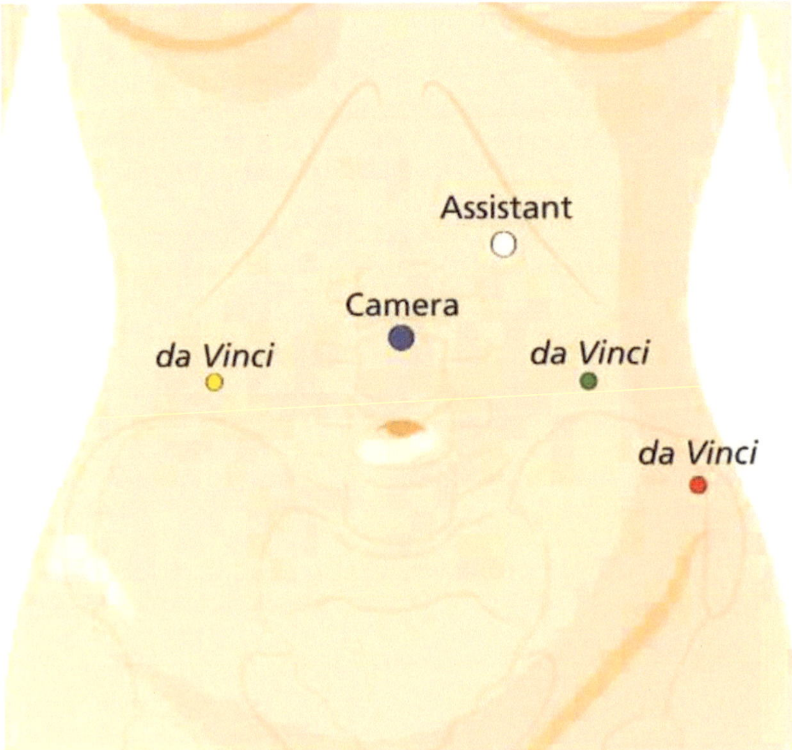

Fig. 2. Port Placement (Courtesy of Intuitive Surgical)

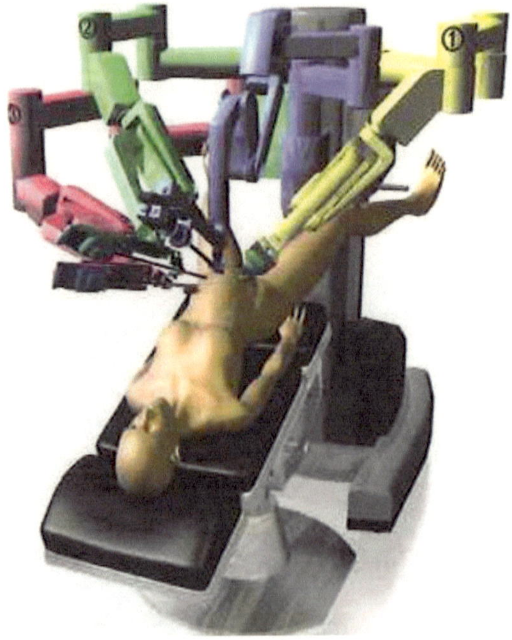

Fig. 3. Da Vinci Robotic System docked (Courtesy of Intuitive Surgical)

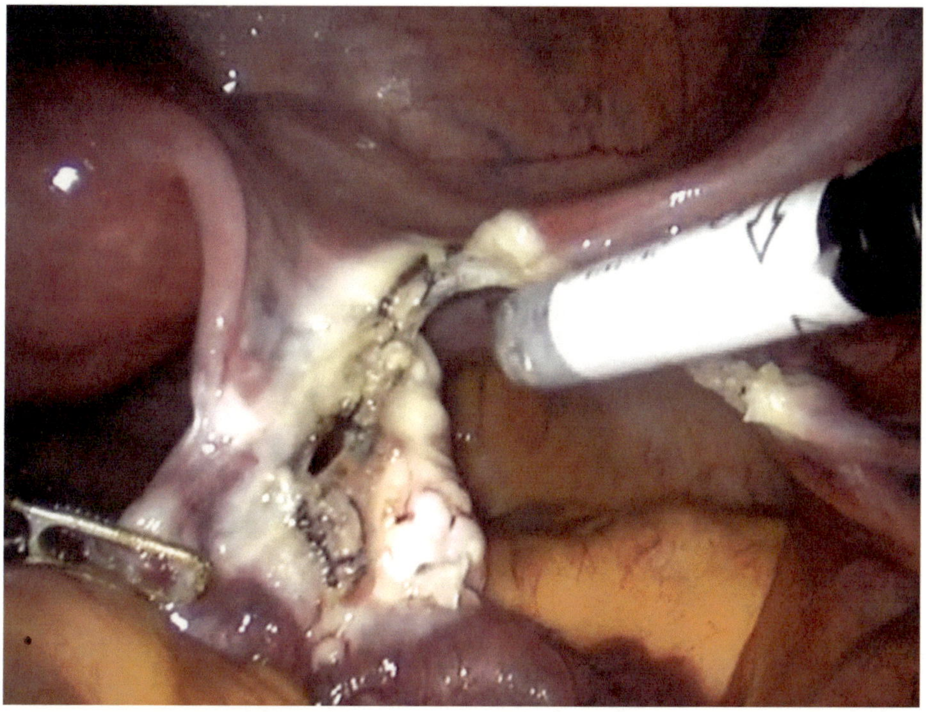

Fig. 4. Securing the round ligament

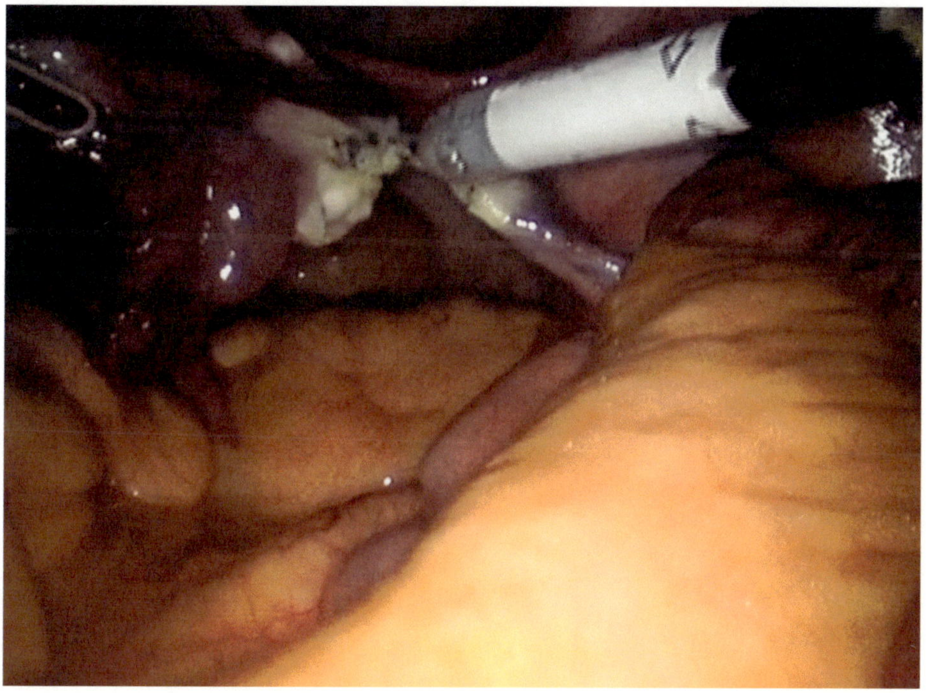

Fig. 5. Securing the infundibulo-pelvic ligament.

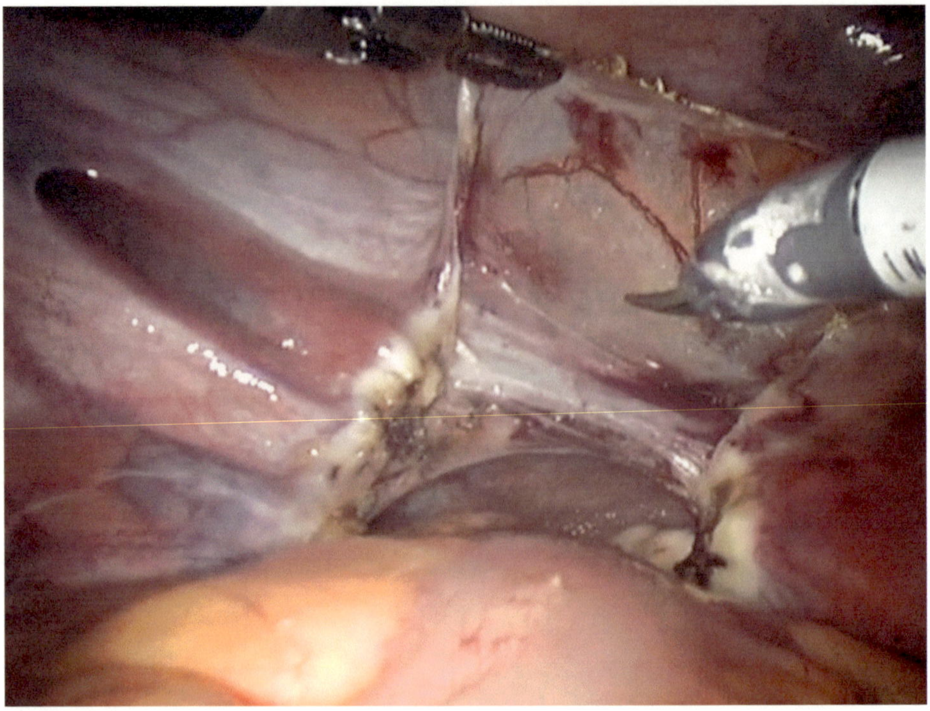

Fig. 6. Opening the broad ligament and developing the vesico-uterine reflection.

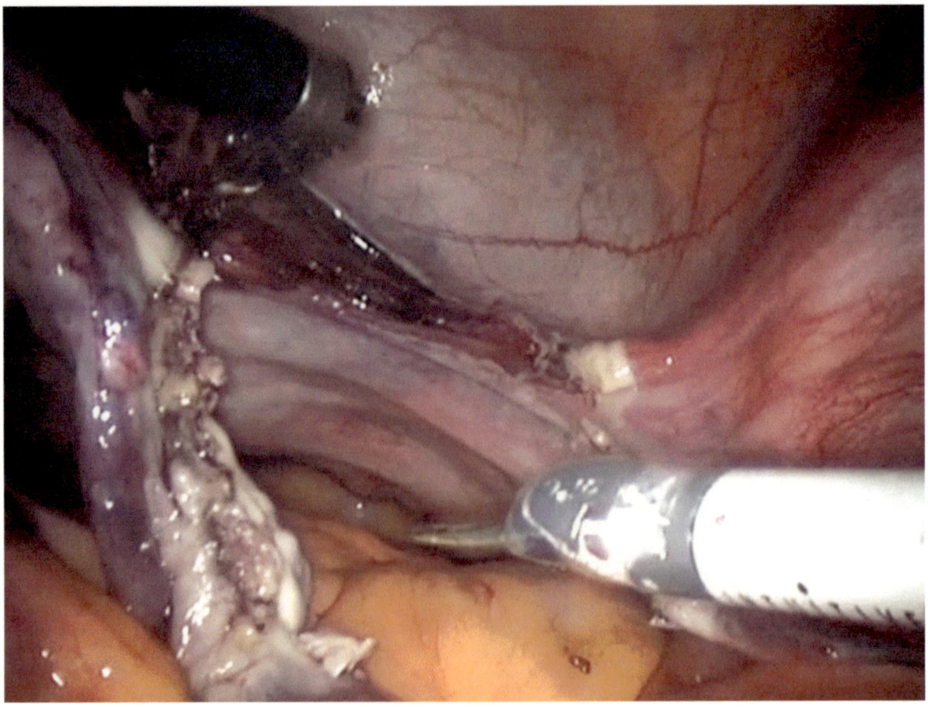

Fig. 7. Securing the ascending branch of the uterine artery

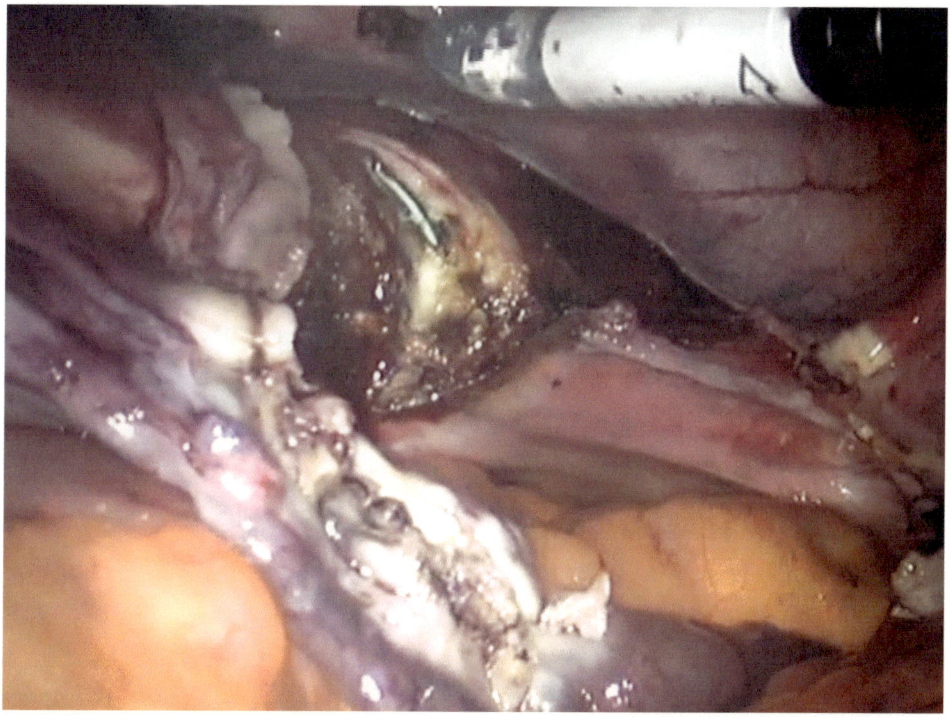

Fig. 8. Performing the colpotomy (green).

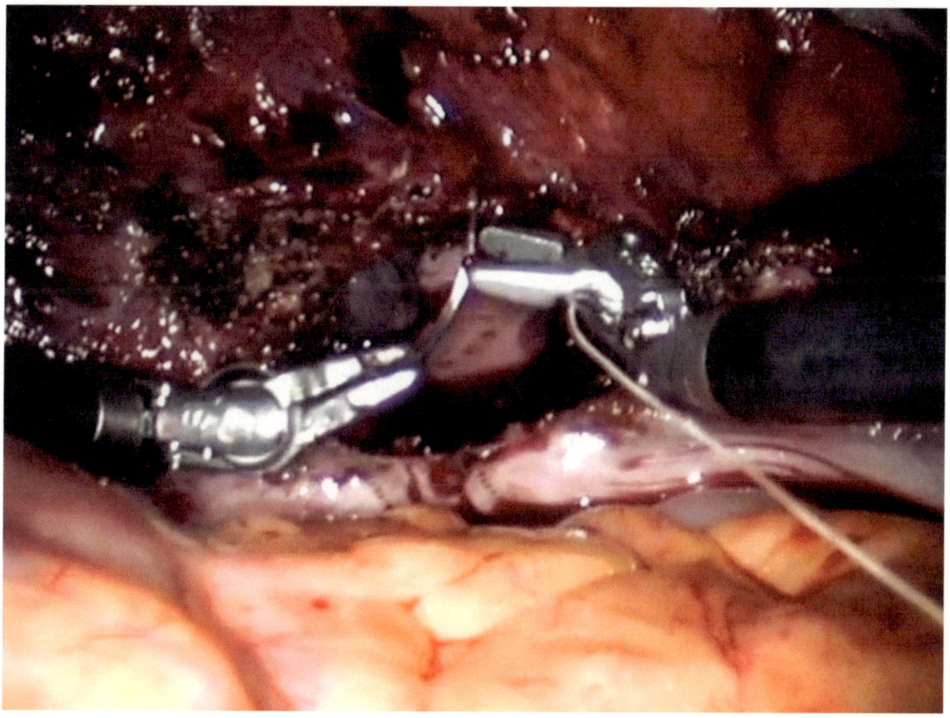

Fig. 9. Vaginal cuff closure.

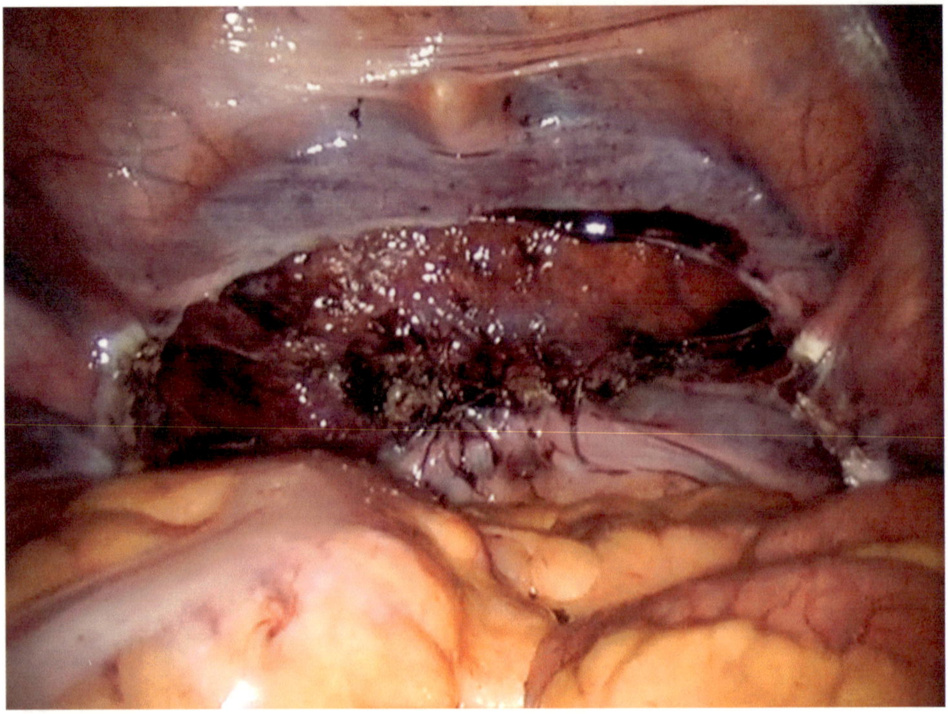

Fig. 10. Completion of the procedure with the vaginal cuff closed.

9

Robotic Surgery for Lung Cancer

Joao-Carlos Das-Neves-Pereira[1], Marc Riquet[2], Françoise Le-Pimpec-Barthes[2], Paulo-Manuel Pego-Fernandes and Fabio Biscegli Jatene.
[1]*Thoracic Surgery Department of University of Sao Paulo and University Paris VI,*
[2]*University Paris V/Thoracic Surgery Department of HEGP*
(Hôpital Européen Georges Pompidou)
[1]*Brazil*
[2]*France*

1. Introduction

Lung cancer is the leading cause of cancer related deaths in developed countries.
Although the best strategy for reducing lung cancer mortality is tobacco cessation, patients harboring lung cancer need specific treatment.
Surgical treatment is the best choice for localized early tumors, without local or distant malignant spread. Pulmonary lobectomy can be performed by open thoracotomy or by minimally invasive techniques as video-assisted thoracic (VATS) or robotic assisted surgery.
VATS lobectomy is a safe, efficient, well accepted and widespread technique among thoracic surgeons, but standard VATS forceps have rigid extremities and do not mimics wrist angulated movements. Furthermore, traditional VATS video-imaging is a simple two dimensional image.
Robotic surgery is performed with telemanipulated flexible effector instruments; some of them can give surgeons tactile feedback; and under three-dimensional (3-D) video-imaging.
Hilar pulmonary dissection for lung cancer can be performed by robotic devices in an efficient and safe way. Scientifically speaking, oncological results need further studies including longer postoperative follow-up to allow comparisons between VATS and robotic techniques; but similarities between these approaches regarding the extension of resected structures as pulmonary parenchyma and lymph nodes suggest that robotic surgery is going to be proved as efficient as VATS for lung cancer.
Learning curve can be one of the biases when comparing results between traditional or VATS lobectomy to robotic surgery.
Costs have been implied as one of the major difficulties in becoming robotic lobectomy more used among thoracic surgeons, but some authors have already studied this issue and concluded that if it is considered the total average costs associated with the resultant hospital stay, "the cost of robotic assistance for VATS is still less than thoracotomy, but greater than VATS alone".
Our nowadays restrict knowledge about robotic lobectomy for lung cancer do not allow us to conclude that it is better, similar or even worse than VATS lobectomy. But we believe that in few years, their advantages are going to be proved, because it allies advantages of both open (precise articulated movements) and VATS (minimally invasive technique);

additionally it fill all the requirements to take part in the modern concept of Fast Track Rehabilitation, also called Enhanced Recovery After Surgery (ERAS).

1.1 Lung cancer surgical treatment

Lung cancer is the leading cause of malignance related mortality in western countries.

They can be divided in two major groups: the small cell and the non small cell lung cancer (NSCLC). In this chapter we are not going to discuss small cell lung cancer because it is considered as a priori spread tumor when diagnosed, and its treatment of choice is based essentially in the systemic therapeutic approaches as chemotherapy, allied or not to radiotherapy.

Although the best therapeutic approach for NSCLC is a multi modality therapy, including radio and chemotherapy, surgical removal remains the cornerstone for early stage carcinomas. The surgery of choice for these patients is the entire lung lobe resection with ipsilateral hilar and mediastinal lymph node dissection.

Lung cancer resection can be performed using several surgical techniques. Location, number and extension of surgical incisions, total or partial muscle sparring techniques, video assisted thoracic surgery (VATS) and the use of robotic devices for camera holding or fine vascular and lymphatic dissections are some of the variables considered when planning lung cancer resection.

1.2 Minimally invasive surgeries

Surgical operations were traditionally performed through open incisions. Following the development of operative and anesthesia techniques and surgical instruments, surgeons has been becoming used in performing minimally invasive procedures. In thoracic surgery, minimally invasive techniques play an important role.

The first phase of minimally invasive techniques in thoracic surgery was based in minithoracotomy, followed by the second phase based in the use of port access instruments

Nowadays minimally invasive thoracic surgeries are based on muscle sparring incisions and VATS with or without robotic assistance.

1.3 Opened versus video assisted lung cancer resection

It is impossible to understand robotic assisted surgery for lung cancer without previously knowing about VATS.

Thoracic surgery has being incorporating VATS devices and techniques progressively in routine dissections since the early 1990s (Lewis RJ; 1993; Kirby TJ and Rice TW; 1993; Walker WS et al; 1993 and McKenna RJ; 1994).

Nowadays, VATS can be considered as an indispensable tool in thoracic surgery. It has been proved that well trained surgical teams can perform VATS resections in a manner as safe and efficient as traditional open surgeries (Gossot, 2008). Some years ago, there was a deep discussion about costs, because some surgeons believed that VATS would be an expensive choice for lung cancer resection. Nowadays, if the whole cost of surgical procedure and hospitalization is considered, VATS has been proved as a cost-effective procedure when compared to traditional opened lung cancer lobectomy.

Early stage NSCLC can be safely and efficiently resected by VATS. Both pulmonary lobe and regional lymph nodes can be dissected and resected by VATS following standard oncological requirements.

Despite some obvious advantages of VATS over open surgery, some movements of surgeon fingers, hands and wrists can not be reproduced by traditional VATS forceps extremities. These instruments have limited maneuverability. Another disadvantage is that tridimensional visualization of operative bed is not possible when using traditional VATS image devices; furthermore these cameras must have a human holder, thus having an unsteady platform.

Recovering fine movements of human fingers, hands and wrist and three-dimensional visualization are some of the advantages of allying robotic devices to VATS instruments. One can ask why not using these robotic devices as being mere traditional VATS instruments in routine VATS operations. The answer can be that surgeon hands movements using traditional VATS instruments do not require a console as a stable platform, nor traditional VATS monitor images devices do so. But robotic dissection instruments and image devices can not be maneuvered in the same way as done in traditional VATS.

In robotic assisted vascular and lymph nodal fine dissection, surgeon hands must be kept over a stable console when manipulating robotic instruments, furthermore binocular visualization devices can be easily installed in this stable platform. These binocular image devices could not be installed in a comfortable way in front of both surgeon eyes during traditional VATS phase, because this traditional VATS dissection is performed besides the patient, away from the console. In this case, binocular devices should be set on the surgeon head, a not very comfortable option.

1.4 Robot assisted lung cancer resection definition

What is robotic surgery?

What kind of operation can be considered as robotic surgery?

Can we perform a "pure" robotic lung cancer resection disposing only of our nowadays available technology?

In fact, there are different robotic devices that can be used, each one, in several ways in thoracic surgery. But traditionally, not all these robotic assisted uses are classified by thoracic surgeons as "robotic surgeries".

In order to exemplify some of the most used robotic devices in thoracic surgery, we can cite the Automated Endoscopic System for Optimal Positioning (AESOP) robotic system and ZEUS of Computer Motion Inc, Goleta, California; and da-Vinci Surgical System of Intuitive Surgical, Sunnyvale, California.

1.5 Camera holding was one of the first and simple tasks of robots in VATS

The simple task consisting in merely hold a VATS camera by robotic arms was one of the first uses of robotic devices by thoracic surgeons. These devices were usually surgeon voice controlled and could target VATS camera to the dissected surgical bed. But the effective dissection was performed using only traditional VATS instruments. These first experiences in the robotic field can not be considered as real "robotic surgeries". This term has been traditionally applied only in cases were robotic devices are used to both hold camera and dissect anatomic structures.

1.6 Robotic fine dissection in VATS

Robotic dissection has been applied in cardiac surgery since the early 2000s. In 2001, Mohr and colleagues published their experience with 148 coronary artery bypass grafting performed by robotic surgery.

But even nowadays, in the field of general thoracic surgery, a pure robotic lung cancer resection is not possible. Robotic assistance is only one phase of two-phase robotic assisted video assisted thoracic surgery. Robotic assistance is the first phase of fine vascular and lymph nodal dissection, without vascular or bronchial ligation and division.

The second phase is still indispensable, because it comprise all the vascular and bronchial ligature and division. Although small vessels can be coagulated by robotic devices, usual vascular and bronchial ligatures for lung cancer resection still require instruments available in the traditional VATS arsenal, but not yet developed for pure robotic uses. One of the examples is the use of traditional VATS mechanical staplers for arterial, venous and bronchial suture and section.

For these reasons we will define robotic surgery for lung cancer as those two-phase procedures, allying the initial robotic assisted vascular and lymphatic fine dissection followed by traditional VATS ligature, division, resection and specimen removal: the robotic assisted VATS lobectomy. Some authors use the term RATS for robotic assisted thoracic surgery.

1.7 Specific anatomic features of thoracic cavity for VATS/RATS

Before talking about robotic surgery for lung cancer, it would be interesting to describe in a few words why video assisted surgical operations in thoracic cavity have some advantages over abdominal video assisted procedures. It can explain why modern thoracic surgery is almost a synonymous of VATS procedures.

Some disadvantages of traditional VATS are also discussed, but it is briefly discussed as how some of them can be resolved or minimized by robotic solutions.

Special characteristics of thoracic cavity compared to abdominal one for robotic/VATS-surgery are the following:

1. One anatomical advantage thoracic cavity for video assisted surgery is that this cavity, differently of abdominal one, does not require gas insufflations in order to achieve visceral visualization. Lung parenchyma is an elastic structure and collapses spontaneously when chest wall is opened resulting in an induced pneumothorax. It is known that some patients with pneumopathies can not be submitted to the CO_2 body cavity insuflation.
2. Another advantage is that collapsed lung remains almost immobile compared to intestinal segments that slide slowly, but continuously. Visceral contact to camera lens became them dirty and difficult visualization, requiring stopping dissection followed by some maneuvers in order to clean leans; and only after these procedures, lens are ready to allow the surgical team to continue operating in the video assisted operative field.
3. Mediastinal movements secondary to contra lateral pulmonary ventilation follow a stereotyped and predictable rhythm, allowing surgeon to avoid unnecessary contacts between lens camera and mediastinal structures. Some robotic devices can subtract of surgeon visualization some undesirable movements as hands tremor, due to robotic software capacity to filter these undesirable movements; based in this concept, we believe that in the future even these repeated ventilation predictable movements will be subtracted by image robotic devices.
4. One clear disadvantage of thoracic cavity operations is that chest wall is composed by muscles, cartilages and ribs, being these two last structures rigid tissues. Traditional VATS effector instruments have limited manoeuvrability due to the rigid shaft axis

fixed to the chest wall by the entry trocar, moreover they should be manipulated between the upper and lower ribs in narrow intercostals spaces. In conclusion, traditional VATS instruments can not recovery fine human finger, hands and wrist movements in the operative field. This disadvantage can be resolved by robotic flexible instruments, which have seven degrees of freedom in the instrument wrist allied to axial freedom of movements. It allows fine vascular and lymph nodal dissection, as will be discussed later.

5. Another disadvantage of thoracic cavity is related to vascular dissections. The pulmonary hilum is composed by structures that can be distant some centimeters one from another, differently of some compact hila, as the renal hilum for example. In thoracic cavity, endoscopic vascular ligature and division of each individual hilum structure can not be performed as an in block ligature. It means that several individual ligature and division must be performed, requiring a number of endoscopic mechanical stapler charges. In addition, for each one of these vascular and bronchial components, endoscopic staplers must be placed in a special and different angle. Nowadays robotic devices can not resolve this anatomical requirement.
6. Another relative advantage of thoracic cavity for video assistance in surgical procedures is that anatomical lung segmentation follows a stereotyped distribution. Chest tomography can determine the exact position of a lung cancer, allowing its endoscopic removal without the need of tactile exploration in order to find the correct tumor placement. In abdominal video operations, intestinal tumors may be firstly found along the probable visceral segment, which some times means some centimeters of tactile exploration.

1.8 Robotic assisted VATS

As discussed above, nowadays, robotic devices still must be allied to VATS instruments in lung cancer resection; no "pure" robotic lobectomy has been described, mainly due nowadays available robotic instruments features that do not permit large vessel coagulation. Despite this limitation, manual dexterity and visualization provided by robotic devices represent some advantages over pure traditional VATS.

Robotic assistance is applied mainly to hilar and mediastinal lymph nodes and vascular (pulmonary artery and vein) fine dissection. Vascular individual dissection of arterial and venous pulmonary branches is the standard initial phase of lung cancer resection surgery, despite of open, VATS or robotic assisted VATS technique.

Although bronchial dissection is not usually performed with robotic instruments, Ishikawa and colleagues (Ishikawa et al, 2006) performed a robotic bronchial dissection, section and end-to-end anastomosis during a experimental robot-assisted VATS right upper lobectomy followed by bronchoplastie in a cadaver in 2006.

Pure robotic lung cancer lobectomy is not yet possible. Even considering only surgical groups with large experience in the use of robotic devices for lung cancer, all of them describe its use only in the first phase of fine dissection of lymphatic and vascular pulmonary structures. As an example, in 2009, Farid Gharagozloo et cols described their large experience with 100 consecutive cases of robot-assisted lobectomy for early-stage lung cancer resection. In 2008, the group of Dr Bernard J. Park, Raja M. Flores and Valerie W. Rusch described their initial experience with 34 robotic assisted VATS lobectomy, and also consider robotic dissection as only one of the two-phase lobectomy.

These groups reported some advantages and disadvantages of robotic assistance in VATS lobectomy.

1.9 Costs comparison between opened, VATS and robotic assisted VATS

One of the most impeditive reasons for not using robotic systems in lung cancer resection is both the associated cost for incorporating this new technology and the specific cost of instruments that may be used in each surgery.

In 2008, Park BJ and Flores RM (Park BJ a& Flores RM; 2008) compared the financial impact of VATS and robotic assisted VATS for lobectomy to those of traditional open thoracotomy.

Park and Flores concluded that although it was confirmed the hypothesis that pure-VATS is less expensive than robotic assisted VATS, robotic assisted VATS had a smaller financial impact in the overall surgical treatment and hospitalization costs than the traditional open thoracotomy.

Authors explain that pure VATS has an increased cost at the first hospital day, but considering the overall hospitalization, it is still less costly than traditional opened thoracotomy, in contrary of some surgeons believed.

1.10 Advantages of robotic assistance

In a few lines we cite some general advantages of robotic assistance for any type of video surgery. These advantages were also observed in lung cancer resection:

- Three-dimensional, stereoscopic binocular video-imaging is one the advantages over traditional VATS images, which are two-dimensionally displayed in the monitor. Da Vinci Robotic System comprises a 3-D scope with 3-chip cameras allowing surgeon a depth perception and optical resolution.
- Magnified video-imaging up to ten times the actual size. This is one advantage over not video assisted procedures, considering that imaging magnification principles can be applied even in non robotic video devices. It is interesting to discuss that in some lung cancer lobectomy steps, it is important having a panoramic vision of intra thoracic structures. Thus, video devices must have the capacity of affording surgeons both magnified images for fine dissection and panoramic vision of whole thoracic cavity.
- Stable robotic camera-holders are one of the advantages of using robotic platform to support video devices. The scope is held by the central four degree of freedom manipulator. We must consider two different points: the skills of human hands compared to the robotic arms in holding the camera and acquiring the best image of operative bed; and the second point that is the requirement of a human being beside the patient to hold the camera. It is well known that well trained humans can optimally perform camera holding and acquisition of an adequate image for surgeon. But the point is that a robotic camera hold can liberate this assistant to perform other tasks, moreover it is important when considering the voluminous robotic devices that are present besides the patient during robotic phase of lung cancer operation.
- Telemanipulated flexible effector instruments: these nowadays available robotic instruments have facilities that represent a recovery of the human movement's degrees of freedom, which were lost during the pure-VATS era. More than a mere recovery of human movements, these robotic instruments provide greater range of motion than those possible for human hands. They have seven degrees of freedom. Three degrees of freedom are conferred by the robotic arm that allow pitch, yaw and insertion

movements; four additional degrees of freedom are conferred by the mechanical wrist located in the interior of thoracic cavity, allowing internal pitch, internal yaw, rotation and grip.
- Downscaling of surgeon movements: fine dissection of pulmonary artery branches, veins and lymphatic structures is facilitated by downscaling. Robotic system is a transducer of surgeon movements in more fine ones in the instruments extremities.
- Indexing is another advantage of robotic systems over the traditional VATS instruments, and will be discussed later.
- Tremor filter: robotic system software is able to filter surgeon hands tremor due to a transducer that are able to reproduce only the desirable movements in the operative field.

1.11 Disadvantages of robotic assistance
- The learning curve has been cited by several authors as a disadvantage of performing robotic assisted VATS. We disagree, because is a characteristic not only applicable to robotic surgery, but to all the new incorporated technologies, including traditional VATS. Melfi and colleagues (Melfi et al, 2002) reported that they believe that the learning curve was relatively short in their experience with robotic assisted VATS, since the surgeons had a solid background in thoracoscopic surgery.
- Costs were already discussed above.
- Large volume of nowadays hardware is one of the disadvantages of robotic assistance for VATS lobectomy. This is a characteristic that requires surgeon team adaptation, because these robotic components limit the free access to the patient by the surgical assistant, usually used performing lobectomy with less voluminous VATS devices (Loulmet et cols, 1999). As discussed later, these components of robotic systems tend to have a decrease in their volume.
- Collision of robotic arms is one of the disadvantages of robotic assistance. But this trouble can be minimized with the optimal placement of port access. Furthermore, in the future, robotic hardware tends to be miniaturized.
- Some authors believe that one of the disadvantages of robotic assisted VATS lobectomy is that two VATS trained surgeons are required in the operative room. Although it is a irrefutable argument, we believe that even for traditional VATS lobectomy it is a prudent measure having two trained thoracic surgeons, always when possible.
- Tactile feedback systems are only in their early development phase, but some surgeons believe that this disadvantage can be minimized with learning curve progression of the surgical team.
- Dissection of lung parenchyma with the nowadays available fine robotic forceps can result in lung tears and bleeding.

2. Technical features

2.1 Robotic assisted video assisted indication
Nowadays, robotic assistance for VATS lobectomy is only indicated for early stage NSCLC. Some services indicate RATS/VATS only for IA stage, other extend this indication for IB or IIA/IIB stage. These stages include tumors classified as T1 or T2 and N0 or N1.
The most large series of robotic assisted VATS lobectomy for lung cancer was reported by Farid Gharagozloo and his colleagues; they used the following inclusion and exclusion criteria in their experience of 100 consecutive cases:

- Inclusion criteria: clinical stage I and II lung cancer (T1 or T2N0; and T1 or T2N1), predicted ability to achieve resection by lobectomy, and the physiologic state of the patient.
- Exclusion criteria: chest wall invasion, endobronchial tumors visible at bronchoscopy, a central tumor, and induction therapy.

Melfi and colleagues (Melfi et al, 2002) suggest five inclusion criteria for robotic assisted VATS lung cancer resection:

1. Lesions with a longer diameter less than five centimeters
2. Clinical stage I status for primary lung carcinomas
3. Absence of chest wall involvement
4. Absence of pleural symphysis and
5. Complete or near complete interlobar fissures.

There is no reference in the literature of robotic assistance neither for T3/T4 nor for N2 stages.

2.2 The choose of the robotic system

Considering only robotic assisted VATS lobectomy, it means excluding the use of robotic devices only as mere camera holders, available articles describe experience only with the use of da-Vinci Surgical System.

2.3 Da Vinci robotic system (Intuitive Surgical, Mountain View, CA)

We describe the Da Vinci robotic system as an example of robotic system already used for lung cancer robotic assisted VATS.

Da vinci roboti system is an assembly of two groups of devices. The first one is the surgeon's viewing and control master console; the second one is the surgical arm cart were robotic instruments and camera are supported and moved.

- <u>The control console:</u> during the first phase of robotic assisted VATS lobectomy, the surgeon control robotic arms and camera from the console, where one surgeon sits comfortably with both hands supported over a stable platform. The surgeon eyes must be accommodated in front of the visualization eyepieces.
- <u>Console robotic arms control:</u> the console facilities allow the surgeon both the telemanipulation of robotic arms with attached dissection fine instruments as allow the optical devices control.
- <u>Console visualization devices:</u> the console eyepiece provides a stereoscopic binocular 3-D visualization of the surgical field. Furthermore, images of the dissected area are magnified.
- <u>The surgical arm cart:</u> robotic arms with attached instruments and camera are moved by the surgical arm cart. Surgeon control movements from the console are processed (for tremor filtration, indexing and scaling) and reproduced by robotic arms in a real time, with no delay. Processed movements are more precise and accurate than real surgeon hands movements.
- <u>Tremor filter:</u> as discussed above, robotic arms process the real surgeon movements in order to filter hands tremor and only transmit effective movements.
- <u>Indexing:</u> while surgeon is repositioning one instrument in one of the robotic arms, the other one can remain steady in the last position the surgeon moved it.
- <u>Movements scaling:</u> Even after tremor filtration, robotic arms also process the surgeon hands movement to transducer them in a more fine scale in the operative field.

Choosing the surgical team

The minimum surgical team includes two thoracic surgeons with experience in VATS lobectomy and one third assistant. During the robotic dissection phase, one of them maneuvers the robotic arms and video system from the non-sterile console and the other two assistants remain in the sterile operative field besides the patient.
These two assistants must be trained in VATS and opened lobectomy, they may be able to perform all the necessary operative maneuvers during the time needed for the console-based surgeon be able to take part in the operative field. In case of severe bleeding requiring conversion to open surgery, these assistants must perform all the urgency maneuvers immediately.

Patient position

Patient position for RATS lobectomy is the same as that for VATS or opened resection: the lateral decubitus.

Positioning robotic devices in operating room

One of the most important things for robotic dissection phase performance is the determination of the optimal position of robotic devices.
Considering that robotic devices can be sometimes placed in a cranial position, it is very important that surgeons and anesthetists must choose together the optimal position for achieving both robotic dissection and anesthetic maneuvers security. Melfi and colleagues (Melfi et al, 2002) suggest that during operation, the main body of the machine should be better placed behind the operative site and that the best position of robotic arms must be established in relation to the side of the lesion.
Robotic arms collision will be discussed below.

Choosing the number, position and length of incisions

One of the incisions can be classified as the main utility incision, also called "service entrance" incision (Melfi et al, 2002).
Utility incision is longer than ordinary ones and is usually used for resected lung specimen removal. Its location is usually chosen based on the resection that is going to be performed. Upper lobe resection requires a more cranial placement and lower or middle lobe operations require a more caudal one.
Other ordinary incisions are used for camera and robotic instruments insertion. It is important to say that compared to traditional VATS lobectomy, trocars must be positioned at a greater distance from each other in order to avoid or at least minimize the risk of robotic arms collision.
When choosing the position and length of incisions, surgeon must consider the angle that will be required for vascular and bronchial mechanical stapling, because small incisions can bleed if staplers are forced through a narrow entry. And not well programmed position of incisions for stapling devices can result in unnecessary prolongation of operative time.

Draping robotic arms and camera

Several components of robotic system must be draped by sterile protectors. In order to avoid bacterial contamination and acquire a high performance skill, the nursing staff must be trained in this task.
Dr Morgan and colleagues described in 2003 (Morgan et al; 2003) that during the initial period of the learning curve with robotic system draping, they had to book the operations later in the day, because sometimes it could took the nurses two hours to drape the robot.

Single-lung ventilation

Single-lung ventilation is required because video assistance for both RATS and VATS requires a pleural space between lung parenchyma and chest wall in order to visualize and manipulate anatomic structures with endoscopic instruments.
In case where the ipsilateral lung parenchyma can not be adequately collapsed, as in some emphysematous patients, lobectomy can be safer and faster performed by opened techniques.

Initial VATS exploration

Before proceeding to robotic fine dissection of vascular and lymphatic structures, an initial VATS exploration is performed with traditional equipment.
This thoracic exploration can recognize situations that would preclude lung cancer lobectomy, as small pleural tumor spread not identified in chest tomography, for example.
It is also used to guide the optimal placement of additional incisions.

Incisions position may avoid robotic arms collision

When choosing additional incisions optimal placement during the initial VATS exploration, surgeons must remember that incisions position may allow free robotic arms movement.
If incisions are placed based only on the optimal position for robotic and VATS dissection, ligature, division and specimens removal, not considering the risk of robotic arms collision, unnecessary time will be add to the surgical procedure in order to resolve or minimize this trouble.

2.4 Robotic assisted mediastinal and hilar lymph node dissection phase

Most used instruments for robotic assistance during dissection phase

Robotic instruments must be personally chosen by the surgeons who will perform the robotic dissection of vascular and lymphatic structures. As in traditional VATS phase, one surgeon can be more familiarized with a specific instrument. For each instrument family, several design and degrees of movement are available. We cite some of the instrument families used for robotic fine dissection phase:
Instruments

- Needle Holders
- Scalpels
- Scissors
- Graspers
- Monopolar cautery instruments
- Bipolar cautery instruments
- Ultrasonic energy instruments
- Specialty instruments
- Clip appliers

Vision equipments

- 2D 5mm endoscope system and accessories
- 3D endoscope system and accessories

Vascular and lymphatic dissection

Lymph nodal dissection: is an important aspect of lung cancer resection. Although there is a wide discussion about the extent of nodal dissection, if node picking have the same diagnostic and therapeutic results compared to radical dissection, it is a consensus that both hilar and mediastinal lymph nodes must be explored during the surgical treatment of NSCLC.

Lymph nodal dissection is one of the procedures that should be performed during the robotic assisted phase of RATS/VATS lobectomy. It can be done before or after lobe removal, but published articles usually describe it before lobe removal.

Arterial branches: are dissected during the first phase of robotic fine maneuvers. DeBakey forceps and electrocautery are the most used instruments during this vascular dissection.

There is no available robotic instrument for pulmonary artery major branches coagulation or ligation. One can say that if arterial branches were hypothetically dissected until a more distal bifurcation, their caliber would be short enough for coagulation with robotic cauteries or robotic clip appliers. But an excessive distal dissection require a longer operative time, expose vascular and parenchyma tissues to further, and perhaps dangerous, dissection and can cause unnecessary bleeding or alveolar air leak. Furthermore, traditional VATS staplers can be easily used for ligature and section of more proximal segments of the arterial pulmonary tree.

Venous structures: are traditionally dissected with VATS instruments only until its more proximal length. In robotic assisted VATS surgeons prefer keeping this principle, too. At this more proximal segment, pulmonary veins have a large caliber when compared to arterial structures, which are usually dissected more distally until segmental branches. More than a mere larger caliber, venous structures are less elastic and resistant to dissection, being more susceptible to small vascular, but bloody, injure.

As arterial vessels, VATS traditional staplers are used to perform ligature and division of pulmonary veins, as discussed later.

VATS lobectomy phase

As discussed below, robotic assisted VATS lobectomy includes a two-phase procedure, being traditional VATS lobectomy the second phase. In this phase, ligature and division of arterial, venous and bronchial structures are performed.

Individual ligation and division of the hilar structures requires temporary repositioning of instrument arm

During the VATS lobectomy phase, endoscopic staplers are used to perform ligation and division of vascular and bronchial hilar structures. Robotic instrument arm must be temporary repositioned in order to allow staplers introduction. Usually, the arm that must be repositioned depends on the lobe that is going to be resected:

- Upper lobectomy: staplers are usually introduced through the posterior incision.
- Middle lobectomy: staplers are usually introduced through the posterior incision.
- Lower lobectomy: staplers are usually introduced through the anterior incision.

Fissure dissection

Robotic instruments allow a fine dissection of vascular and lymphatic structures, but can perforate lung parenchyma causing minor bleeding and alveolar air leak. For this reason, for fissure completion, surgeons prefer using traditional staplers and VATS instruments.

Traditional VATS instruments are more adequate to dissect lung parenchyma and can be used in order to achieve a faster and safer fissure dissection when compared to robotic fine instruments.

Surgeons can perform fissure dissection before or after vascular ligature, but usually it is dissected last, during the VATS phase.

Resected lobe specimen removal

As discussed above, resected lobe is removed through the main utility incision, because it is the incision with the longer length.
Some surgeons prefer performing a previous traditional VATS wedge resection containing the primary lung tumor in order to reduce the whole lung volume. This simple maneuver is believed to allow the specimen removal through narrower utility incisions. Oncologically saying, in-bloc resection of anatomical structures harboring a carcinoma is theoretically preferable, but no scientific study has been performed comparing oncological results between these two techniques. Furthermore, some authors believe that extending some few centimeters the length of the utility incision does not add any important morbidity to the surgical procedure.
If extending the utility incision or performing a previous VATS wedge resection is controversial. But authors agree that the use of protective VATS bags is essential for the specimen's removal. More than only protecting chest wall against tumor cell implants, it facilitates specimen sliding through the orifices, requiring minimal chest wall incisions.

3. Other robot platforms not used in lung cancer resection

Robotic assisted VATS lobectomy for lung cancer uses extra cavity and steady platform for camera holding and for robotic arms support. Moreover, instruments axis are rather rigid than flexible. We believe that these three features of nowadays available robotic systems for thoracic surgery will evolve to more miniaturized, flexible, intra cavity (or endoluminal) "intelligent self moving" devices.
We believe that miniaturized robots will probably be controlled from the outside cavity, but the surgeons will be able to move them freely in the intra cavity operative field.
We must ally the concept of Natural Orifice Transluminal Endoscopic Surgery (NOTES) to the available robotic assisted VATS techniques.
Some devices are already used in other surgical procedures, based in technologies that can be incorporated in robotic systems for VATS assistance.
NeoGuide's Endoscopy System: One example of technology that can be incorporated aiming more movement free miniaturized robotic devices is the NeoGuide's Endoscopy System used for colonoscopy. Eickhoff (Eickhoff et al, 2007) and colleagues carried out an initial clinical trial using this device. It consists in a computer-assisted colonoscope, which changes its shape to adjust it to the colonic silhouette directed by a computer algorithm.
Based in the concept of Natural Orifice Transluminal Endoscopic Surgery (NOTES), we can suppose that combined endoscopic and thoracoscopic will be used in the future for bronchial dissection, or even ligature and section of airways structures.
I-SNAKE and CardioArm and Endosamurai: 'I-Snake' is a flexible Imaging-Sensing Navigated and Kinematically Enhanced (i-Snake) Robot equipped with special motors, multiple sensing mechanisms and imaging tools at its 'head'.
The flexible i-Snake robot can act as the surgeon's hands and eyes. It can be guided along intra luminal or intra cavity anatomic structures. CardioArm and endosamurai are other available flexible promising robotic device to be used in body natural or surgeon accessed cavities (Mummadi & Pasricha; 2008).

4. Controversies about robot in lung cancer

Although robotic assistance can increases maneuverability, dexterity and afford a 3-D and magnified visualization, clinical outcomes advantages and costs remain controversial.
It is realized by surgeons who perform robotic assisted VATS lobectomy associated to hilar and mediastinal lymphatic dissection that robotic assistance can add advantages in these procedures when fine dissection is required. In cases where patients have a complete pulmonary fissure, blood vessels are easily visualized and dissected; VATS instruments can perform vascular and bronchial dissection in a fast, efficient and safe manner.
It seems that a sub group of patients with incomplete fissures or with pathologic lymph nodes in the hilum or inter lobar fissure can benefit of robotic assistance for arterial dissection (Farid Gharagozloo et al, 2009).

5. Perspectives

We summarize some items we believe are the most important points to be developed in robotic assisted VATS lung cancer lobectomy:

1. Smaller robots hardware
2. Miniature robots including intra cavity and flexible free devices
3. More advanced devices with better tactile sensation
4. New design of dissecting forceps oriented for lung cancer surgery
5. Collision detection and untangling for surgical robotic manipulators
6. Finally, we believe that learning curve is a fair and severe judge of new incorporated technologies in all human activities.

5.1 Are we in the road until a real pure robotic lung cancer resection?

In conclusion, it is intuitive that continuous technological advances will allow surgeons performing pure robotic lung cancer resection one day.
Robotic systems will confer the capacity to resect lung cancer through even smaller incisions, resulting in lesser chest wall tissue manipulation and less painful procedures. In the other hand it is also clear that analgesic techniques and drugs are being developed as well; and it will be possible to offer patients painless surgical treatment of lung cancer based on these new options.
But the concept of pursuing tissue integrity is one of the surgical science cornerstones and can misbalance the equation in favor of minimally invasive procedure, allying NOTES concepts to robotic assisted lung cancer treatment.
Finally, we believe that best pure robotic lung cancer treatment would be a friendly robot helping humans stop smoking.

6. References

Eickhoff A, van Dam J, Jakobs R, Kudis V, Hartmann D, Damian U, Weickert U, Schilling D, Riemann JF. Computer-assisted colonoscopy (the NeoGuide Endoscopy System): results of the first human clinical trial ("PACE study"). Am J Gastroenterol. 2007 Feb;102(2):261-6.

Gossot D. Technical tricks to facilitate totally endoscopic major pulmonary resections. Ann Thorac Surg. 2008 Jul;86(1):323-6.

Ishikawa N, Sun YS, Nifong LW, Chitwood WR Jr, Oda M, Ohta Y, Watanabe G. Thoracoscopic robot-assisted bronchoplasty. Surg Endosc. 2006 Nov;20(11):1782-3.

Kirby TJ, Rice TW: Thoracoscopic lobectomy. Ann Thorac Surg. 1993; 56:784-6.

Lewis RJ. The role of video-assisted thoracic surgery for cancer of the lung: wedge resection to lobectomy by simultaneous stapling. Ann Thorac Surg. 1993; 56:762-8.

Loulmet D, Carpentier A, d'Attellis N, Berrebi A, Cardon C, Ponzio O, Aupècle B, Relland JY. Endoscopic coronary artery bypass grafting with the aid of robotic assisted instruments. J Thorac Cardiovasc Surg. 1999 Jul;118(1):4-10.

Morgan JA, Ginsburg ME, Sonett JR, Morales DL, Kohmoto T, Gorenstein LA, Smith CR, Argenziano M Advanced thoracoscopic procedures are facilitated by computer-aided robotic technology.. Eur J Cardiothorac Surg. 2003 Jun;23(6):883-7; discussion 887.

McKenna RJ. Lobectomy by video-assisted thoracic surgery with mediastinal node sampling for lung cancer. J Thorac Cardiovasc Surg. 1994; 107: 879-82.

Melfi FM, Menconi GF, Mariani AM, Angeletti CA. Early experience with robotic technology for thoracoscopic surgery.. Eur J Cardiothorac Surg. 2002 May;21(5):864-8.

Mummadi RR, Pasricha PJ. The eagle or the snake: platforms for NOTES and radical endoscopic therapy. Gastrointest Endosc Clin N Am. 2008 Apr;18(2):279-89; viii. Review.

Park BJ, Flores RM, Rusch VW. Robotic assistance for video-assisted thoracic surgical lobectomy: technique and initial results. J Thorac Cardiovasc Surg. 2006 Jan;131(1):54-9.

Park BJ, Flores RM. Cost comparison of robotic, video-assisted thoracic surgery and thoracotomy approaches to pulmonary lobectomy. Thorac Surg Clin. 2008 Aug;18(3):297-300, vii.

Walker WS, Carnochan FM, Pugh GC. Thoracoscopic pulmonary lobectomy. J Thorac Cardiovasc Surg. 1993; 106: 1111-7.

10

Robotic Surgery in Ophthalmology

Irena Tsui[1], Angelo Tsirbas[1,3], Charles W. Mango[2],
Steven D. Schwartz[1,3] and Jean-Pierre Hubschman[1,3]
[1]*Jules Stein Eye Institute, University of California, Los Angeles*
[2]*Weill Cornell Medical College*
[3]*Center for Advanced Surgical and Interventional Technology*
USA

1. Introduction

Innovations in ophthalmology have developed rapidly in recent years with the advent of small incision surgery and the engineering of more efficient phacoemulsification and vitrectomy machines(Georgescu, Kuo et al. 2008; Hubschman, Bourges et al. 2009). We feel that these latest developments lend themselves to the mechanization of ocular surgery, and the next major advancement in ophthalmology will probably be the integration of robotics. The potential benefits of robotic surgery in ocular surgery include increased precision, elimination of tremor, reduction of human error, task automation and the capacity for remote surgery.

In increasing complexity and with distinct demands, ocular procedures can be grouped as extraocular surgery, intraocular anterior segment surgery, or intraocular posterior segment surgery. Intraocular surgery currently requires state of the art operating microscopes. Although the requirement of specialized microscopes and visualization systems presents a challenge to the adaptation of robotics in ocular surgery, robotic surgery has the capacity to include new visualization devices such as digital microscopy and/or endoscopy, which would be an advantage over conventional operating microscopes.

The purpose of this chapter is to present the unique issues of ocular surgery in the application of robotics and to summarize the progress which has already been made towards the goal of robotic ocular surgery for clinical patient care. We will also discuss the previous and current ocular robotic prototypes and the utilization of surgical motion sensors to assess the mechanical requisites of eye surgery.

2. Early ocular surgery robotic prototypes

One of the first ocular robotic systems was described by Guerrouad and Vidal in 1989. (Guerrouad & Jolly 1989; Guerrouad & Vidal 1989; Guerrouad & Vidal 1991; Hayat & Vidal 1995). It was called the Stereotaxical Microtelemanipulator (SMOS) and included a spherical micromanipulator mounted on a x, y, z stage, which allowed 6 degrees of freedom. This prototype was fabricated and performance tests were completed. Yu et al developed in 1998 a patented spherical manipulator, similar to Guerrouad and Vidal, for intravascular drug delivery, implantation of microdrainage devices and the intraretinal manipulation of microelectrodes. These tasks were successfully carried out with minimal tissue damage(Yu, Cringle et al. 1998) (Figure 1).

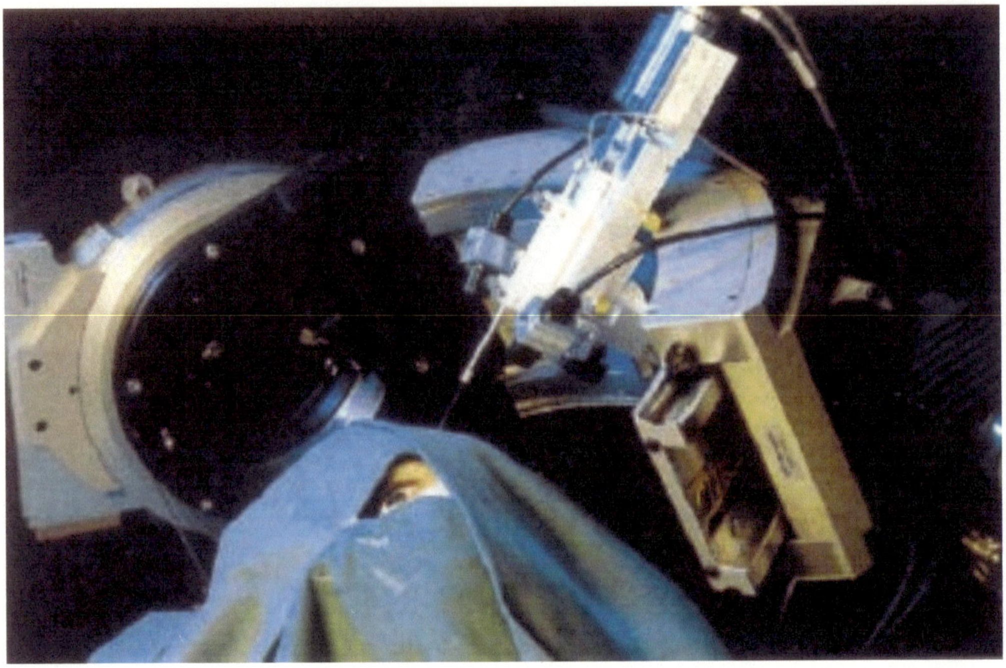

Fig. 1. Picture of one of the earliest ocular robotic prototypes in position related to the head. From Yu, D. Y., S. J. Cringle, et al. (1998). "Robotic ocular ultramicrosurgery." Aust N Z J Ophthalmol 26 Suppl 1: S6-8.

These first prototypes already had an adapted remote centre of motion for intraocular surgery as well as a relatively good range a motion but they were too premature to raise a tangible interest for further development.

In 1997, Steve Charles and collaborators described a new telerobotic platform which was called Robot Assisted MicroSurgery (RAMS)(Charles S 1997)(Figure 2). This lightweight and compact 6 DoF master-slave system demonstrated 10 microns of precision and a wide range of motion. The slave robot arm (2.5 cm in diameter and 25 cm long) and the master device were built with associated motors, encoders, gears, cables, pulleys and linkages that caused the tip of the robot to move under computer control and to measure the surgeon's hand precisely. The 3 joints of the arm were torso joint rotating about an axis aligned with the base axis. This design allowed low backlash, high stiffness, fine incremental motion and precise position measurement. The complexity of the software control as well as the lack of mechanical remote center of motion were the main limitations of this model.

In 1997, a laboratory in Northwestern University needed to measure the intraluminal pressure inside feline retinal vessels as well as extract retinal blood samples for research purposes. The retinal vessels ranged in internal diameter from 20 to 130 microns. The researchers were unable to achieve this goal with human dexterity, and therefore designed another one of the earliest ocular surgery robotic prototypes(Jensen, Grace et al. 1997). The prototype used the Stewart based platform which had already established its place in machine tool technology (Figure 3).

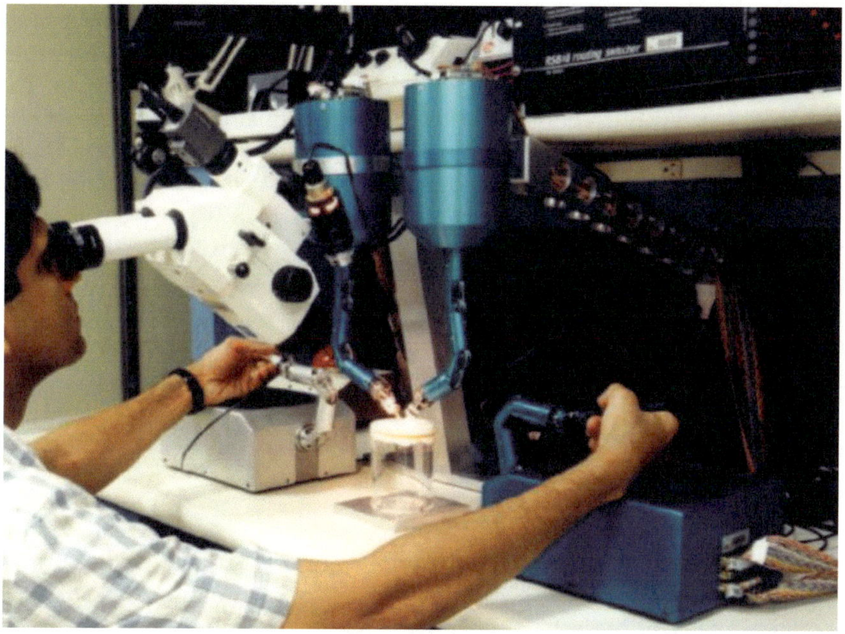

Fig. 2. RAMS master slave robotic system. From Charles S, D., H, Ohm T (1997). "Dexterity-enhanced tele-robotic microsurgery." Proc. IEEE int conf adv Robot.

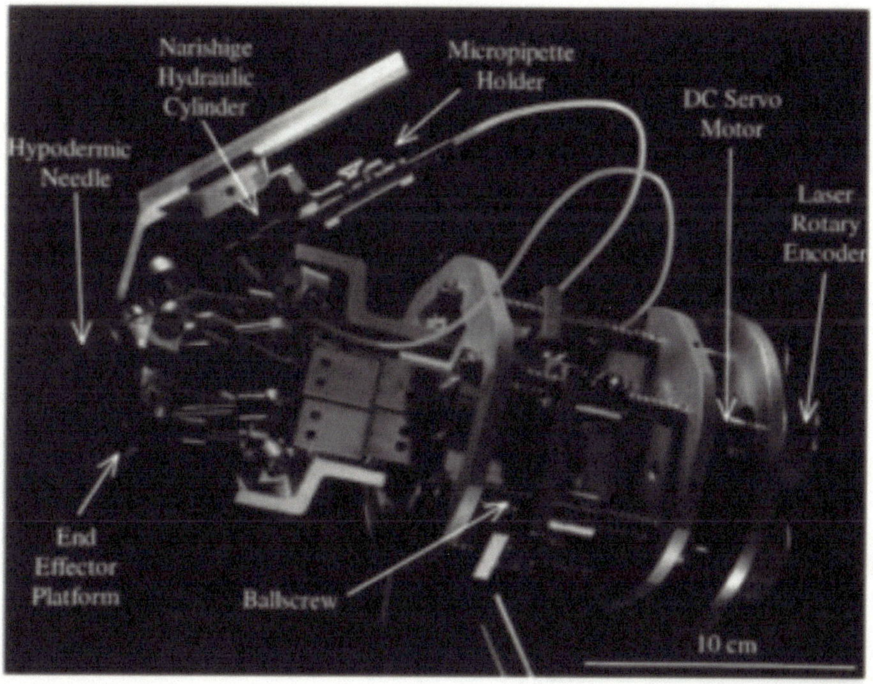

Fig. 3. Photograph of the robotic manipulator based on a stewart platform design. From Jensen, P. S., K. W. Grace, et al. (1997). "Toward robot-assisted vascular microsurgery in the retina." Graefes Arch Clin Exp Ophthalmol 235(11): 696-701.

Advantages of the effector platform design in this early prototype were its inherent stiffness, ability to pivot, and capacity to perform large displacements. Ball screws were rotated using DC servo motors and laser rotary encoders tracked their motions. The device was capable of operating in 6 degrees of freedom with both translational and rotational motion (x,y,z, pitch, roll, and yaw). The operator controlled the slave arm by using a handheld trackball and two buttons, and the intended direction of motion was entered into the computer software before performing it. This control mechanism which was practical at the time for laboratory research purposes may not be the best input system today because the motions needed for modern day eye surgery are more complicated and the robot effector in ocular surgery needs to respond more quickly. Nonetheless, the constructed device was successfully used to cannulate and take samples from retinal blood in anesthetized cats for laboratory use.

3. Current ocular robotic prototypes

3.1 *Da Vinci* surgical system

At present, the Food and Drug Administration approved *da Vinci* Surgical System (Intuitive Surgical, Sunnyvale, CA), is the most commonly employed robotic platform in human surgery (Figure 4). It is being used routinely in fields such as general surgery, urology, gynecology, and cardiac surgery(Diaz-Arrastia, Jurnalov et al. 2002; Hemal & Menon 2004; Katz, Van Praet et al. 2006; Kumar & Hemal 2006; Kypson & Chitwood 2006). This design consists of three robotic slave arms that are controlled by the surgeon via a remote console. Image capture is achieved with a dual-channeled endoscope on one of the arms, and a binocular viewfinder on the remote console allows stereoscopic viewing. In 2006, our team started to evaluate the possibility of performing ocular surgery with the *da Vinci* Surgical System(Bourla, Hubschman et al. 2008).

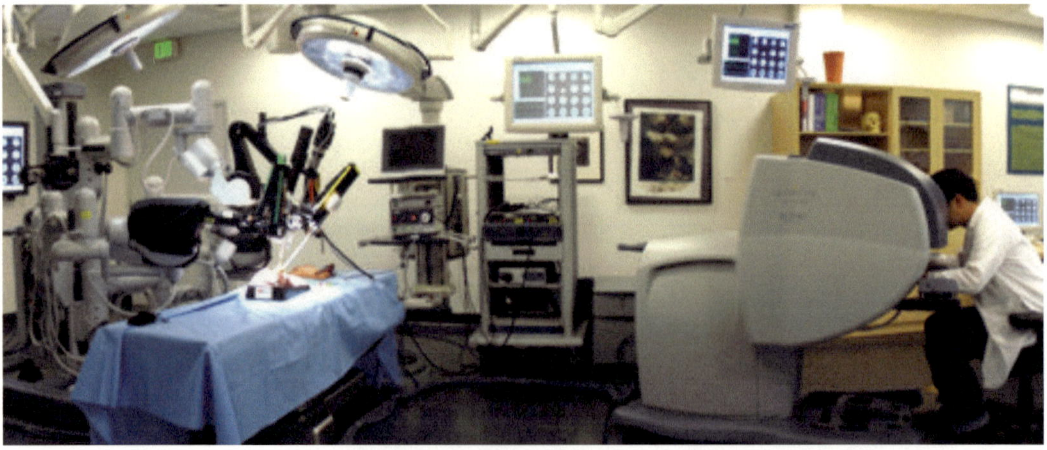

Fig. 4. The *da Vinci* surgical master (right) and slave (left) platform at the CASIT Center for Advanced Surgical and Interventional Technology at the University of California, Los Angeles.

3.1.1 Extraocular surgery

A typical scenario in ocular surgery is closing a partial thickness corneal laceration after surgical or accidental trauma. This relatively simple to perform maneuver is most similar to surgery on other parts of the body. Therefore, we elected to start testing the *da Vinci* Surgical System in ocular surgery with the task of closing a full thickness corneal and scleral laceration created on an enucleated porcine eye (Tsirbas, Mango et al. 2007). Portions of corneal wound closure such as passing the needle in a smooth arc through the tissue and throwing knots squarely were successfully carried out using *da Vinci* Surgical System (Figure 5). There was human assistance with steps such as loading the needle and cutting the suture.

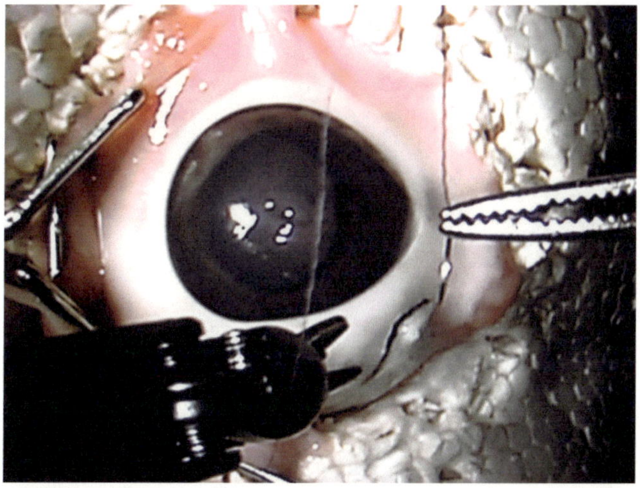

Fig. 5. A porcine eye with a full thickness scleroconjuntival wound is being sutured using the *da Vinci* surgical platform.

These early experiments used 10-0 nylon suture, which is the standard for corneal wound closure; however, the smallest suture typically used with the *da Vinci* needle holders are 7-0 Prolene suture in cardiac surgery. There was some bulkiness of the *da Vinci* needle holder when compared with traditional ocular surgery needle holders. Future work should include miniturizing the needle holders for ocular surgery as well as incorporating additional components to automate tasks which were performed by humans such as loading the needle and cutting the suture.

Visualization is important in all surgery, but paramount in ocular surgery and prior to these experiments it was unknown whether adequate visualization for ocular surgery could be achieved with the original design of the da Vinci endoscope. An important conclusion was that the mounted endoscope provided adequate image capture and depth perception for extraocular surgery.

3.1.2 Intraocular anterior segment surgery

Cataract surgery, the most common ocular surgery procedure performed in the United States, was attempted robotically with the *da Vinci* Surgical System. The feasibility of performing intraocular cataract surgery in enucleated porcine eyes was assessed with the commercially available *da Vinci* Surgical System combined with standard ocular surgery instruments.

An important principle in modern day cataract surgery is to create a biplanar self-sealing wound through the clear cornea and to manipulate this opening as little as possible intraoperatively in order to maintain constant pressure inside the eye for the purposes of controlling hemostasis and maintaining the shape of the eye. This self-sealing wound was difficult to achieve with the *da Vinci* system because wound gape constantly let fluid egress out of the eye, allowing the eye to collapse and lose its spherical shape.

The major problem was that the remote center of motion of the *da Vinci* surgical arm was preset and located 9 cm away from the surface of the eye (Figure 6). The major emphasis of these initial trials of cataract surgey using robotics was that to make instrument movement safe during intraocular surgery, the remote center of motion (or pivot point) must be at the surface of the eye.

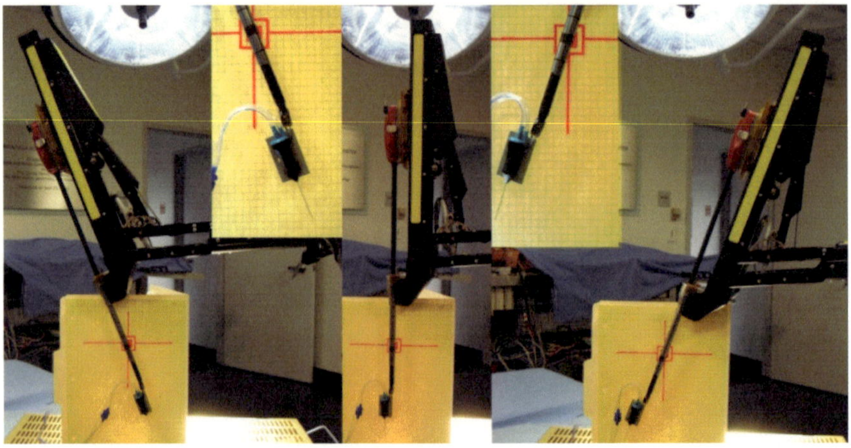

Fig. 6. Visualization of the Remote Centre of Motion (RCM) and its distance from the tip of the forceps.

To augment visualization during cataract surgery, retroillumination is a valuable technique that increases contrast between two transparent tissue planes. This is carried out by aligning the viewing microscope to be co-axial with the light source which allows light to be reflected out of the eye and illuminate ocular tissue from behind. This optical phenomenon of retroillumination was not possible using the *da Vinci* endoscope for visualization because the comparatively bulky endoscope arm and illumination source could not be lined up coaxially. Nevertheless, the dual channel endoscope offered a sufficient optical resolution of the surgical target to perform anterior segment eye surgery.

On the other hand, a bimanual teleoperated robotic penetrating keratoplasty (PK) has been succesfully performed with the *da Vinci* in porcine and human eyes with no difficulties. The precise placement of continuous sutures was facilitated by the wrested-end forceps. The anatomic contours of the orbital rim and nose did not limit the range of surgical motions(Mulgaonkar, Hubschman et al. 2009).

3.1.3 Intraocular posterior segment surgery

Intraocular posterior segment surgery, which is more complex than anterior segment intraocular surgery, was attempted robotically(Bourla, Hubschman et al. 2008). Pars plana vitrectomy is the most common intraocular posterior segment surgery performed in the United States. The *da Vinci* Surgical System was used to perform pars plana vitrectomy using standard 25-gauge vitrectomy instruments (Figure 7 and 8). The commerically available vitrectomy handpieces were adapted with magnets so that they could be stored for easy and independent pick up by the robotic slave arm forceps.

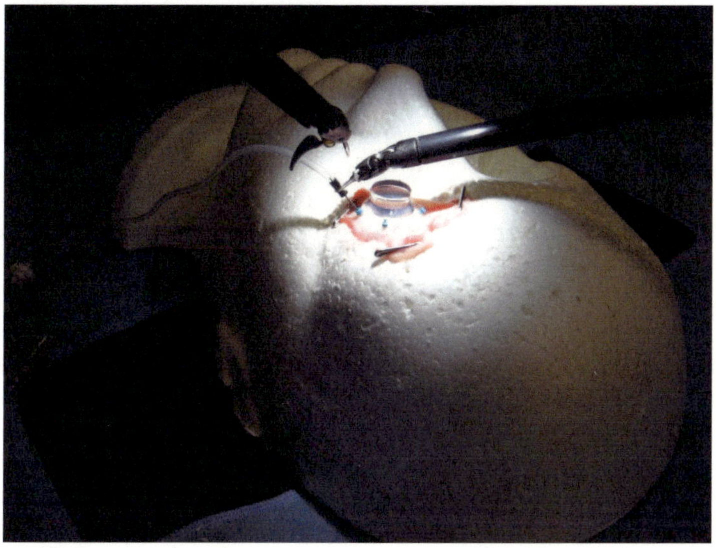

Fig. 7. The *da Vinci* surgical system was used to insert 3 trans-scleral cannulas which is necesaary for minimally invasive vitrectomy surgery. In addition to axial motion, the wrist-like tips of the robotic instruments have roll, pitch, yaw and grip to facilitate delicate manipulations.

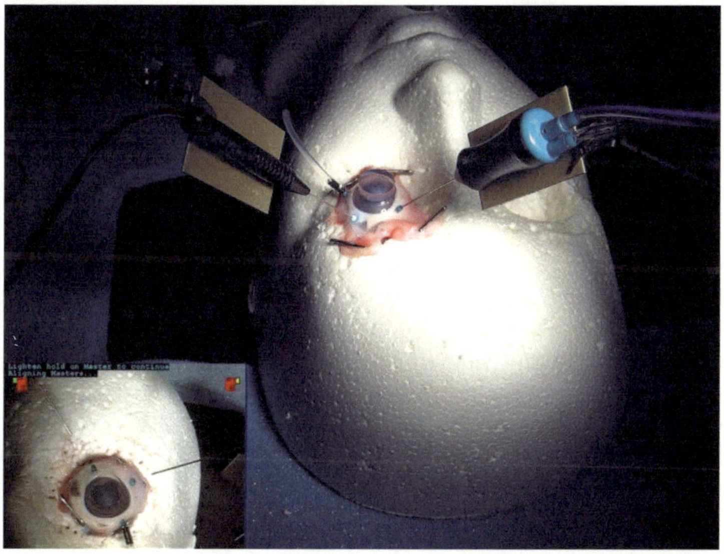

Fig. 8. Insertion of the modified 25-gauge vitreous cutter and endo illuminator with the robotic arms. Left corner - high magnification view through the robotic endoscope.

In our experiments, wound entry using a 25-gauge vitrectomy system was easier than in cataract surgery because of surgically inserted ports which facilitated and guided instruments into the eye. However, the remote center of motion (or pivot point) still needed to be located at the surface of the eye to control intraocular maneuveability and avoid distortion of the globe. As discovered during trials of anterior segment surgery, this was not possible with the *da Vinci* Surgical System because its pivot point was preset 9 cm from the tip of the instrument.

The image quality of the endoscope, although adequate for external eye surgery was not to the standards of microscopes typically used for intraocular surgery. Also, the limited field of view of the endoscope required constant repositioning when entering the eye for vitrectomy surgery, which was tedious and impractical.

Furthermore, vitrectomy surgery needs specialized microscopes, lenses, and image inverters to make intraocular visualization optically possible. Lack of this telescope system with the *da Vinci* Surgical System made posterior segment intraocular surgery impossible to achieve.

3.1.4 *da Vinci* surgical system summary

With the above earliest attempts at extraocular surgery, intraocular anterior segment surgery, and intraocular posterior segment surgery, there were general observations made regarding the use of the *da Vinci* Surgical System in ocular robotic surgery. Wrist turning movements seemed intuitive and facile to perform, and x-y planar movements using robot arms were well suited for ocular surgery when kept in a limited surgical field .

In conclusion, using the *da Vinci* Surgical System, extraocular surgery was carried out successfully, although imperfect due to the large size of the instrument tips and incomplete automation. Intraocular surgery, both anterior and posterior segment procedures, were difficult and limited due to the preset pivot point on the *da Vinci* instrument arms being external to the eye. Future work in ocular robotic surgery will need to include improving visualization systems such as with digital microscopy or endoscopy and more importantly incorporating an adapted remote center of motion during intraocular procedures.

3.2 Hexapod surgical system

To overcome the remote center of motion problem for intraocular surgery posed by the *da Vinci* Surgical System, we sought to modify this macrorobot with the addition of a microrobotic platform. We chose to combine the *da Vinci* system with the Stewart based manipulator, described above, because it had six degrees of motion and was originally designed for robot-assisted cannulation of retinal vessels with success (Jensen, Grace et al. 1997).The platform had a parallel manipulator with a fixed based and used an octahedral assembly of struts.

The Stewart platform was customized to fit onto the arms of the *da Vinci* Surgical System, and the combined device was named the Hexapod Surgical System (Figure 8). Its major advantage over the *da Vinci* Surgical System alone was the ability to place the remote center of motion at the site of ocular penetration using automated software. As described above, this was the major limitation of the *da Vinci* system alone which prevented further progress towards the application of robotics in intraocular surgery.

The remote center of motion, controlled by software on the Hexapod Surgical System, was able to constantly reposition the pivot point of the intraocular instruments to be located at the entry point. Each actuator was also equipped with a linear potentiometer type sensor to facilitate feedback control by the computer. As an additional safety measure, tasks performed with the Hexapod Surgical System were limited to joystick movements that maintained the remote center of motion at the ocular surface.

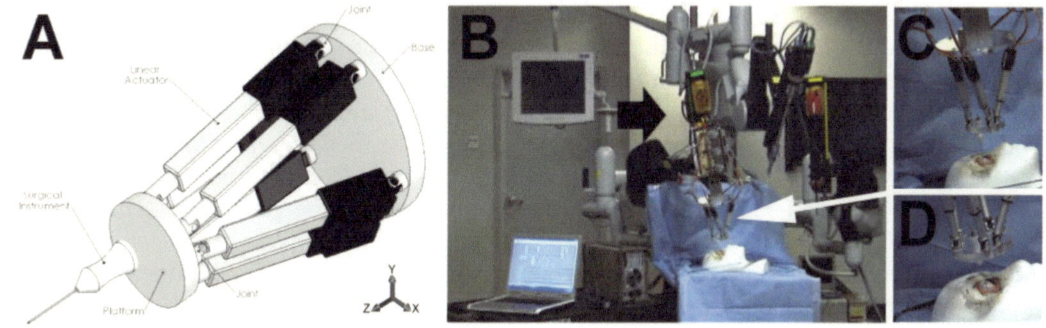

Fig. 8. The Hexapod Surgical System (HSS) consists of a Stewart Platform (A). The protype (B) was built based on six linear actuators changing length when remotely given a command voltage. The HSS is able to integrate the *da Vinci* robot (C) to adapt a second RCM to the needs of intraocular microsurgery (D). The probe held by the Hexapod Surgical System easily entered the targeted sclerotomy when remotely actuated by using a dedicated joystick that could be adapted to the *da Vinci's* command console (B,C,D).

Experiments were designed to assess the range of motion of the Hexapod Surgical System in vitro as well as while penetrating the eye during simulated vitrectomy in enucleated porcine eyes (Mulgaonkar, Hubschman et al. 2009). Briefly, platform rotations around the desired range of motion of instruments were simulated using MATLAB code to predict the required change in leg length by the inverse kinematics calculation. A vitreous cutter or any other intraocular instrument could be positioned on the Hexapod Surgical System's platform.

The results showed that maximum translations with the Hexapod Surgical System were 10 cm (x, y-planes) and 5 cm (z-plane). Mean translation and angulation stabilities at the tip of the probe were 1.2 mm and 1 mm, respectively. When a vitreous cutter attached to the Hexapod arm was inserted into porcine eyes through 20-gauge sclerotomy sites, there was minimal tension observed at the site of ocular penetration indicating that the remote center of motion could be maintained in the correct location.

The major limitation of the Hexapod Surgical System causing it to be not adequate for modern eye surgery was its limited translation and angulation ability. Essentially, the instruments were confined to a 30 degree cone inside the eye. In retinal surgery, it is important to have access to the periphery where there is often pathology such as retinal tears or vitreous traction. This range of motion might have been large enough for the original intent of the Stewart platform, namely retinal vessel cannulation, but it was not adequate for more general applications of posterior segment intraocular surgery such as pars plana vitrectomy. The problem was that the ball bearing joints which connected the legs of the Stewart platform were spherical, allowing only 30-40 degrees of maximum swivel. This range of motion was further decreased as the remote center of motion was placed futher away from the center of the Stewart platform.

In summary, combining the *da Vinci* Surigcal System with the Stewart platform to create the Hexapod Surgical System solved the problem of a dynamic remote center of motion in intraocular surgery. This novel device also demonstrated a high level of precision and dexterity, but its major limitation was a restricted range of angulation when used inside the eye (Mulgaonkar, Hubschman et al. 2009).

3.3 Surgical microhand

An advantage of ocular robotic surgery over traditional ocular surgery is the ability for increased dexterity beyond the limits of human adroitness. Towards this goal, we wanted to design dedicated microinstruments to be used in robotic intraocular eye surgery. The first instrument specially designed for ocular robotic surgery at the University of California, Los Angeles, was a pneumatically operated micromanipulator, called the microhand (Figure 9). It consisted of balloon-based joints and interconnecting silicone phalanges (Hubschman, Bourges et al. 2009).

The motion of the microhand was driven by compressed air and pneumatic actuation technology. This was ideal for intraocular posterior segment surgery because vitrectomy consoles used this same technology to power vitreous cutters. In the future, the microhand and currently available vitrectomy system could be combined into one piece of equipment, both using the same pneumatic actual technology.

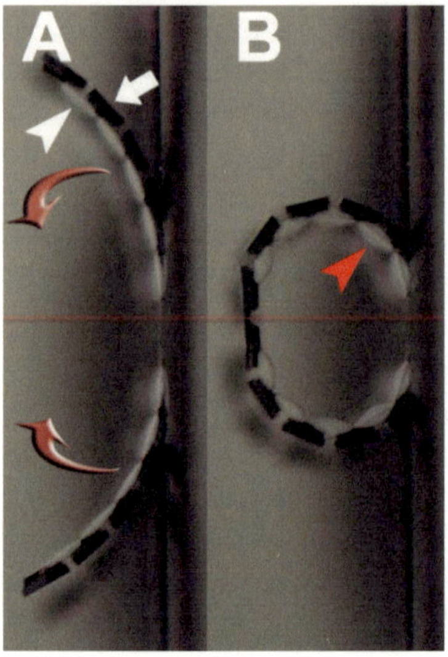

Fig. 9. The Microhand forceps is a four-fingered Microhand articulated by six silicone phalanges (A, white arrow) and joined by inflatable balloons (A, arrow heads). When balloons are inflated (B, red arrow head), fingers are incurved (A, red arrows and B) and face themselves along the central axis (red line). From Hubschman, J. P., J. L. Bourges, et al. (2009). "'The Microhand': a new concept of micro-forceps for ocular robotic surgery." Eye.

The microhand designed for ocular surgery trials had 4 mm-long x 0.8 mm-wide fingers with 6 micron thick inflateable balloons. When compressed air was introduced into the microhand, the balloon joints inflated and the attached silicone phalanges made out of plane motions. Each finger was a a six-phalange and six-balloon system which curled in response to compressed air, mimicking the action of a human finger (Figure 9). The microhand device was designed to achieve a large lifting force which was measured by using coil-shaped metallic weights of known mass.

The microhand was tested for ocular surgery use on flat-mounted porcine eyes to assess its functional capacity. Retinal tissue was manipulated by displacing it a pre-set distance without damage by carefully controlling the amount of pressure created with compressed air. A 65 psi (448 kPA) air pressure was necessary to pinch the retina, and the applied force for this maneuver was estimated to be less than 5 mN. The promising results of these studies was not only a novel application of the previously developed surgical microhand, but it also allowed a way to quantitate pressure exerted on ocular tissues which will be important when piloting ocular robotic surgery in the future.

3.4 The steady hand manipulator

Russel Taylor and his team at the Johns Hopkins University developped a steady-hand robotic system for microsurgery(Taylor, Jensen et al. 1999; Mitchell B 2007). This robotic system, described for the first time in 1999, was designed to extend a human's ability to perform small-scale manipulation tasks requiring human judgment, sensory integretion and hand-eye micromanipulation. With this device, the intraocular surgical tool is held simultaneously both by the operator's hand and the specially designed actively controlled robot arm. The robot controller senses forces applied by the surgeon on the surgical tool and uses them to provide smooth, tremor-free, precise and scaled motion of the arm. The device includes an adapted RCM for intraocular surgery and 5 degrees of freedom (Figure 10). The first prototype has been recently optimized and tested on a biological model. The successful cannulation of an 80 micron vein was rapidly and reliably achieved with minimal dammage to the surrounding tissues.

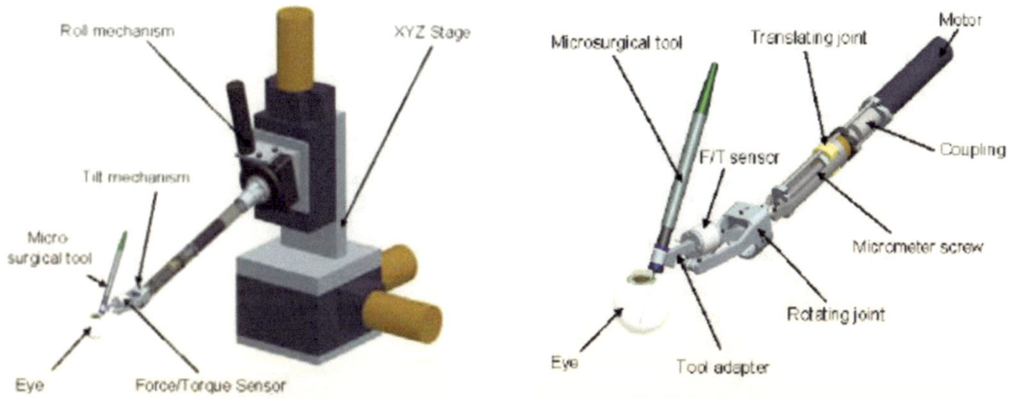

Fig. 10. Robot mechanical system: general view (left) and tilt mechanism (right). From Mitchell B, K. J., Iordachita I, et al (2007). "Development and application of a new steady-hand manipulator for retinal surgery." Proc IEEE Int conf Robot.

3.5 Japanese ocular robotic prototype

As already indicated, intraocular posterior segment surgery was the most demanding of ocular procedures and the most difficult to translate into robotic surgery. Recently, Ueta et al. demonstrated success with intraocular posterior segment surgery with a custom built micromanipulator prototype (Ueta, Yamaguchi et al. 2009). The controle console communicated with the slave arm in real time with a custom computer console. The high-definition video camera was capable of 2010 x 1096 pixel resolution with steroscopic image capture using a beam splitter. The surgeon obtained a three-dimentional view of the operating field using a prism lens viewer.

This robotic instrument was constructed with a pair of spherical guides, allowing x-axis and y-axis planar motion as well as the ability to push and pull, which allowed for z-axis movement with 5 degrees of freedom. The remote center of motion was set at the entry point of the eye to reduce stress on the eye. Ophthalmic surgical instruments such as a microscissor, microforcep, microneedle, and microcannula were attached at the tip to perform intraocular posterior segment procedures.

Experiments were carried out to test pointing accuracy using graph paper as well as to assess the feasibility of performing posterior vitreous detachment, retinal vessel sheathotomy, and retinal vessel microcannulation in porcine eyes. The group reported success with all these procedures, except for retinal vessel microcannulation. They attributed the achievement of this task to be limited by visualization difficulty given the lack of contrast of retinal vessels in enucleated porcine eyes.

4. Surgical motion sensors

As progress continued towards applying robotics to ocular surgery, it became important to better define the range of motion and other spatial parameters of ocular surgery. Motions that are natural and innate for human hands to perform needed to be precisely measured to custom design robots to mimick the same movements. Therefore, we wanted to determine the range of motion required to carry out common intraocular surgical tasks. This was done with electromagnetic sensors which were capable of quantifying microscopic translational and angulational movements. Experiments were carried out using enucleated porcine eyes (Son, Bourges et al. 2009).

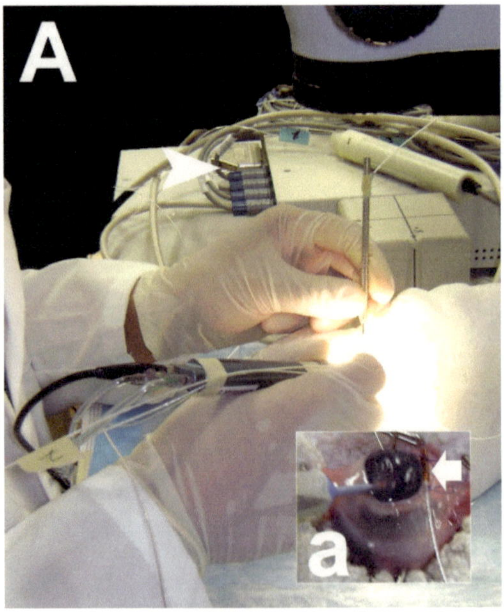

Fig. 11. (A) Porcine eyes were operated on with intraocular surgical instruments which were affixed to sensors connected to the control unit (white arrow-head). (a) To record motion at the entry site of instruments into the eye, a sensor was tightly sutured to the limbus (white arrow).

Electromagnetic sensors (MicroBird, Ascension Technology, Burlington, VT) were adapted to be surgical motion sensors by attaching them to instruments used in cataract surgery (i.e phacoemulsification handpiece, cataract chopper) and vitrectomy surgery (i.e. vitreous cutter, intraocular lightpipe) (Figure 11). These intruments were chosen to mimic typical bimanual surgical techniques in anterior segment and posterior segment surgery.
A reference sensor was sutured to the limbus of the porcine eye to detect and measure the motion relative to the eye during these procedures. Experienced ophthalmologists performed successive trials of cataract surgery and vitrectomy on porcine eyes as the x,y, and z coordinates of the intraocular instruments were continuously tracked. Maximal angulation areas of instruments were also determined for each surgical step.
The results of this study showed that robotic ocular surgery devices which hold instruments should be designed to allow a minimum translation of 3.65 cm, 3.14 cm, and 2.06 cm respectively in the x, y, and z-planes. A minimum angulation of 116 degrees and 106 degrees were needed intraocularly in the x and y-planes (Figure 12). This information is useful to assess currently available instruments as well as design upcoming instrument prototypes for intraocular robotic surgery.

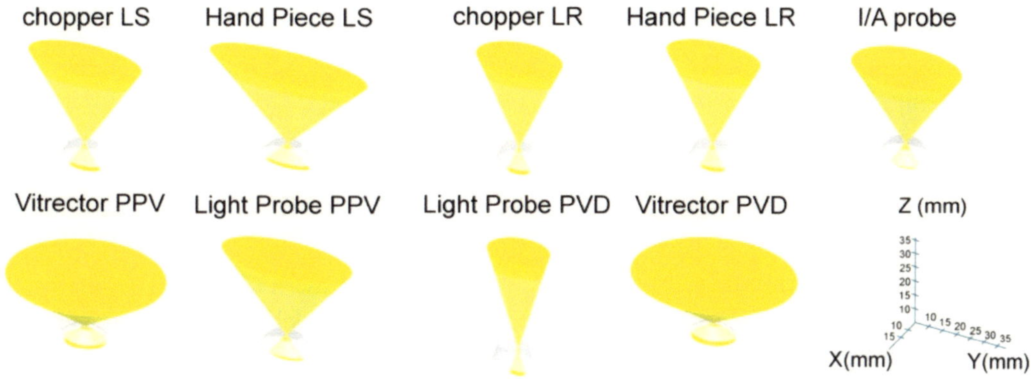

Fig. 12. The maximal angulation of each tool during various surgical steps (yellows areas) and standard deviations (gray areas) are plotted around a mean calculated position.

5. Further applications

Applications of robotic surgery include training and educating physicians in a safe, controlled, and feedback oriented way. Furthermore, with ongoing advancements, remote telesurgery and surgical automation may soon become a reality in the field of ophthalmology.

5.1 Training surgeons

Surgical training is an important part of ophthalmology residency, and there is much debate about the ideal way to safely and effectively teach ocular surgery (Goh 2009). There is no standardization of surgical experience during ophthalmology residency and in particular many training programs are not able to offer in depth experience in retinal procedures (Shah, Reddy et al. 2009).
Robotic ocular surgery would be an ideal adjunct to the methods now used to teach ocular surgery. Current means of ocular surgeon training rely on wet lab practice on porcine eyes

(Henderson, Grimes et al. 2009) and the use of computerized surgical simulators (Solverson, Mazzoli et al. 2009). Present day surgical skill assessment would include tools such as motion sensors and video grading which would lend itself to training physicians with robotic ocular surgery(Ezra, Aggarwal et al. 2009).

5.2 Telesurgery

In the *da Vinci* Surgical System, the control module was spatially separated from the robotic arm module. This made the idea of telesurgery possible. Telesurgery is the concept of the surgeon sitting in one location and operating on someone via a robot in another location.

In 2001, the first transatlantic robotically assisted remote surgery was performed on an animal model (Marescaux, Leroy et al. 2001), and this was followed by a transatlantic robot-assisted laparoscopic cholecystectomy in a human being (Marescaux, Leroy et al. 2002). Over the last several years, telesurgery has been demonstrated successfully on multiple occasions (Marescaux & Rubino 2004). Ocular robotic telesurgery may also be feasible in the future, bringing emergency eye care to remote locations.

5.3 Autonomous robots

In the distant future, we may see surgical robots with artificial intelligence and the resulting capacity to make surgical decisions and act on them without the input of a human being. More likely, in the coming years, we may see robots with the ability to perform a routine task independent from the controlling surgeon.

6. Conclusions

Ocular robotic surgery poses unique challenges such as intraocular accessibility, instrument refinement, and visualization. The diversity of ocular procedures requires a myriad of new instruments and surgical techniques, and the application of robotics to ocular surgery in humans will likely evolve in stages. Rapid progress in ocular robotic surgery has been made in recent years with the evaluation of the *da Vinci* Surgical System, the development of the Hexapod Surgical System, the creation of the surgical microhand, the utilization of surgical sensors, and the refinement of micromanipulators.

Advantages that robotic surgery offers include increased precision, improved range of motion, elimination of tremor, ability to maneuver in a confined anatomic space, reduced error, increased predictability, and increased surgeon safety. Future work will continue to integrate traditional surgical techniques with new devices to bring the advantages of robotics to the field of ophthalmology.

7. References

Bourla, D. H., J. P. Hubschman, et al. (2008). "Feasibility study of intraocular robotic surgery with the da Vinci surgical system." Retina 28(1): 154-8.

Charles S, D., H, Ohm T (1997). "Dexterity-enhanced tele-robotic microsurgery." Proc. IEEE int conf adv Robot.

Diaz-Arrastia, C., C. Jurnalov, et al. (2002). "Laparoscopic hysterectomy using a computer-enhanced surgical robot." Surg Endosc 16(9): 1271-3.

Ezra, D. G., R. Aggarwal, et al. (2009). "Skills acquisition and assessment after a microsurgical skills course for ophthalmology residents." Ophthalmology 116(2): 257-62.

Georgescu, D., A. F. Kuo, et al. (2008). "A fluidics comparison of Alcon Infiniti, Bausch & Lomb Stellaris, and Advanced Medical Optics Signature phacoemulsification machines." Am J Ophthalmol 145(6): 1014-1017.

Goh, E. S. (2009). "Maximising safety of cataract surgery training: improving patient safety by reducing cataract surgery complication rates." Int J Health Care Qual Assur 22(5): 535-46.

Guerrouad, A. and D. Jolly (1989). "Automatic analysis of weariness during a micromanipulation task by SMOS." IEEE Conference Proceeding 3: 906-907

Guerrouad, A. and P. Vidal (1989). "SMOS: stereotaxical microtelemanipulator for ocular surgery." IEEE Conference Proceeding 3 879-880.

Guerrouad, A. and P. Vidal (1991). "Advantage of computer aided teleoperation (CAT) in microsurgery." IEEE Conference Proceeding 1: 910- 914.

Hayat, S. and P. Vidal (1995). "Conception of information tools to assist the surgeon when he carries out radial keratotomy with a micromanipulator." IEEE Conference Proceeding: 3-5.

Hemal, A. K. and M. Menon (2004). "Robotics in urology." Curr Opin Urol 14(2): 89-93.

Henderson, B. A., K. J. Grimes, et al. (2009). "Stepwise approach to establishing an ophthalmology wet laboratory." J Cataract Refract Surg 35(6): 1121-8.

Hubschman, J. P., J. L. Bourges, et al. (2009). "'The Microhand': a new concept of micro-forceps for ocular robotic surgery." Eye.

Hubschman, J. P., J. L. Bourges, et al. (2009). "Effect of Cutting Phases on Flow Rate in 20-, 23-, and 25-Gauge Vitreous Cutters." Retina.

Jensen, P. S., K. W. Grace, et al. (1997). "Toward robot-assisted vascular microsurgery in the retina." Graefes Arch Clin Exp Ophthalmol 235(11): 696-701.

Katz, M. R., F. Van Praet, et al. (2006). "Integrated coronary revascularization: percutaneous coronary intervention plus robotic totally endoscopic coronary artery bypass." Circulation 114(1 Suppl): I473-6.

Kumar, R. and A. K. Hemal (2006). "The 'scrubbed surgeon' in robotic surgery." World J Urol 24(2): 144-7.

Kypson, A. P. and W. R. Chitwood (2006). "Robotic cardiovascular surgery." Expert Rev Med Devices 3(3): 335-43.

Marescaux, J., J. Leroy, et al. (2001). "Transatlantic robot-assisted telesurgery." Nature 413(6854): 379-80.

Marescaux, J., J. Leroy, et al. (2002). "Transcontinental robot-assisted remote telesurgery: feasibility and potential applications." Ann Surg 235(4): 487-92.

Marescaux, J. and F. Rubino (2004). "Robot-assisted remote surgery: technological advances, potential complications, and solutions." Surg Technol Int 12: 23-6.

Mitchell B, K. J., Iordachita I, et al (2007). "Development and application of a new steady-hand manipulator for retinal surgery." Proc IEEE Int conf Robot

Mulgaonkar, A. P., J. P. Hubschman, et al. (2009). "A prototype surgical manipulator for robotic intraocular micro surgery." Stud Health Technol Inform 142: 215-7.

Shah, V. A., A. K. Reddy, et al. (2009). "Resident surgical practice patterns for vitreoretinal surgery in ophthalmic training programs in the United States." Ophthalmology 116(4): 783-9.

Solverson, D. J., R. A. Mazzoli, et al. (2009). "Virtual reality simulation in acquiring and differentiating basic ophthalmic microsurgical skills." Simul Healthc 4(2): 98-103.

Son, J., J. L. Bourges, et al. (2009). "Quantification of intraocular surgery motions with an electromagnetic tracking system." Stud Health Technol Inform 142: 337-9.

Taylor, R., P. Jensen, et al. (1999). "A Steady-Hand Robotic System for Microsurgical Augmentation " The International Journal of Robotics 18 1201-1210.

Tsirbas, A., C. Mango, et al. (2007). "Robotic ocular surgery." Br J Ophthalmol 91(1): 18-21.

Ueta, T., Y. Yamaguchi, et al. (2009). "Robot-assisted vitreoretinal surgery: development of a prototype and feasibility studies in an animal model." Ophthalmology 116(8): 1538-43, 1543 e1-2.

Yu, D. Y., S. J. Cringle, et al. (1998). "Robotic ocular ultramicrosurgery." Aust N Z J Ophthalmol 26 Suppl 1: S6-8.

11

Robot-assisted Laparoscopic Central Pancreatectomy with Pancreaticogastrostomy (Transgastric Approach)

Chang Moo Kang, M.D.
Department of Surgery, Yonsei University College of Medicine, Korea

1. Introduction

The pancreatic surgeons need to consider patients' quality of life when treating benign and borderline malignant tumor of the pancreas because the patients' long-term survival is highly expected following successful pancreatectomy. Ideally, function-preserving minimally invasive surgery is thought to be quite adequate approach for them. Pancreaticoduodenectomy (PD) or extended distal pancreatectomy (EDP) with splenectomy was traditional treatment option for the benign and borderline malignant tumors locating in the pancreatic neck portion. Central pancreatectomy (CP) was just selectively applied in the past because of its frequent combined-morbidity.[1, 2] Recently, revisiting role of CP seems to be lightened by several authors.[1-5] With the development of laparoscopic experiences and instruments, only a few reports of conventional laparoscopic central pancreatectomy have been published by some expert surgeons[6-7]. However, the several disadvantages of conventional laparoscopic surgery, such as limited range of motion, fulcrum effect and two-dimensional operative view, could not encourage liberal attempts of various pancreas surgeries. Recent advances in computer technology are providing surgical robot system especially with multi-articulated joint and three-dimensional (3-D) operating view[9]. This surgical system is thought to provide more precise, safe, and effective laparoscopic performance, which might result in expanding the indication for minimally invasive surgery in benign and borderline malignant tumors of pancreas. Herein, we demonstrate a case of robot-assisted laparoscopic central pancreatectomy with pancreaticogastrostomy (transgastric approach) in neuroendocrine tumor of the pancreas locating in neck of the pancreas and briefly discuss the feasibility and benefit of this procedure.

2. Case presentation

<u>Patient:</u> A 64-year-old female patient visited our institution (Yonsei University Health System) for incidental discovery of pancreatic mass during routine medical check-up. Abdominal CT scan showed about 1.5cm sized hypervascular mass in the proximal body of the pancreas (Figure 1). Blood laboratory examinations were normal and tumor markers (CEA, CA19-9) were also within normal range without any clinical symptoms Preoperative clinical diagnosis was non-functioning neuroendocrine tumor tumor of the pancreas. We

planned for minimally invasive and function-preserving surgery (robot assisted central pancreatectomy).

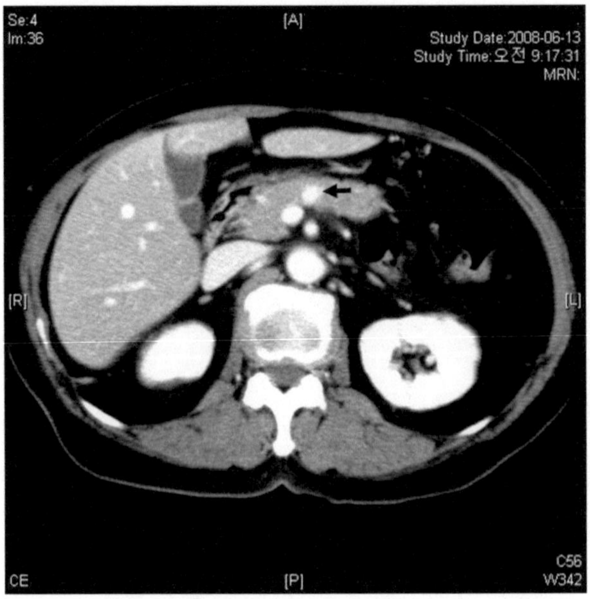

Fig. 1. Abdominal CT scan. About 1.5cm sized hypervascular mass was noted near the neck of the pancreas (arrow)

<u>Surgery</u>: The patient was placed in supine position with her head and left side slightly elevated. Four ports were placed for robotic arms and another one for assistant surgeon (Figure 2). After dividing the gastrocolic ligament, pancreatic neck mass could be well visualized. Intraoperative ultrasound was perform to identify the exact tumor location (Figure 3) Careful dissection was carried out by use of wrist function of robotic arms and 3-D good visual surgical field between SMV-SV confluence and pancreas containing mass to ensure space for pancreas division (Figure 4-A). After completion of making window

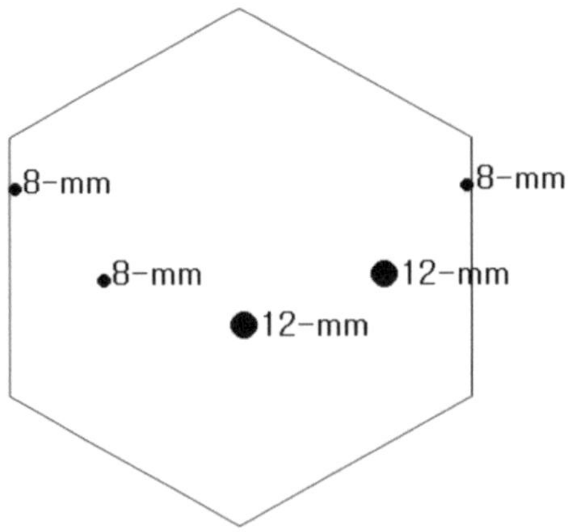

Fig. 2. The ports placement. The left-sided 12-mm port was used for assistant-surgeon and endo-GIA application.

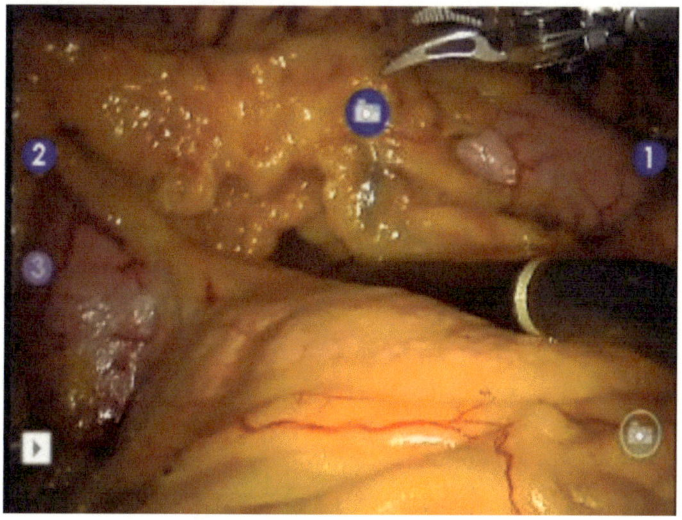

Fig. 3. intraoperative laparoscopic ultrasonography is applied to identify the exact location of the pancreatic tumor.

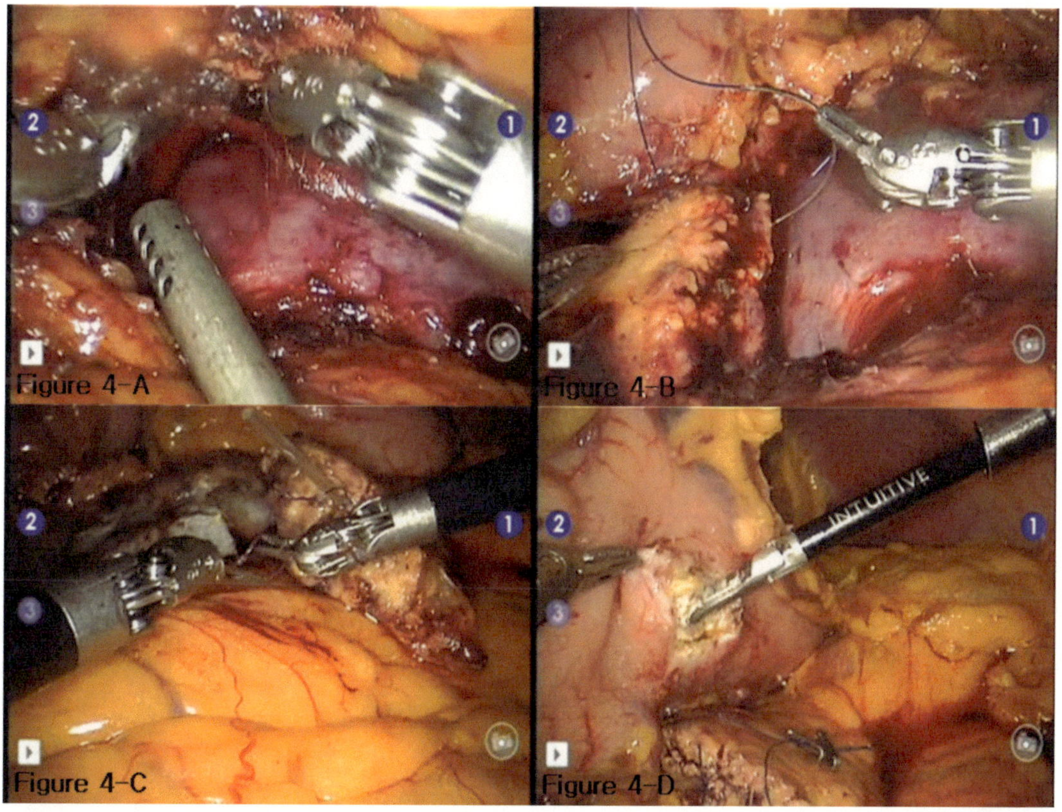

Fig. 4. Intraoperative surgical view

through the avascular space between pancreas and portal vein, endo-GIA was applied to divide proximal part of pancreas. For the safety of proximal pancreatic stump, several additional figure of eight interrupted suture were applied (Figure 4-B). The dissection between pancreas and splenic vessels was continued distally to ensure distal resection margin and to facilitate pancreatigogastrostomy. Distal part of pancreas was divided by harmonic scalpel. The stable operative field and articulating movement of instrument in robotic system were very appropriate for identify the pancreatic duct and preparing for reconstruction in remnant pancreas. The short pancreatic stent was inserted into the pancreatic duct and fixed as usually done in open surgery (Figure 4-C). Two stay sutures were placed at both upper and lower border of the pancreas to retract remnant distal pancreas into the stomach. And, appropriate size of gastrotomy for pancreas-invagination was made at posterior part of stomach (Figure 4-D). Anterior gastrotomy corresponding to posterior gastrostomy site was made (Figure 5-A). Pancreas-invagination through transgastric approach was done and serial interrupted sutures (4-0 PDS) were placed between pancreas and gastric posterior wall (Figure 5-B and 4-C). Wrist-like movements and good visual field provided by robotic system played important role in this procedure. After completion of pancreaticogastrostomy, anterior opening of gastric wall was safely closed by continuous suture (Figure 5-D). Resected specimen was delivered through small vertical extension of camera port site. Two-armed closed suction drains were placed around surgical field.

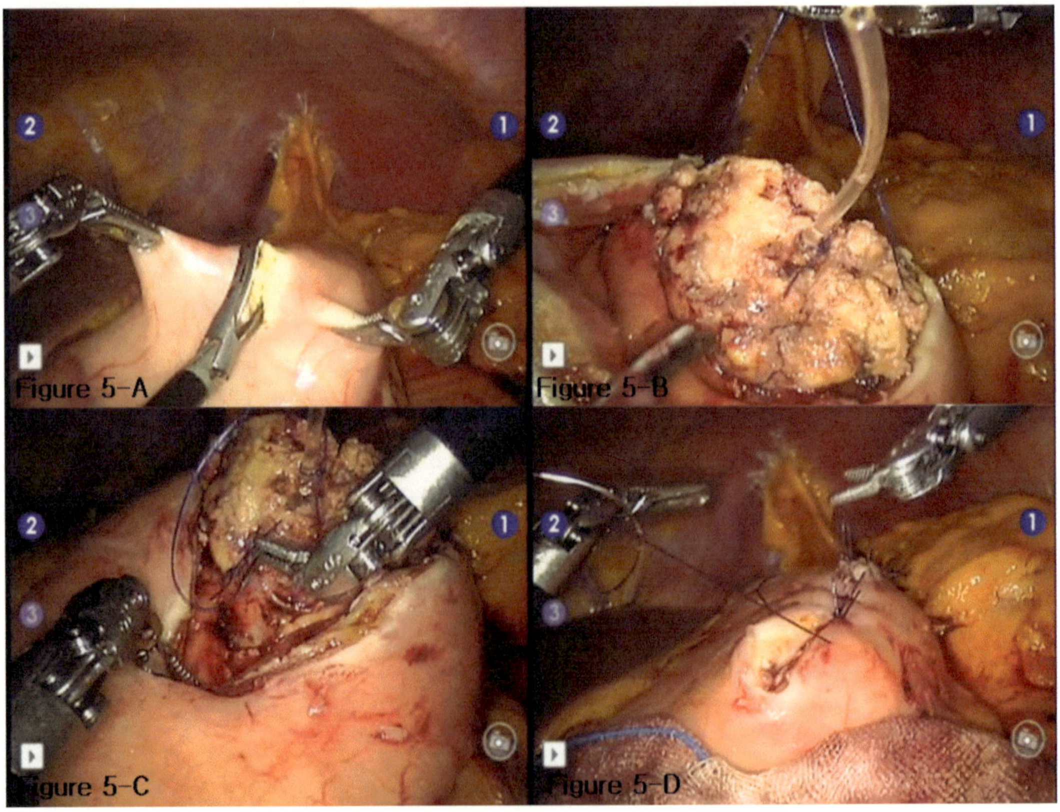

Fig. 5. Intraoperative surgical view

Postoperative course: She had no nasogastric tube after surgery. Oral intake was started on postoperative seventh day after surgery. She experienced transient pancreatic leak but surgical drain can be removed in eighth day postoperatively. She could go home on postoperative 12th day.
Pathology: Grossly resected pancreas was measured 4x2.5x2cm in size and about 1.2cm sized ill-defined solid pinky and brown mass was confined to the pancreas parenchyma (Figure6). Pathologic examination was reported as well-differentiated endocrine tumor of the pancreas without mitotic figure and low proliferative index (Ki-67 expression < 2%).

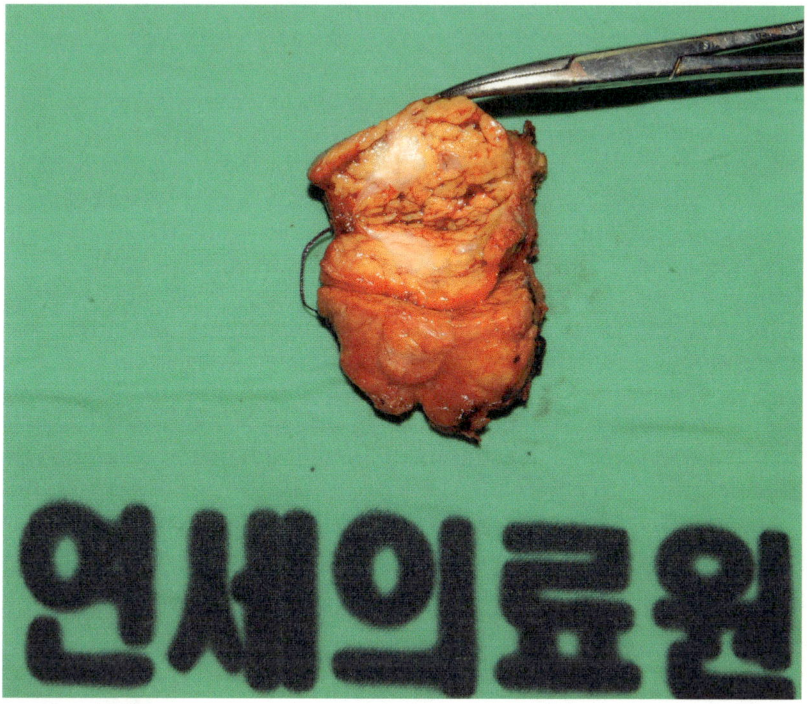

Fig. 6. Surgical pathology

3. Discussion

Since Guillemin and Bessot firstly reported central pancreatectomy in 1957,[9] only a few authors described this technique in the management of pancreatic tumor in the pancreatic neck area. The theoretic benefit of central pancreatectomy is preservation of remnant pancreas parenchyma enough to reduce an incidence of endocrine and exocrine insufficiency, conservation of spleen to maintain immunologic function, and continuity of biliary drainage which is thought to be more physiologic than choledochoenterosotmy after pancreaticoduodenectomy. By reconstruction of pancreaticogastrostomy following central pancreatectomy, conserving continuity of upper gastrointestinal tract can be another advantage of this procedure. Despite of controversy in reconstruction of remnant pancreas (pancreaticojejunosotmy vs. pancreaticogastrosotmy), potential advantages of pancreaticogastrostomy has been advocated.[10-13] Recently, Bassi, et. al[14] introduced their surgical technique, " open pancreaticogastrostomy after pancreaticoduodenectomy". Even though their original work was published as pilot study, it seem that this technique is easy and safe due to excellent exposure of surgical field comparing with conventional anastomosing the remnant pancreas to the gastric posterior wall from the outside of the stomach.

When treating benign and borderline malignant pancreatic pathology near the neck or proximal body of the pancreas, function-preserving minimally invasive surgery is theoretically appropriate treatment option for them. Although there are a few clinical report of laparoscopic CP, we need to admit that this procedure should require far advanced laparoscopic technique and experiences. Only a few expert surgeons in the world are believed to be qualified for this fulfillment for laparoscopic central pancreatectomy. However, we used da Vinci surgical robot system to complete central pancreatectomy with transgastric pancreaticogastrostomy. By the help of surgical robot system, more effective and safe surgical procedure could be obtained. Endo-wrist instrument and good 3-D visualization enhanced precise and secure performance during surgical procedure. Especially, dissecting of the pancreatic neck portion, preparing remnant pancreas for pancreaticoenterostomy, and final pancreaticogastrostomy were performed safely as usually done in open surgery. This transgastric approach basically provided excellent surgical field for intracorporial robot movement. Additionally, three dimensional views of operative field and wrist-like movement of effector instruments provided by da vinci robot system were enough to fulfill the safe central pancreatectomy and reconstruction of pancreaticogastrostomy. We believe surgical performance in this robot surgery would be almost similar to open surgery. The patient experienced postoperative pancreatic leak (Grade A[15]), however, which was successfully managed by conservative management in usual manner. Additional small extension of umbilical wound was enough to deliver resected specimen. Follow up observation revealed good cosmetic effect from this procedure (Figure 7). Currently, total five patients underwent robot-assisted central pancreatectomy

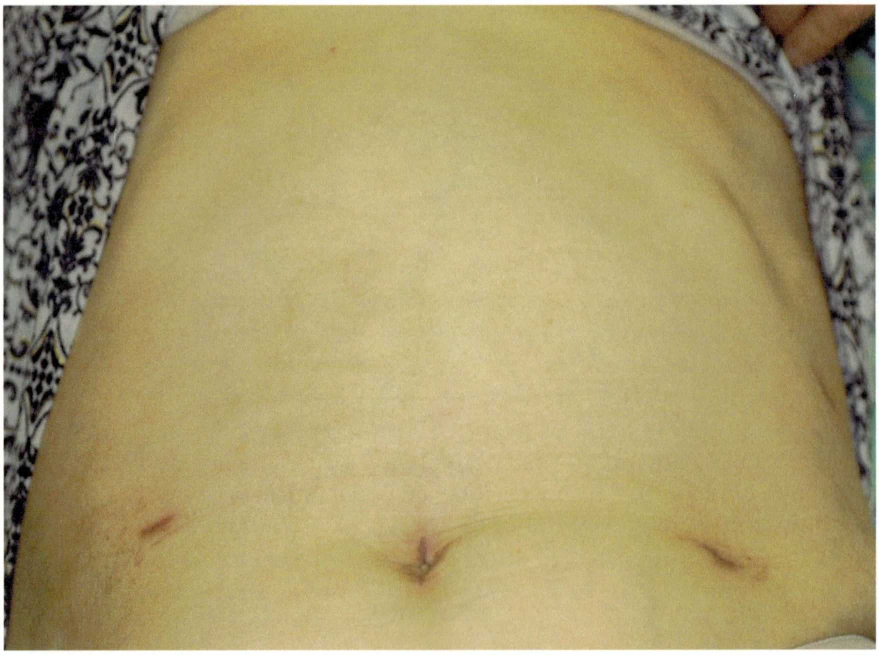

Fig. 7. Postoperative wound

for benign and borderline malignant tumors in our institution during the last one year. Asymptomatic patients with benign and borderline malignant tumor of the pancreas are expected to be discovered more frequently due to easy accessibility to medical care and improvement socioeconomic status. Therefore, the role of functiong-preserving minimal invasive surgery would be emphasized and robot-assisted surgery may be quite appropriate approach for safe and effective function preserving minimal invasive surgery. More experiences including clinical follow-up information is mandatory.

4. Conclusion

Based on our initial experience of robot-assisted central pancreatectomy and transgastric pancreaticogastrostomy, it is thought to be safe and ideal for well-selected patients with benign or borderline malignant tumor of the pancreatic neck area. No one deny the real benefit and effectiveness of laparoscopic surgery over conventional open surgery in general surgical field. In this point, we would like to say the surgical robot system could play a role to compensate conventional laparoscopic surgery particularly in case where the pure laparoscopic approach would be technically difficult. Therefore, it is thought that the surgical robot system is able to extend surgical indication for function-preserving minimally invasive surgery. We need to accumulate more experiences of robot surgery in pancreas to address the real benefit of robot in far advanced laparoscopic era.

5. Reference

[1] Roggin KK, Rudloff U, Blumgart LH, Brennan MF. Central pancreatectomy revisited. J Gastrointest Surg 2006; 10(6):804-12.

[2] Christein JD, Smoot RL, Farnell MB. Central pancreatectomy: a technique for the resection of pancreatic neck lesions. Arch Surg 2006; 141(3):293-9.

[3] Crippa S, Bassi C, Warshaw AL, et al. Middle pancreatectomy: indications, short- and long-term operative outcomes. Ann Surg 2007; 246(1):69-76.

[4] Aranha GV, Shoup M. Nonstandard pancreatic resections for unusual lesions. Am J Surg 2005; 189(2):223-8.

[5] Muller MW, Friess H, Kleeff J, et al. Middle segmental pancreatic resection: An option to treat benign pancreatic body lesions. Ann Surg 2006; 244(6):909-18; discussion 918-20.

[6] Orsenigo E, Baccari P, Bissolotti G, Staudacher C. Laparoscopic central pancreatectomy. Am J Surg 2006; 191(4):549-52.

[7] Sa Cunha A, Rault A, Beau C, et al. Laparoscopic central pancreatectomy: single institution experience of 6 patients. Surgery 2007; 142(3):405-9.

[8] Lanfranco AR, Castellanos AE, Desai JP, Meyers WC. Robotic surgery: a current perspective. Ann Surg 2004; 239(1):14-21.

[9] Guillemin P, Bessot M. [Chronic calcifying pancreatitis in renal tuberculosis: pancreatojejunostomy using an original technic.]. Mem Acad Chir (Paris) 1957; 83(27-28):869-71.

[10] Nanashima A, Sumida Y, Abo T, et al. Comparative study of anastomosis in pancreaticogastrostomy and pancreaticojejunostomy after pancreaticoduodenectomy. Hepatogastroenterology 2007; 54(76):1243-6.

[11] Ohigashi H, Ishikawa O, Eguchi H, et al. A simple and safe anastomosis in pancreaticogastrostomy using mattress sutures. Am J Surg 2008; 196(1):130-4.
[12] Sledzinski Z, Kostro JZ, Zadrozny D, et al. Results of pancreaticogastrostomy after pancreaticoduodenectomy in 159 consecutive cases. Pancreatology 2008; 8(1):36-41.
[13] Wente MN, Shrikhande SV, Muller MW, et al. Pancreaticojejunostomy versus pancreaticogastrostomy: systematic review and meta-analysis. Am J Surg 2007; 193(2):171-83.
[14] Bassi C, Butturini G, Salvia R, et al. Open pancreaticogastrostomy after pancreaticoduodenectomy: a pilot study. J Gastrointest Surg 2006; 10(7):1072-80.
[15] Bassi C, Dervenis C, Butturini G, et al. Postoperative pancreatic fistula: an international study group (ISGPF) definition. Surgery 2005; 138(1):8-13.